A THOUSAND ROUTES THROUGH
NAVARRE

A THOUSAND ROUTES THROUGH NAVARRE

JAVIER PAGOLA LORENTE

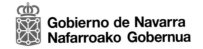

Gobierno de Navarra
Nafarroako Gobernua

TITLE: A thousand routes through Navarre

TEXT: Javier Pagola Lorente

TRANSLATION: Traductores e Intérpretes del Norte, S.L. (TRINOR)

PHOTOGRAPHS: Gema Arrugaeta, Azpilicueta y Domench, Carlos Cánovas, José Ramón Carmona, Jesús Caso, Javier Ederra, Xabi Landa, Larrión & Pimoulier, Nicolás López, José Ignacio Moreno, Jorge Nagore, Paco Ocaña, Luis Otermin, Xabi Otero and Archivo de la Institución Príncipe de Viana (for more details, see page 231)

Editorial co-ordination: Servicio de Comunicación del Departamento de Presidencia e Interior

Design and page layout: Bega Comunicación

Films: Ernio Navarra

Printed by: Castuera Industria Gráfica

ISBN: 84-235-2005-6

Depósito legal: NA. 1.211/2000

Promoted and distributed by: Fondo de Publicaciones del Gobierno de Navarra (Departamento de Presidencia e Interior)
C/ Navas de Tolosa, 21
E.31002 Pamplona

Phone and fax: 948 42 71 23
E-mail: fpubli01@cfnavarra.es

Navarre has always been a land of a thousand routes. Its geographical location between continental Europe and the Iberian peninsula has made it an inevitable crossroads where different cultures, languages and religions have mixed. One of them is the route of all routes: the Pilgrim's Way to Compostela, favoured by the monarchs of Navarre in the Middle Ages and which today maintains its monuments, and above all the spirit, of the thousands of pilgrims and travellers who follow it every year. The people of Navarre also have a strong feeling for this route and value it as one of our strongest signs of identity. There are also other, lesser, routes —rugged and secluded paths—that lead to the farthest corners of our territory, areas where an enormous variety of natural surroundings can be enjoyed at their best and where the authentic roots of the Navarrese people are best preserved. These thousand routes are there for whoever wishes to follow them and enjoy the surprises that Navarre holds at every step along the way.

This book sets out to help the reader enjoy to the full his or her journey to the most prominent places in Navarre, whether they be familiar to him/her or not. If you turn the pages without having visited the place described, the text will outline its history, natural heritage and legends associated with it, plus comments by famous writers and travellers who have visited it. If you already knows the place, this book will provide you with a compendium of basic ideas to help look at it from a new, more meaningful perspective.

The masterful prose of Javier Pagola, pervaded with the accuracy of an experienced reporter and the feeling of someone who deeply loves what he is describing, gently guides the reader and unravels the knowledge, sentiment and magic contained in the vision he puts across of each place. The photographs chosen will also bring you closer to the reality described.

The book's 24 chapters are 24 attractive proposals to get to know different parts of this varied and appealing land. It is true that everything that appears in it is Navarre, but unfortunately not all Navarre appears. The extent of the book means that only certain places have been selected, and consequently others have been left out or referred to in passing, places perhaps just as deserving of space.

The aim of this book, dear reader, will be fulfilled if you accept the invitation in each chapter to become interested in and get to know the area described, or if you re-read these pages after visiting the place, where some of the routes of Navarre are sketched, some of the thousand routes that Navarre puts before you so that you can delve deeper into its richness and variety.

Bay of Biscay

SAN SEBASTIÁN

PAU

France

Guipúzcoa

Irún
Bera-Vera de Bidasoa
Zugarramurdi
Lesaka
Etxalar
Urdax
Saint Jean de Pied de Port
Señorío de Bértiz
Arizkun
Elizondo
Ituren
Irurita
Zubieta
Oloron-Ste.-Marie
Leitza
Puerto de Belate
Lantz
Luzaide-Valcarlos
Quinto Real
Orreaga-Roncesvalles
Embalse de Irabia
Selva del Irati
Puerto de Belagoa
Río Bidasoa
Embalse de Eugui
Orbaitzeta
Belagoa
Sierra de Aralar
San Miguel de Aralar
Río Arakil
Irurtzun
Zubiri
Garralda
Ochagavía
Foz de Mintxate
Mesa de los Tres Reyes
Altsasu
San Donato
Valle de Ultzama
Río Erroki
Río Irati
Isaba
Álava
Sierra de Urbasa
Sierra de Andía
Río Arga
PAMPLONA
Foz de Txintxurrenea
Río Salazar
Roncal
Huesca
Monasterio de Iranzu
Embalse de Alloz
Astrain
Monreal
Aoiz
Foz de Arbayún
Navascués
Burgui
Foz de Burgui
Río Urederra
Puente la Reina
Puerto del Perdón
Obanos
Idocin
Alto de Loiti
Foz de Lumbier
Monasterio de Leire
Río Ega
Monasterio de Irache
Eunate
Yesa
Monasterio de Azuelo
Estella
Mendigorría
La Valdorba
Liédena
Sangüesa
Javier
Monjardín
Artajona
Aibar
Pantano de Yesa
Torres del Río
Los Arcos
Larraga
San Martín de Unx
Viana
Río Ega
Tafalla
Ujué
Peña
Petilla de Aragón
LOGROÑO
Olite
Lodosa
Río Ebro
Pitillas
Laguna de Pitillas
Río Arga
San Adrián
Río Aragón
Monasterio de la Oliva
Marcilla
Río Arga
Bardenas Reales
La Rioja
Corella
Cintruénigo
Tudela
Monasterio de Fitero
Río Alhama
Río Queiles
Zaragoza
Cascante
Monasterio de Tulebras
Cortes
Río Ebro
Canal Imperial

Navarre

Towns
Church/monastery
Natural park
Castles
Shrovetide carnivals
Mountain pass
Gorge
Pilgrims' Way to Compostela

SUMMARY

The name of Roncesvalles (or Roncesvaux) was carried all over Europe through the *chansons de geste* and pilgrims' tales. It is a name which evokes the historical defeat of Charlemagne, the legendary fate of Roland, and memories of a Hospital which was famous throughout Christendom. The Collegiate Church had rich domains which, although much has been confiscated, have left us the legacy of a sanctuary which radiates holiness, a collection of buildings of great beauty, a point of reference for European unity, a welcome refuge on the route to Santiago de Compostela, and the renewed resources of around a thousand hectares of forest.

RONCESVALLES

History and Legend

At an altitude of nine hundred metres, just where the peaks of the Western Pyrenees begin to rise up and create a harsh Alpine landscape, it is a surprise to find a wide plain stretching out over fifteen square kilometres. In the whole mountain range it would be difficult to find similar scenery, offering from a distance the sight of a ring of mountains with rocky outcrops silhouetted against the sky, while their tree-lined slopes drop down to a plain covered with small woods, pastures and fields which can only be cultivated from late spring to early autumn, because they can be covered with snow for weeks at a time.

Winters are long and harsh; the peaks are covered in mist and the horizon closes in; it rains intensely and the snows are slow to disappear. Yet blizzards seem increasingly to be a thing of the past, and modern technology has put an end to the harshest aspects of the winter season and the problems of being cut off and isolated. In fact now people even welcome the sparkle and the fun of falling snow. Benito Urtasun, a writer who comes from this area and who particularly loves this plain, describes the strong contrasts from one season to another and transmits the feeling of overwhelming joy at the prosperous days when "The sun shines and the countryside seems to have been created anew. Dew lies like pearls sown across the slopes and meadows, and the flowers seem to don new colours every day. The kindly, smiling spring comes late, but keeps its tender innocent delights well into summer. Summertime brings mild temperatures, a northern breeze and the pure forest air. Autumn, too, is a season of quiet peace, when migrating birds draw many to the hides and the forest takes on a thousand hues, melting to a golden brown with the last pleasant rays of the sun."

The spectacular peaks of Ortzanzurieta and Astobizkar mark the northern limit of this plain, across which flow the upper stretches of the river Urrobi. Between these mountains lies the Lepoeder pass and below them, the Ibañeta pass. Two ancient routes, trodden by imperial armies and now, as in olden times, by numerous pilgrims on their way to Santiago, cross these passes. The oldest of these routes goes through the narrow Luzaide pass and was a Roman road which continued towards the south and which offered shelter about half way along the plain in the little *domus pausatoria* of Iturisa, of great interest to archaeologists.

In the Middle Ages the whole plain belonged to the Count of Erro, and José María Jimeno Jurío has suggested that this might explain its enigmatic name. This plain between the mountains would have been *Erro-zabal* in the local language —the place where the Erro valley widens. This name, transposed from Basque into the Romance tongue, would have given *Rozavalles*, a name which appears in documents of 1050.

Before 1132, the year in which the Sanctuary and Hospital of Roncesvalles were erected on their present site, the latter replacing the earlier hospital on the Ibañeta pass, there was already a village in the heart of the plain called 'Villa' or 'Burgo de Roncesvalles'.

[PREVIOUS PAGE] *The collegiate church of Roncesvalles appears in the foreground next to the basajuanberro wood. in the distance, burguete stands in the middle of the wide plain.*

Much later this village was given the pleasant sounding diminutive name of Burguete.

Aingiruen Erregina,
Orierriagan xarririk,
aingiruen konpañian
gloria guztiz beterik.

This poem, written in praise of Santa María de Roncesvalles, by the canon Juan de Huarte at the beginning of the XVIIth century, gives the Basque name for the place where the Collegiate Church is situated. *Orreaga* would have referred to an area of the plain with many juniper bushes. In a similar way, another village which grew up at the other end of the plain in 1269 was and still is called Espinal. Another name for the area, apparently of Latin origin, is *Auriz*, which was the name used until the XIIth century for the Ibañeta pass, and which then became Auritz, the Basque name for Burguete, and which in turn gave rise to *Aurizberri* (New Auriz), the Basque name for Espinal.

A HISTORICAL SKIRMISH BECOMES A LEGENDARY BATTLE

Cervantes, in Don Quixote, puts the following words into the mouth of a farm labourer from Toboso, who sings a romance traditional among Sephardi Jews:

Mala la hubisteis franceses,
en esa de Roncesvalles.

[A bad time you French had of it in that business at Roncesvalles].

It was at dusk on the 15th of August, in the year 778. The exact site of the battle has been the subject of much discussion. After a detailed examination of sources and history books, the historian Jimeno Jurío concludes that it took place in the defile, which leads down to the north from the Ibañeta pass towards Luzaide, and which, for that reason has been called Valcarlos or the Valley of Charlemagne since the XIIth century.

This action must have been a skirmish rather than a battle. Charlemagne was returning, disappointed, from an expedition to Saragossa and had just destroyed the walls of Pamplona. A band of Basques, allied with some Arabs, waited to ambush the royal army in the beech forests of Girizu and Ibañeta. They watched the long column of knights and foot soldiers go past. When the rearguard had crossed the highest point of the pass a horn sounded and rocks and arrows started to rain down on soldiers who must have cursed the rough, narrow terrain of the route over the pass.

In the garden of the Collegiate Church of Roncesvalles a monument commemorates the battle with the inscription *Vascones in summi montis vertice surgentes*, a phrase taken from the chronicles written around 830 by Eginhardo, whose accounts are biased in favour of the Emperor. On the Ibañeta pass, another monument bears a sword and two maces in memory of Roland.

The tragic memory of this humiliating ambush, recorded by Arabic and Carolingian chroniclers, was made even worse when, in

824, Frankish troops sent by Charlemagne's son and successor were defeated at the very same spot. This narrow pass had become an accursed place for the Carolingians.

Later, epic literature distorted the facts to create beautiful legends :

> *Morz est Rollant, Deus en ad l'anme es cels.*
> *Li emperere en Rencesvals parvient.*

'La chanson de Roland', preserved in a text dating from the end of the XIth century, is the oldest French *chanson de geste*. Its four thousand lines tell the tale of the Twelve Peers of France and Roland, Charlemagne's nephew, who fights against the Saracens and is betrayed by his step-father, Ganelon.

In the heat of battle, Roland sounds his horn Oliphant and the effort bursts the veins in his temples. He tries several times to break his sword Durandal against stones of marble, but in vain. Roland dies and his soul is carried to Paradise by Saint Gabriel. The emperor returns to Roncesvalles and orders all the bodies to be buried in a grave. There follows a last battle on the plain of Roncesvalles, in which Charlemagne is victorious, subsequently pursuing the Moors as far as Saragossa.

It appears that before the Oxford version, the earliest existing version of the *Chanson*, the epic of Roland was already known in the kingdom of Pamplona. In the Royal Palace in Estella the capital of a XIIth century column depicts the battle between Roland and the giant Ferragut. And in an early XIVth century manuscript in the Archives of Navarre there is a fragment of the 'Cantar de Roncesvalles' whose spelling and other characteristics suggest that it was composed locally.

A beautiful cycle of legends of Roland, with armies of maidens, flowering lances and stones moist with tears was illustrated in the stained glass of Chartres Cathedral, and became part of the canon of chronicles, ballads and great poems such as Ariosto's 'Orlando Furioso'. In the XIXth century Garay de Monglave composed the beautiful Basque poem '*Altabizkarko kantua*', set to music by Benito Lertxundi.

The road to Santiago

The most famous 'guidebook' for mediaeval pilgrims, the *Codex Calixtinus*, dating from the mid XIIth century, mentions the site of the

"…*A short distance from Roncesvalles there is a stone cross, which was known in ancient times as the Pilgrims' Cross*", wrote Becquer.

battle of Roncesvalles, Charlemagne's cross where the pilgrims knelt to pray towards Galicia, and the choice of routes available to the pilgrims from San Juan de Pié de Puerto (St Jean Pied-de-Port): towards Ibañeta on the high route through Cize and Bentartea, or up the valley of Valcarlos, and gives information on the many hospitals and shelters, thus giving the lie to dark legends of wild people, thieves and murderers.

In 1071 there was already a chapel and hospital on the site where the modern hermitage of San Salvador de Ibañeta now stands at the top of the pass. To guide pilgrims in an area of almost daily fog the bell was rung repeatedly from sunset to midnight.

The pilgrimages to Compostela began at the end of the IXth century and reached a peak in the XIIth century when the bishop of Pamplona, Sancho de Larrosa, chose Ibañeta "on which the inhabitants of those parts bear witness to the deaths of many thousands of pilgrims, some buried by blizzards, and most devoured by wolves" to found the Hospital of Roncesvalles in 1127. Five years later the hospital and church of Santa María were moved to a more sheltered spot below the head of the pass where the Collegiate Church now stands. From here the canons of Saint Augustine administered their rich domains in several European countries, and offered a warm welcome to thousands of people who followed the road across the mountains. A XIIIth century poem in Latin relates their medical and charitable work :

> *In hac domo pauperum pedes abluuntur,*
> *barbae cum rasoriis eis auferuntur,*
> *lavatis capitibus, capilli tolluntur…*

They opened their doors to everyone, Christians, pagans, Jews and heretics alike. Travellers would have their feet washed, their beards trimmed, and their hair cut. They could sleep in soft clean beds. The sick were carefully tended, and did not leave until they had fully recovered. Those who died were buried there. Many grateful pilgrims made donations to the Hospital when they left.

Although the number of pilgrims and the resources available for them had diminished, an average of 20,000 meals a year were still being provided in the XVIIth century, without taking into account those given to the poor and beggars. The Constitutions of the XVIIIth century determined that the Hospital should give those going to Santiago "a decent bed for three nights, with five lunches

and dinners, bread and wine and a regular portion of roast meat or pollack, and a cheese roll with half a pint of wine for breakfast on the day they are to continue their journey." Even half way through the XIXth century Pascual Madoz mentioned in his Dictionary that "Roncesvalles is one of the most famous sanctuaries in Christendom, the most important after Jerusalem, Rome and Santiago de Compostela."

Seizure of lands and the wars of the XIXth century marked a period of crisis for the Collegiate Church. This had the effect, however, of strengthening popular religion and the springtime processions when the sanctuary, a centre of pastoral care now run by secular diocesan priests, was visited by the faithful bearing crosses and wearing traditional tunics, accompanied by the sound of bells and hymns to the Virgin Mary. The Navarrese from the north beyond the passes also come in procession on the Wednesday before September 8th and their massed voices join to sing beautiful melodies in Basque.

A brotherhood dating from the Middle Ages and consisting of 3,500 Navarrese from nearby villages (and others who have moved away) still exists, but the Collegiate Church can no longer feed the growing number of travellers who pass this way. However, it does welcome them and provides the comforts of a warm shower, a bed for the night, the pilgrim's credentials and a blessing, in Latin, dating from the XIth century. 12,630 people spent the night here in 1996. During the summer of 1993 (one of the years dedicated to St. James) there were nights when as many as one thousand pilgrims gathered in Roncesvalles, and it is possible that twice as many will come during 1999, another holy year. The prior estimates that over the year they receive visits from fifty tourists for every one pilgrim. That makes a total of over half a million visitors.

THE HISTORICAL MONUMENTS AND BUILDINGS OF RONCESVALLES

Between Burguete and Roncesvalles the road runs in a straight line beneath a shady arch of ashes and beeches. Surrounded by leafy trees, a Gothic cross welcomes the visitor. The upright part of the cross, aged by moss and lichen, carries a barely legible inscription

[OPPOSITE PAGE] *The Collegiate Church, built at the beginning of the XIIIth century, is of early Gothic style from the Isle de France.*

The apse of the church and the front part of the Chapter look eastwards over the gully of Arañosin. The tower has a fortress air about it.

in Renaissance relief. It is set on three stone steps and recalls the romantic 'Travels' of Gustav Adolf Bécquer: "A short way from Roncesvalles there is a stone cross, which was formerly known as the Pilgrims' Cross. It was placed there by some pious hand, undoubtedly as a place to rest. I sat down at the foot of the cross, and breathed in deeply the pure, gentle mountain air. This was where the pious pilgrim knelt, dressed in his coarse tunic and carrying his rough wooden staff, overcome with a profound feeling of worship at the sight of the Sanctuary. Nothing has changed. There is the plain, the Pyrenees … This is the Roncesvalles of chivalrous tales, of wonderful traditions, the Roncesvalles of ballads and romantic poetry."

The XIIth century chapel and cemetery of the Holy Spirit is the oldest of all the buildings that make up Roncesvalles. It is situated above a crypt where pilgrims or soldiers who died crossing the Pyrenees were buried. The last time it was restored the remains found in the crypt were analysed; some dated from the Xth century, and all corresponded to males between 18 and 35 years old. The chapel is covered by a ribbed vault, and in the XVIIth century outer arches were built to enclose its square perimeter. Nearby is the church of Santiago with its ogive style and, on the other side of the road is a strange Gothic building, *Itzandegia*, with its powerful buttresses.

The collegiate church of Santa María, built on the orders of King Sancho VII (*el Fuerte*) at the beginning of the XIIth century, is in early Gothic style, brought very early on from the Isle de France. Its main door opens onto the Road to Santiago and it has a crypt decorated with painted Gothic murals. The central nave is twice the width of the two lateral naves and above the dividing arches there is a triforium crowned by scalloped windows. The flying buttresses, probably the first to be used in a Gothic building in Spain, are hidden by a grandiose wooden structure which supports a heavy roof consisting of 50 tons of lead, steeply sloped to ensure that snow does not accumulate on top. The tower, looking like a fortress with its defensive parapets and openings for projectiles, is of a more advanced Gothic style. The polygonal apse allows light to filter through five magnificent stained glass windows, which were made in Munich and placed in 1945. The church has an underfloor heating system designed to combat the extremely low winter temperatures efficiently: a chamber was excavated under the tiles to house the three miles of piping required.

Roncesvalles after a snowfall. To the right, the burial chapel of the Holy Spirit, the oldest building of all the historical monuments.

In the presbytery, on a small chest designed to hold relics, and beneath a silver canopy which is an exact copy of the one in Gerona cathedral, sits a statue of Santa María de Roncesvalles. One of the most beautiful examples of Marian imagery in Navarre, this statue combines sculpture and silverwork imported from French workshops in Toulouse. It was carved from cedar wood at the beginning of the XIVth century and was covered with silver, according to a much repeated but not necessarily very accurate tradition. An appreciation of this statue centres less on its formal beauty and more on the expression, especially in the long narrow eyes which gaze at the Christ-child with a mixture of tenderness and melancholy. A legend from the Baroque period tells how this statue was hidden to save it from being profaned during the Islamic invasions, and how it then miraculously appeared following the night-time visit of a stag with two dazzling stars shining from its antlers.

The right-hand nave gives onto the cloister, a sober XVIIth century building which replaced the earlier Gothic passages which gave way under the weight of the snow in 1600.

Situated towards the east is the Chapel of San Agustín, stands a chapter house built during the XIVth century in imitation of the 'Barbazana' chapel in Pamplona cathedral. A modern stained glass window made by José Maumejean in 1906, shows the battle of Navas de Tolosa, in which king Sancho el Fuerte (the Strong) was victorious. The tomb in the centre of the chapel has held the monarch's remains since 1912, the celebration of the seventh centenary of his joint victory against Miramamolín.

The recumbent statue of the king which covers the tomb is a Gothic sculpture, a portrait possibly made of the king in his lifetime and of great interest for the study of the clothing and symbols of the period. It also gives an idea of the temperament and physical appearance of the king, who was apparently a giant more than two metres tall, a fact confirmed by the analysis of his femur and by the chronicles of the time: "You should know that the king was the most handsome man in the world and a whole hand taller than other men."

The museum of Roncesvalles has three very valuable pieces of silverwork: a XIIIth century Gospel with rich silver covers, an enamel reliquary made in Montpellier in the XIVth century and known as 'Charlemagne's chess board' and a Gothic filigree chest. One of the outstanding paintings in the collection is a Mannerist style picture of the Holy Family painted by Luis de Morales. The library contains four early books or *incunabula* and there are valuable collections of diplomatic and musical documents in the archives.

The Information Office is located in a tastefully restored XVIIth century mill. Cereal crops were previously grown on the plain of Roncesvalles and the Collegiate Church continually received payments and donations in kind, making it necessary to be able to mill the grain at the site.

BURGUETE AND ESPINAL, VILLAGES ON THE ROAD TO SANTIAGO

The villages of Burguete and Espinal grew up in the Middle Ages on the Pilgrims' Way to Santiago and consist mainly of one long street with solid stone buildings on either side. Their situation near the border with France, together with wars and disputes with neighbours, sometimes "with drums beating and weapons drawn", meant that these villages have had a troubled history, and the traditional wooden roofs meant that the nightmare of horrific fires was a common occurrence. As a result, no mediaeval buildings or churches have survived. The lintels of most of the houses date from the XVIIIth century or later. However the most notable thing about the houses is the typical architectural style of the Pyrenees: whitewashed stone and steeply sloping roofs covered with flat tiles. The streets are clean, full of flowers in season, and the high standard of service matches the rich heritage of the villages, both of which have their own *frontón* (the high walls of the *pelota* court), the scene of exciting matches.

A new parish church, designed by the architects Esparza and Ayestarán and built of pink stone, was inaugurated in Espinal in 1961. The church is in keeping with the style of the other buildings, and although it might seem to be just another, rather larger, house, in fact the house of God is open to all and decorated with beautiful mosaics. No-one knows how the church of Aurizberri was able to save its greatest treasure, a finely worked silver-plated processional cross, from the constant depredations of war.

Tomb of King Sancho VII 'el Fuerte'. The recumbent statue is Gothic, and is of great interest for the study of the clothing and symbology of the period.

The cemetery of Burguete recalls the libertarian verses of Georges Brassens who wanted "to be buried in the graveyard of his village." Death is a great leveller and there is no sense in reflecting social distinctions on tombs, as if one could establish a 'standard of death' to match the 'standard of living'. Everyone buried here, rich and poor alike, is given the same respect. The Christian names are not even recorded, only the surname, or the name of the house, carved on the circular gravestone of each family tomb. The cemetery in *Auritz*, designed by the architect Miguel Gortari, was inaugurated in 1960. The gateway, made of iron and cement, is in the shape of a Greek *alpha*, representing the beginning of eternity. A great cement cross stands over this place of rest, marking its furthest boundary.

There is a greater tradition of tourism here than in any other part of Navarre, and the manufacture of furniture now complements an economy based on forestry and livestock. There are Pyrenean cows and sheep, whose milk is used to make delicious cheeses. The Pyrenean mare, the *pottoka*, crossed with stud horses from Brittany, produced the 'Burguete Breed', a medium-sized horse which is very strong, and much sought after at fairs for cultivating crops in Valencia.

The potato chosen for sowing is the great agricultural speciality of the region. One hundred and thirty-one families from Espinal, the valleys of Aezcoa and Salazar and the mountain villages of Codés have joined together to form OPPOSA, which stands for the 'Western Pyrenean Potato Producing Organisation'. In 1996 they produced and sold eight million kilos of potatoes, a crop of great importance since it helps to support the population of the area.

Navarre is a green area, as a third of its surface (around 346,000 hectares) is covered with woods and forests. The Pyrenean section is almost continuous leafy woodland area, with rims and tongues of conifers. The beech rules the roost in the mountains of Navarre, indeed the region is home to a third of all the beech forests of Spain. The Irati forest is the one of the most attractive; it has excellent quality beech and spruce trees with a small area of virgin vegetation of extraordinary scientific interest: the Reserve of Lizardoia.

THE POWER OF THE
FOREST

When Anton Dvořák expressed his love of the Bohemian woods in music for piano and cello, he called his collection of languid melodies 'Silent forests'. Solitude and silence are the sensations you get on entering these dense woods. The animals of the wood are nimble, and even the (sometimes conspicuous) birds appear to be silent. You may hear the steps of someone walking, the crunching of a branch, the noise of a brook, the roar of a power saw, the dripping of the rain or the unleashed fury of a storm.

Visual sensations are even richer. In winter, the bare trees reveal a landscape turned into a shining mirror by the snow. When the snow melts, the frogs leave their jelly-like eggs in the ponds. Some delicate flowers appear among the withered leaves, announcing the arrival of Spring long before the first light green leaves appear on the beech trees. Hundreds of young plants fight for sunlight, and branches shoot out from tree trunks and filter the sun's rays through their foliage. The wood has a fresh and damp feel through the hot days of summer. In its clearings you can find raspberries and wild strawberries, cranberries in the shade, and delicious wild mushrooms among the ferns and hollows. When Autumn arrives an orgy of colours breaks out and bellowing animals announce battles of love, first the deer and then the bucks. Doves fly overhead, dogs bark and the dry, crisp sound of rifles rings out in the air.

In his novel *Bajo los robles navarros* (Under the oaks of Navarre) the writer Félix Urabayen picked up the spirit of the "woods who sang their song" and distinguished the 'melodies' of each 'tribe' of vegetation:

"The beech is the legend. Its smooth, strong bark resists the elements without turning a hair and the trees advance *en masse*. Their strength lies in numbers, not in the hardness of a trunk nor the proliferation of leaves at the top, not even in a honey-coloured mop, always waving in the wind. Bunched tightly together, they climb the mountain, take over embankments, crawl up clearings until they take root on the summit, and surround the forgotten river beds and hollows. The beech makes the most of its ancestral authority to rule the forest by a majority of votes … The beech is above all sober; it only asks for a little humidity for its straight, slim trunk to grow, a decisive trunk which pushes its foliage upwards with great, almost mystical determination. The trees are beautiful when the sun's rays play different patterns on them. They are grey, greenish black, reddish, brownish, blue, but always smooth, silky and shiny, like young nymphs sprinkled by love.

The beech's companion and long-suffering, but never tender, lover is the pine. The beech corrects the over-violent impulses of its companion, making it sociable and providing it with a springy, calm and nutritious soil. It is true that the pine is an excellent husband, a vegetal Adam which sweats sap in the inevitable process of Genesis: a thick, warm sweat which perfumes the entire wood. It quietly, slowly and conscientiously softens the rain to turn it into spray like a wise seed-sower. When it oozes with satiety, it creates springs.

[PREVIOUS PAGE] *At the foot of Mount Adi, at a sheltered spot near Urkiaga, that most Navarrese of rivers is born: the Arga.*

The oak was the first of all trees, like the Basque language was the first of all languages. When the old beech trees had still not even sprouted, when the pines still struggled to approach, the Lord of the Pyrenees was the oak. This sacred tree reflects austerity, nobility and strength. It is a country gentleman who has come on hard times, but still preserves his lordly air, the presence and pride of his lineage. Arms and crowns come from the oak, and also coats of arms and the shield on which the first King of Navarre was raised. Our first dreams were rocked in a cradle made of white oak. May our last anguish be buried for ever in an oaken coffin."

Scientific data back up this lyrical story. In prehistoric times almost the whole of Navarre, except a few dry areas in the south, was covered by forests. These were of different kinds: beech, birch and hazel-nut, and in the low areas, where most human settlement has taken place, oaks and evergreen oaks.

Farmers moved into the oak forests, leaving the high ground where the beech grows and where they could not stay all year round, even though in summer they led their flocks to the great clearings at high altitude. On the more comfortable plains man has cultivated the land so much that it is more difficult to come across oak groves than beech. The oak, however, has a characteristic which is not shared by the beech: it is capable of holding water beneath it. This is why large groups of oaks remain in marshy land or on certain slopes where agriculture cannot flourish. Thick undergrowth is found around the oak, giving protection to a rich variety of wildlife.

The beech, part of the scenery of Navarre for the last six thousand years, is more recent than the oak in this area, and quickly takes over hill slopes, creating woods and forests of enormous ecological value. It prefers the mist to the downpour, it likes to feel the dampness of the fog in its leaves, although likes to keep its roots near the surface dry. It grows very slowly and adapts its posture to the surroundings, but when it reaches a hundred years of age it develops faster and reaches up to forty metres high. It ages at around three hundred years. The beech is rather selfish regarding the small plants around it, but when it sheds its leaves it returns almost all the nutrients it extracted to the soil, as well as protecting it against erosion and maintaining water reserves which it releases little by little into springs and streams.

At the end of the century, a thorough analysis of the situation was made with aim of reviewing forestry policy. The survival of the woods and forests of Navarre is guaranteed, and over the last three decades over 70,000 hectares of forest cover has been recovered. The quality of drinking water is ensured by the presence of leafy woodlands in the basins. The air of Navarre is clean and does not contribute to the greenhouse effect or climatic changes because its woods and forests absorb a quarter of the carbon dioxide emissions from the area's fuel. The forestry sector generates about 6,000 permanent jobs and has the merit of keeping people in rural areas. Navarre is searching for solutions to the drop in profitability of the timber trade and has created special areas in its woods for hunting, mushroom-collecting and obtaining energy from biomass. However, ecological values and the continued attraction of leisure, sport and tourism are leading to a greater appreciation and protection of these natural spaces by the population in general.

The Irati forest and its surrounding area covers about 10,000 hectares of trees and belongs to the Salazar and Aezkoa valleys. It is the largest in Navarre. It is comparable to the best in Europe in terms of quality, and the mixed forest of beech and spruce is the most western in the Pyrenees. Two streams, the Urbeltza and Urtxuría, join forces below the hermitage of the *Virgen de las nieves* (Virgin of the Snows) to form the river Irati, which, when it emerges from the forest, leaves a magnificent oak grove on either side of its course: Tristuibartea, a natural reserve with highly-developed trees, and Aritztoki, between Olaldea and Garralda, "the best white oak wood in the whole Iberian peninsula" according to the Ecological Guide of Navarre.

The small Irati reservoir, built to provide electricity, appears like a crystal island in the middle of the wood. Excursionists are familiar with the joy of covering its nine kilometres, on foot or mountain bike. At the narrow end of the reservoir there is a path along the left bank. Walking along, you have the impression of walking through a green tunnel while enjoying wonderful views over the three banks of the reservoir.

Irabia has miles and miles of walks with singularly beautiful scenery; the *Monte de La Cuestión*, one of the natural treasures of Navarre; the reserve of Lizardoia, with 20 hectares of virgin forest untouched by human hand where giant beech and spruce grow up to 40 metres high. The trees die and fall as a result of their own weight and become a 'decomposition laboratory' where moss, fungi and woodpeckers abound (particularly the white-backed variety, an ornithological jewel).

Irati was untouched for centuries thanks to its distance from population centres and the fact that its forests have only been commercially exploited in recent times. Wood and pastureland were exploited, the wood for building being floated down river as trunks, and later as rafts (*almadías*). For military reasons, from the 18th century onwards the Government allowed the Navy to cut trees free of charge. This was done selectively, and by preference used the spruce trees It became large scale at the start of the 20th century, as shown in the photographs of the Marquis of Santa María del Villar, a document of incalculable value. Squads of woodcutters used hand saws and axes, hauling the trunks with mules and oxen. Domingo Elizondo, who emigrated from the area and made his fortune in Argentina, founded the 'Irati S.A'. company in 1907. It was an innovative timber,

hydroelectric, chemical and transport group which undertook engineering projects still in use today, also pioneering distilling techniques and an electric tram linking Pamplona with Sangüesa and Aoiz.

Basoillarrak khantatzen dizu
Iratiko shoruan;
ihurk elezakezu pentsa
nik zer düdan goguan:
gauak oro igaraiten tüt
maitearen onduan.

This romantic poem, in which the love-struck young man swears he spends sleepless nights remembering his loved one, mentions the capercaillie, an emblematic bird for the protection of Nature, one which no longer has its "singing places" in the Irati forest. The most spectacular wildlife are the deer which the solitary, silent walker will easily find along any path. Birds and music join forces in a traditional song which associates the imposing mount Orhi with beautiful melodies, such as 'Orhiko txoria' or 'Belatzarena', in which the *txirula*, a short recorder-type flute, produces the effect of the majestic flight of a kite in a sequence which seems to be taken from a lectern of Gregorian melodies.

The Irati forest is a haunt of legends. Its silent solitude, interrupted by obscure crunching and unidentifiable noises, has given rise to one of the most popular

The beech likes to feel the dampness of the mist in its leaves, although it prefers to keep its surface roots dry. Moss covers it.

myths of the area, that of Basajaun, a tall figure with long hair and amazing strength. He walks proudly with a stick in his hand and is more agile than the deer. The hill walker should not try to flee when Basajaun calls, and even less confront him because that would be madness. The only way of keeping him on your side is to obey his orders without question. You thus become inoffensive and even a protector and guide to Basajaun, Lord of the Wood.

Popular imagination has created another legend in Irati, one told to the writer Madrazo at the end of the 19th century. A man was sleeping in the shade of a beech tree at sunset. He was woken by the vigorous shaking of a blast of wind which passed over him leaving a stench of death in the air. He awoke up from his slumbers and, as in a nightmare, saw a chorus of fairies in a clearing holding aloft a human skeleton in/like a shroud. The figure's skull had a sinister shining crown on top. Who was that Queen? It was Doña Juana de Albret, who died of poisoning and whose burial place is uncertain. Even in 1929 a Guide to Navarre says that "when the wild wind shakes the leaves of Irati, the fearful people hide in their

houses, because the spirits and witches run through the wood at breakneck speed, carrying a shroud which has a skeleton on whose head a regal crown sits."

Entering Irati from Aezkoa, at the deepest part of the gorge of Txangoa, where there are iron, copper, mercury, zinc, silver and lead mines exploited since Antiquity, the factory of Orbaiceta is located, the heir of a medieval forge. King Carlos III of Spain bought it in 1784 and built a large dam using the current of the Legarza river. The factory, which produced artillery shells and iron ingots, did not take its raw material from the exhausted mineral deposits of the area but from the mines of Biscay province. The factory is not far from the French border and suffered from war, looting and fire, and closed down in 1873. Having been restored, it is now an attractive example of industrial

archaeology. The original layout of buildings around the square is still maintained, presided over by a church with a neo-classical façade. Inside the factory two casting furnaces, workshops, stores and an excellent channelling of the river have been preserved among the remains of vaults and imposing walls.

In Autumn the Irati forest, like all the other beech and oak woods, forms a magnificent splash of colour.

is the sheep-fold of Azpegi, with its huts covered with *oholak*, boards cut from oak which used to be abundant on the steep roofs of the mountain houses.

The 'Urkulu' is rather obscure, both in sound and meaning. Maybe the term can be translated into Spanish as 'orgullo' (pride). The summit of the mount is crowned by a cylindrical tower (*trophaeum*), built by the Romans in the First Century BC as a tribute to their legionnaires. It reflects their influence on the area and serves as a lookout post for the path, by then part of the Pilgrim's Way to Compostela.

From this vantage point the view is spectacular, although the sight of the green pastures on either side of the mountain is relaxing. These areas have firm, strong-sounding names: Orión, Idopil, Organbidea and Soraluze. They are very ancient pastures where the shepherds have raised their flocks since Neolithic times, and where many tombs can be found: first dolmens, then cromlechs. Nearby are the grasses of Errozate which cover the slopes with an ever-changing tapestry, and at its foot the cave of Arpea, a sanctuary of pre-Christian worship.

Prehistoric traces, linked to the high-altitude pastures, are found in many Megalithic stations, more so as the Pyrenees get closer to the Cantabrian Sea. For example, the sixteen circles of Ilarrita on the platform of Okabe, on the clear heights of Abodi, near Lindux (an excellent bird observatory), on the plain of Ohiarzabal scented with hawthorns and gorse, in the peacefulness of Sorogain overlooked by the majestic mount Adi, or in the plateaux of Argintzo, from where the gentle scenery of the Baztán valley can be seen. Each dolmen, each tomb has its own name, more often than not euphonic: Arxilo, Gaztanbidea, Bortubizkarra, Mairubaratza…

On the fringe of these woods and pastures is the peak of Mount Adi, often covered by a veil of clouds. Its conical shape and bare summit, surrounded by trees on the slopes below, makes it look like one of those ideal mountains that everyone has in their mind. A path leads to the hill of Urkiaga between beech trees and larches, skirting the unclear frontier territory of the Alduides (the term comes from the Basque *Aldubide*, which means 'high path'). It is an historical name much older than that of 'Quinto Real', referring to the tribute to the Crown of one in every five pigs which grazed on the mountain.

The source of the 'most Navarrese' of all rivers, the Arga lies in a sheltered corner near Urkiaga. If flows down a shadowy slope and on the way moistens heather, cranberries, and *L. Campestris* as far as

From Urkulu to Quinto Real

Ascending the gorge of Txangoa from the factory at Orbaiceta, you reach a magical scene, a landscape at the mercy of the *zeharaize*, the twisting north-west wind, a landscape unchanged for thousands of years.

To the right is the Natural Reserve of Mendilaz, a magnificent example of Pyrenean mountain beechwood on an abrupt, rocky limestone terrain with poor, discontinuous soil. The broken relief of wide depressions and deep chasms makes it difficult to gain access to this protected area where the wood, with trees over 100 feet high, is home to beautiful wildlife. It has not been exploited at all in the last few decades, and seems to have been exploited very little in previous years.

The path splits into two around mount Urkulu. Near the fork

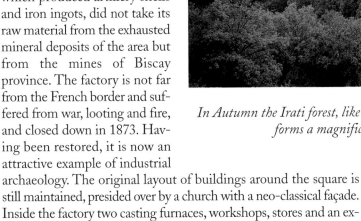

[PREVIOUS DOUBLE PAGE] *A beech forest in winter. The bare trees reveal a landscape that the snow turns into a shining mirror.*
[OPPOSITE] *Ochagavía is the gateway to the largest forest in the Pyrenees. Meadows and trees stand alongside each other near the village.*

The old factory at Orbaiceta and its foundry made use of the current of the river Legarza. Following restoration work it is now an attractive example of industrial architecture.

Olaberri, where the Royal Factory of Iron Munitions was located. The river is then dammed by the reservoir at Eugui to ensure the water supply to Pamplona and its surrounding area. The lake makes the Pyrenean mountain pass even more beautiful, it is a sun-kissed golden pond. Its clear waters reflect the blue sky and the green of its banks. Before sunset its surface looks like a silver sheet shining in the twilight and on windy nights the sun glistens on its rippled surface. The lake's marshy flora and its wildlife make this engineered space a natural one, and some pairs of ducks breed in the mud. At the water's edge you can see alders and hazel-nut trees, and alongside the large country houses there are ash-trees with straight branches and rough-barked, hundred-year-old chestnut trees . The ubiquitous beech opens up ferns in the clearings and small pastures dotted with the white spots of the *latxa* sheep. Mounts Erregerena and Legua Acotada are close by, and join up to the Quinto Real range.

LA BAJA NAVARRA (LOWER NAVARRE, IN FRANCE)

The Pyrenees join as much as they separate. On either side of the range ways of life and culture survive despite the fact that rivalries, violence and conflict lasted for centuries, especially over pasture rights. These were not settled until an artificial border was drawn in 1856, a border which has lost its significance with the disappearance of Customs posts.

There are people and territories which say they are Navarrese on both sides of the range. From Medieval times until the Modern Age they were united under a single kingdom and they remain linked today, now by economic and social ties, but particularly by sharing the same language.

The Navarre to the north of the Pyrenees (*Ultrapuertos*) is called *Baxenafarroa* by the locals, which most people interpret as a 'low' geographical area, as opposed to the 'high' Navarre of the Iberian peninsula. Some people also translate it as "the Navarre where there are plenty of woods." After a steep drop from the summits, the slopes become gentler and the plunging, narrow rivers flow into a pleasant profile of rolling hills. A damp, temperate climate determines the livestock-raising nature of the area, with scattered *caseríos* (farmhouses) and small villages, where the *frontón* (Basque ball game court)

and the church are always at their heart. Religious wars destroyed a good part of their heritage, although there are beautiful country churches like the Romanesque one at Bidarrai. The church at Baigorri has a triple interior gallery and oak-carved balustrades.

The administrative and political organisation of the "tierras d'aillent puertos" (lands beyond the mountain passes) partly coincided with that of the rest of Navarre. There were territorial trends and a variety of similar municipal boundaries, and the Albret kings transferred the model of the Pamplona court to Donapaleu. Baja Navarre, however, was never a *merindad* (administrative area in Navarre), rather a federation of baronies, towns and cities, and nine "lands": Amikuze, Arberoa, Armendaritz, Baigorri, Garazi, Iholdi, Irisarri, Ostibarre and Orzaize. The capital was, and still is, the delightful town of San Juan de Pie de Puerto (St. John at the Foot of the Pass — 'Donibane Garazi' in Basque), which still conserves its Citadel, a Gothic church and an ancient street with stone houses from the 16th and 17th centuries.

Garazi (or 'Cize') is the canton which has the privilege of being the birthplace of Basque literature. The rector of the hamlet of Eiheralarre, Bernart de Etxepare, was the author of the first book in *Euskara* (Basque): *Linguae Vasconum Primitiae* in 1554, a collection of religious, erotic poems and others praising the Basque language:

> *Garaziko herria*
> *benedika dadila.*
> *Heuskarari eman dio*
> *behar duien tornuia*

This literary culture of the Basque language, a living language in the area, has continued to the present day in Baja Navarra, through the voice of a popular *bertsolari* (a 'story-telling through song' poet) 'Xalbador'. Folk songs and colourful folklore, which have their high point in Mardi Gras and in summer, brighten up the life of a land which has suffered a high level of emigration in the last two centuries, but one which shows its will to live by renewing its tourism and modernising its economy through the creation of co-operatives.

In his *Historia de los heterodoxos españoles* Menéndez y Pelayo calls Navarre "classic witchcraft territory", and the Renaissance traveller, Cristóbal de Villalón, writes in his notes: "the moment we entered Navarre I was warned that the women of that land were enchanting sorceresses who had made pacts and established communication with the devil..." We shall journey through a bewitched land on the border between fantasy and reality, first visiting an *Akelarre* (witches' cave) and meadow, and then a palace in the forest, the Señorío de Bértiz.

ZUGARRAMURDI
Akelarre and Witches' Caves

In the northern Pyrenees, catching a glimpse of the Cantabrian Sea and holding out a hand to coastal Laburdi (part of the French Basque Country), lie the villages of Urdax and Zugarramurdi, with their typical white farmhouses (*casonas*) among the evergreen meadows. These are villages of farming and tourism. The advent of the European Union has blurred even more an administrative frontier that years ago was a notorious area for contraband.

The name Urdax goes hand in hand with the 'Premonstratense' (from Prémontre in France) Monastery of San Salvador, which started life in the Xth century as a hospital run by Augustine canons and was a halt for pilgrims making their way to Santiago de Compostela. The Abbott was a member of the Cortes (Parliament) of Navarre, and the monastery's economy was linked to the activity of the blacksmiths. The canal that drove the old forge's hammer flows in front of the façade. The old abbey church is now the Parish Church, and houses now occupy the XVIIth-century red stone cloister built by the stonemason Martín de Zubieta; paradoxes of time in a municipality that only belatedly managed to free itself from monastic suzerainty. The canons called the serfs of Urdax *bordeantes* (outsiders) instead of local residents, and not only did the Abbots issue and carry out censures and excommunications, but it was also necessary to obtain their authorisation to marry.

There are two important prehistoric sites here: the Alkerdi cave, with its non-figurative cave paintings, and the cave at Berroberría where there is abundant evidence of human habitation, and which was relatively continuous from the Magdalenian period (12,500 BC) until the end of pre-history. The cave at Ikaburu is a great tourist attraction, and is the mythological home of the *lamias,* mythical characters that were half-woman and half-fish. Stalactites and stalagmites, grey with lime and shiny with magnesium, are to be found along the galleries where the waters of the River Urtxuma sing. The long roots of the oak trees overhead hang from the roof of the hollow like reddish-coloured cables.

The *caserío* (Basque farmhouse and its outbuildings) of Axular is very near Ikaburu. The greatest classical writer in the Basque language, Pedro de Aguerre, was born here and also took it as his nom de plume. He was the Parish Priest in the neighbouring village, Sara, and he wrote only one book, *Gero*, dated 1643, with an ascetic theme in which he demonstrates an admirable knowledge of both Greco-Latin tradition and the Natural Sciences. It is written in clear concise prose defending Basque as an ancient language, but nevertheless one that is suited to the culture: "It seems as if the Basque language is currently ashamed, that it is strange, that it neither dares show itself in public nor is it capable, great or adequate. This is because some of its speakers still do not know how to read or write. If as many books had been written in Basque as in Latin, French or other foreign languages, Basque would also be as rich and as perfect as they, and if this is not the case, the Basques themselves are to blame, not the language. Basque is different from other lan-

guages, but it does not follow that it is inferior in quality. On the contrary, it appears that other common languages have been mixed together, whilst Basque has maintained its original pure state."

Through the oral tradition of the area, folklore has linked the name *Axular* with witchcraft and the occult. He is the 'man who lost his shadow'. He went to Salamanca to study witchcraft at the school of the Devil. When the Devil asked him to pay the price of the class, this being his soul, a new day was dawning. Having quick reflexes, Axular started to run, but he wasn't quite fast enough: Satan, red with anger, had to conform with being left holding the heel of the priest's shoe and his soul in his fingers. The cunning and superiority of human ingenuity had outstripped the sophisms of Evil. Jaun Benat, the legendary rector of Bera, or the historical sorcerer Joanes de Bargote both personify this same figure of priest-wizard in the area's folklore.

The ethnographer José María Satrústegui has collected local variants and stories relating to the same legend. In Baztán it is told that Axular only recovered his soul on celebrating mass, and more precisely at the moment of the consecration on raising the chalice, the culminating moment when the Satanic force that gave him no respite was overcome.

In the River Bidasoa area, the priest-sorcerer is the Parish Priest of Bera, Jaun Benat, who flew to Rome on a cloud steered by the Devil. In payment for the journey, the Devil required an invitation to dinner. For fear that he would poison the meal, the priest asked his mother to serve only walnuts and nothing more. The time set for the dinner arrived, and so did the Devil, on time. Jaun Benat told him to sit under the table. Showing him the walnut, he cracked it, ate the nut and threw the shell to the Devil. "A dry dinner is this", said the horned one with the long tail, to which Jaun Benat retorted, "It is what I eat."

Agapito Martínez Alegría gathered the oral tradition related to the 'Brujo de Bargota' (Sorcerer of Bargota) in the Valley of Codés, who rode his horse through the clouds, appeared with snow on his hat in the middle of the summer, and who could camouflage himself from indiscreet eyes by wrapping himself in mysterious clothing which made him invisible. Sometimes a hand with six or seven fingers would emerge from under his cloak. One day, at the market in Viana, a vendor of earthenware cooking pots made fun of his clothes. He shook his cloak violently and a flock of partridges flew out. A group of weeders were making their way through the market place carrying their hoes over their shoulders. They threw themselves on the partridges and after many frantic blows with their hoes not a cooking pot was left intact.

The figure of the Wizard, in Basque *itxixo* (*sorgiña* in the feminine form) was born in the imagination of the people as the personification of the occult dressed in the robes of a priest, representing the duel between good and evil. He is a man who is initiated in witchcraft and who has the power to fight the Devil. Lucifer pursues his soul, but in vain. He will be saved and go to heaven.

Zugarramurdi originated as a group of *caseros* (tenant farmers) dependent on the Monasterio de Urdax. Near the centre of the vil-

[PREVIOUS PAGE] *The river Olabidea has carved a majestic tunnel in the rock with high galleries. One of these is called Sorginleze (the witches' cave).*

lage are the caves and the Berroskoberro meadow, the famous 'Akelarre', the field of goats that gave its name to the 'sabats', or meetings of the witches and wizards. The area is one of remarkable beauty: the Olabidea brook (Infernuko Erreka) has dug out a magnificent natural tunnel 120 long and 12 metres high, and two elevated galleries. One of them is *Sorginleze*, the witches' cave.

In the year 1610, through the 'Auto de Fe de Logroño', the Spanish Inquisition tried 31 people from Baztán, Urdax and Zugarramurdi, two of them women in their eighties. Only a few of them were saved after confessing their guilt and pleading for mercy with tears in their eyes. Thirteen died, unable to survive the hardships they suffered in prison. On 7th December, six of them were burned alive, and then five more at the stake before some thirty thousand spectators gathered in the Town Hall square. They had confessed to, or were accused of, being possessed by the Devil, celebrating Black Mass, provoking storms in the Bay of Biscay to endanger the ships that sailed to St. Jean de Luz, casting spells on the fields and animals, practising vampirism and eating corpses.

On re-reading the declarations of the accused at the trials and other XVIth and XVIIth century documentation, Fernando Videgáin reconstructed the ritual of an 'akelarre' (sabat).

The meeting was preferably held on the eve of a major Christian festival or on a Friday "because it is a greater revilement and insult to Our Lord Jesus Christ due to their joy that Judas betrayed him for 30 denarii, and on that day he was crucified and killed."

Before leaving home, the participants anointed their left foot, knee, chest and cheek with a greenish-black, foul-smelling ointment made from the brains and bones of corpses boiled up with deadly-nightshade or "with skinned dead toads burned on the embers and the hearts of children all mixed together." Some flew over the chimneys on their broomsticks, others preferred to walk, accompanied by toads. They arranged to meet at a road junction, and having changed into different animals, all flew together from there.

When they arrived at the meadow or the cave, the Devil's seat of honour was set in pride of place. The Devil appeared as a person or as a billy-goat "and has a terrifying voice... and when he talks he sounds like a mule... and his face is melancholic, and he always looks angry."

Some days there was a reception of novices who renounced God and their faith. The Devil marked the new arrival on the shoulder

Mountain streams cut through the slopes and then continue their flow through lively, fresh and clear water courses.

with his fingernail, and then with the sign of the toad in the left eye. Later the Black Mass was celebrated with a hard black host like the sole of a shoe, and instead of the *pax*, Lucifer allowed his genitals to be kissed whilst breaking wind "with a very horrible smell." A banquet followed, in which "they exhumed the bodies of deceased witches and creatures and ate them roasted, boiled or raw." The most appetising part was the heart and that was reserved for the Devil. A minority found a morsel of the dead to be tasty and exquisite, the meat of men being better than that of women. But the majority confessed that the corpse made their stomach turn until they vomited.

After this ceremony, they danced around the fire and indulged in a sexual orgy started by the Devil and continued by all. In Zugarramurdi the most popular woman with the Devil was Estefanía de Iriarte, whom Satan "lay on the floor face down or put against a tree and there used her body, her own husband beating the rhythm on his drum. The queen of the *akelarre* was Graciana de Barrenechea, in charge of deciding who should unite with the Devil and when. According to María de Goizueta, the contacts were made "in the usual parts and those behind, and when from the front, the same pleasure could be felt as if he were a man, despite some pain due to his large hard member, and when from behind there was more pain than pleasure." When the cock crowed at dawn the *akelarre* broke up and the spells ended.

These stories and testimonies, and the tragic fortunes of the dozens of people who were slandered, imprisoned, tortured, condemned without proof and exterminated, seem barbaric to us in the present day. As Julio Caro Baroja writes: "When a man confesses that he has seen a witch fly with his own eyes, all that he says should be taken with a pinch of salt. But the trouble is that declarations of this type are repeated over and over again, both in the writings of the time as well as in those that followed." They were dark, irrational times, even for cultured people who should have kept a cooler head. Some sentences were based on the testimonies of nine and ten-year-old children or on the ill will and unbalanced and lying imagination of certain witnesses. The victims of the accusations were people of low social status, usually ignorant, illiterate peasants who became mentally unbalanced through fear even before falling into the hands of the law, and even more so when tortured. The Basque language used by both the witnesses and defendants was not known to the majority of the judges who had to rely on incompetent interpreters. The periods of mortality caused

by epidemics and the years of bad harvests were unjustly attributed to propitiatory victims. Not all the judges were credulous or unjust, and in general the ecclesiastical judges of Navarre were more reasonable than their civil counterparts.

Two books of opposing disposition determined the attitude of the judges. *Malleus maleficarum*, published in 1487 by Kraemer and Spranger, which put forward credulity and the hard line, was opposed by the influential work of Martín de Arles de Andosilla from Peralta, who in his treatise *De Superstitionibus*, written in 1510, underlined the sceptical and moderate attitude of the most enlightened.

The historian Florencio Idoate and the anthropologist Caro Baroja have provided an interesting 'local' perspective on the subject of witchcraft, an activity that affects all villages some time or other. The Basque word *sorgiña,* meaning witch, is related to *sortiarium* in Latin. In the same way as in other rural communities in Europe, what is commonly called witchcraft has held great importance in this land. The mountainous regions are the classic witchcraft zones of Navarre; maps show this clearly. The phenomenon is feminine; there are more witches than wizards. In rural society there were many women, above all old women, who were considered to be witch doctors or sorceresses. Among Basque speakers, the idea that the woman who mixed potions, made ligatures to prevent reproduction or provoked storms was of enormous importance at the end of the Middle Ages, and she is found to be involved in the feuds of different factions and families.

So what lay behind the legend of the Akelarres? Without doubt the survival of pagan practices, the desire to escape from the considerable hardships of everyday life, and a yearning for fun and enjoyment. But those peasants did not hold Black Masses, nor did they scorn the Church.

The folkloric figure of the witch has existed throughout time: a young blonde woman who rides her horse at a gallop from her farmhouse at midnight. Alternatively, she is an old woman who changes into a cat and comes down the chimney. She may be the *sorgiña,* who is able to cast the evil eye, *begizko,* put a spell on a mattress, predict the future or move the south wind, *haize egoa.* People still hang a thistle flower on their front door to safeguard them from the witches. They drive them away in the same way: the sign of the cross, the north wind, daylight or laurel leaves.

A PALACE IN THE FOREST: SEÑORÍO DE BÉRTIZ

Bértiz is often written 'Vertiz'. The form of the valley, very long and narrow stretching towards the pass or watershed, has meant that it is believed to be an ancient *vertex.*

The Baztán river, which changes its name to 'Bidasoa' on leaving Bertizarana, bathes the southern edge of the Señorío de Bértiz, a nature reserve of some 2,040 hectares that offers many attractions: dense luxuriant woodland, palatial architecture and a botanical garden that is worth visiting at any time of the year. Seen from the nearby hills, where the gentle landscape of meadows and fern-covered ground is evidence of extensive human intervention, Bértiz appears to be just what is, a *Señorío* (noble manor) surrounded by woodland. As if to cap this image, the last owner finished it off with a whim, building a modernist palace on top of the prominent, almost conical Aizkolegi peak. The palace was an exquisite gift for his wife and a magnificent observatory looking out over a wood of beech, oak and chestnut trees. On clear days the Bay of Biscay can be seen from the terraces.

Records on the nobility dating back to the XIVth century, included Pedro Miguel Bértiz, named Merino de las Montañas in 1398, as well as the squire Micheto de Bértiz, to whom King Carlos III ('el Noble') awarded the shield, still on display in the valley, for his brilliant diplomatic work. It shows a mermaid emerging from the sea with a mirror in one hand and a comb in the other. The wood was the scene of hunts and falconry, and it is known that in 1637 there were two houses on the estate.

During the first half of the XXth century, the *Señorío* belonged to Pedro Ciga y Mayo, a lawyer with a vast fortune from his marriage to Dorotea Fernández Morales and his business activities in the Rif. Ciga bought Bértiz in 1899 for a sum of 650,000 pesetas in gold. Ciga was a conservationist who understood how to improve and update its natural heritage. During the first few years of his occupation, he exploited the estate rationally until he had written off a large part of his investment. Subsequently, he gradually reduced felling and thus increased the number of trees in the wood, at the same time as creating an interesting garden at the entrance to the manor. According to the biologist Natxo Esquisábel, "many different species of trees and flowers were selected by Ciga himself, who sought the most outstanding stock in several different countries with the result that his gardens and plants were the source of great pride… One day, some nuns went to ask him for some flowers to decorate the church. Ciga replied that not one single flower was to be cut in the gardens and gave them a thousand pesetas to buy all the flowers they needed."

Ciga was named Honorary President of the animal and plant protection societies that existed in Navarre at the beginning of the century, for whom he acted like a generous Maecenas. The Ciga family used Bértiz as a residence only during the summer, and they spent two weeks in the Aizkolegi palace in July. On his death in 1949, Pedro Ciga bequeathed his estate to the Diputación Foral de Navarre (the regional Administration) on the condition that it be conserved in the same state. On 28th March 1984, it was declared a *Parque Natural* (nature reserve) for the enjoyment of people for educational, research and recreational purposes.

The warm, damp climate of the area explains the lush vegetation and the acclimatisation of exotic species, of which more than 120 can be seen in the botanical garden. This garden also has an ornamental pool with artificial waterfalls and little rustic bridges. Among the trees there is a spruce, a cedar from Libya, a ginkgo with fan-shaped leaves which is considered a living plant fossil, a redwood tree, white poplars, Lawson cypresses, yews, the great Araucaria or monkey-puzzle tree from the Land of Fire, the bare cypress a relic of the Tertiary age, the Japanese *sugi* and *hiba,* the *ocozol* from which the Mexicans obtain liquid amber (a balsamic resin) and also the famous varnish tree, Spanish firs and tulip trees. There are also some outstanding shrubs: the Chinese camellias —green and black tea for infusions are obtained from their button-like flowers, the *cefalotejo*, the small *cicas* palm, a species native to from Java, thorny lemon trees, *osmantos*, rhododendrons and azaleas. But the great surprise in the garden is the miniature bamboo jungle, with its amazingly thick canes. At the back of the palace there are some curious examples of *lagerstroemia*, and there is a pool with a fountain and white lilies floating on it on the open esplanade that runs along the façade. A path leads along past a modernist chapel with delicate glasswork and large flowerpots containing plants of botanical interest, and then towards a Belle Époque balcony overlooking the river.

Every year the 'Baztandarren Biltzarra' festival brings the 15 villages of the Baztán valley together.

wild in the Bertizarana valley (*Catálogo de las plantas que espontáneamente crecen en el valle de Vertizarana*"), compiled a herbarium in which he classified 2,500 botanical specimens. He made notable findings: he found mosses that had never been seen before, and discovered that one Alpine plant and another from North America, which were thought to be different, were in fact exactly the same species. He also published a dictionary of Basque plant names (*Diccionario de los nombres euskaros de las plantas*) of great ethnographic and philological interest. In 1877 he was made a member of the French Botanical Society, and in 1879 he entered the Sociedad Linneana de Madrid where he was considered to be the most eminent cryptogram expert in the north of Spain.

Pío Baroja based a character in his novel, *El caballero de Erlaiz,* on this learned figure. The biographer and scholar of his work, Eduardo Gil Bera states that his neighbours considered the scientist to be eccentric, even mad. "They believed him to be perturbed... He went out to gather plants in all weathers, always carrying his brass box, iron walking stick, adze, hammer and chisel. They saw him collect rough stones and weeds, search deep into the crags of the rocks, climb to places where nobody ever went and hack off a piece of rock covered in lichen with his hammer and chisel to take it away as if it were a treasure... in short, he could not be right in the head."

Lacoizqueta was ahead of his time: he accurately indicated the location of the marble deposits in the area, which were only exploited many years after his death; he made interesting recommendations regarding agricultural crops and forecast future public works: a railway route that he did not know about and the opening of a long tunnel in the Velate Pass, a deep-cut natural obstacle, which was only built a hundred years later.

More than 90 per cent of the surface area of the Señorío de Bértiz is populated by trees. It represents an exceptional reserve of Cantabrian beech and oak groves. The majority of the wood is made up of beech trees with straight trunks, but there are also splendid oaks, holly trees and a fringe of chestnuts. Near Aizkolegi there are areas that have been replanted with larches.

Whilst the discreet walker may spot roe deer, foxes and squirrels, the tracks of wild boar, martens and rodents, or the movements and eggs of the amphibians and reptiles, the real wealth lies in the birdlife: 50 different species of bird have been located here, 37 of which also nest in the wood.

A dozen mountain streams wind their way through the slopes towards the valley. Some of them bear euphonic names, reminding us of fauna that has now disappeared: *Artzaiturri* the bear and *Otsobidea* the wolf. The three largest, which flow throughout the year, contain eels, salmon, loach, miller's thumb, gudgeon, *chipa* and trout, all typical species found in oxygenated, clean spring-water.

LACOIZQUETA, THE BOTANIST FROM BERTIZARANA

In the beautiful area of Bertizarana, it is fitting to remember the wise self-taught botanist, José María de Lacoizqueta, who was born in the neighbouring village of Narbarte. He became a forerunner and pioneer in the complex field of cryptogram taxonomy during the second half of the XIXth century. The house where he was born, *Lakoizketa,* (cider press house) was reputed to be the best farmhouse on the road from Bayonne to Pamplona.

Lacoizqueta, the author of the catalogue of plants that grow

THE BAZTÁN VALLEY

Baztán is the largest municipality in Navarre with an area of 374 square kilometres, 82 per cent of which is common land. The valley has fifteen villages and is dotted with numerous residential areas and *caseríos* which give rise to a network of more than four hundred kilometres of roads. Baztán is organised under the 'Régime of Universality', the oldest system of local government in Navarre, and "the whole valley is like one town hall, one town council, the same as one household." From an administrative point of view, it is divided into four districts: Basaburua, Baztangoiza, Elizondo y

Stone walls and fences break up properties and the always-green landscape at Arriaotz.

Erberea, and is governed by the Area Council and the General Council.

The people of Baztán declared their freedom from the nobility comparatively early on, and a document drawn up in 1440 confirms its collective sovereignty. This civil state had several important consequences: it strengthened territorial organisation, contributed towards demographic balance by preventing more inhabitants coming into a valley with limited resources, and made it possible for some of the people of Baztán to make their fortune at Court in Madrid and on the New Continent. But Baztán was not an egalitarian society: there were *vecinos* (inhabitants), but there were also *moradores* (residents) who had no political or personal rights to the use of common land, and there was also an excluded group, the *Agotes*, who were probably the descendants of leprous Aryan Visigoths from France. The reason why the coat of arms, a chessboard chequered in black and white, adorns a very great number of houses is explained by this collective sovereignty "as proof that the valley's bravery saw war as a game and that it would defend the King to the death", as Juan de Goyeneche wrote in 1685. Some people believe that the armorial was given to the people of Baztán by Sancho VII el Fuerte, and in the Town Hall in Elizondo there is a standard which it is assured dates back to the battle of the Navas de Tolosa. In Amaiur, where there was once a castle, there is now a monument in memory of the last defenders of the Kingdom of Navarre's independence: they surrendered, exhausted and starving, on 19th July 1522.

Baztán's landscape is a mosaic of pastures and stonewalled fields framed by mountains and soft peaks; gentle slopes where the *metas* (haystacks), ferns, huts and hermitages contrast with the big rambling stone farmhouses in the hamlets with their flowers and trained vines on the façades and small kitchen gardens. A few medieval 'tower-houses' that belonged to the titled families still remain, and the huge eighteenth-century palaces built by 'Indianos' (emigrants who made their fortune in America) take one by surprise.

Baztán also holds surprises for ramblers: the beautiful hidden waterfall, *Xorroxin* in Gorostapolo de Erratzu; the prehistoric sites in which 60 dolmens have been catalogued; the nature reserves of *Itxusi* with its large colony of tawny vultures, and *Irubetakaskoa* with a unique alder grove on the hillside. The gastronomic delights of the valley include *txuri ta beltz*, a stew of lamb intestines, and the *Baztan zopak*, both traditional fare on the eve of the festivities of the patron saint.

Baztán is like a cathedral of our folklore. The musicologist Padre Donostia collected hundreds of traditional songs in the valley, among them the Christmas carol, *Belenen sortu zaigu*. The repertory of dances is also extensive: the *mutil-datza,* danced in a ring in an anti-clockwise direction to fifteen different tunes, and the *sagardantza,* danced in carnivalesque costume with the dancers holding apples. Once a year, the *Baztandarren Biltzarra* festival brings the 15 villages together in Elizondo, each one represented by a float. Baztán has its own highly estimated variation of the game of Pelota called *laxoa,* which is played wearing a leather glove.

H ere there is a land whose waters flow out into the Bay of Biscay, a damp land that has preserved some vestiges of prehistoric and protohistoric civilisations. In contrast, hardly any evidence of Romanisation remains, and there is practically no recognisable trace of the Arabs. Christianity arrived late. Only with the arrival of the Gothic period did the region begin to take on any historical personality. It is essentially Basque. It is a land with an abundance of apples, cider and milk. Its old foundries, which consumed vast quantities of timber, cleared the woods of trees", wrote the ethnographer, Julio Caro Baroja, in his celebrated house at Itzea, alongside the river Bidasoa.

BORTZIRIAK
The five mountain villages

In the north-eastern corner, near the Bay of Biscay, there is an ancient geological area, that of 'Las Cinco Villas' (*villa* is the name given to a large village), which is no less than four hundred million years old. It is one of the oldest patches on Navarre's corrugated skin. When it was formed in the Palaeozoic era, it was an islet that emerged from the Tetis Sea where sediment had gradually accumulated, and on rising and folding at the beginning of the Tertiary age, sixty-five million years ago, the Pyrenees were born.

In a landscape with its green carpet of vegetation, the naked crag of the *Peñas de Aya*, the only granite outcrop in Navarre, stands out to the west. It is a 'batholith', the name given to a large granite mass. In memory of Pluto (Hades), the Greek God of the Underworld, it is said that granite is a plutonic rock of deep origin. The granite of the magnificent Peñas de Aya cliffs, formed at a temperature of around 600 degrees, is surrounded by a ring of slate and seams of different minerals, all of which have been exploited since olden times. On the slopes of the province of Gipuzkoa, at the foot of the Peña, the Romans discovered the Arditurri mines, which had previously been worked by the local people. The historian Jimeno Jurío tells us that "the Romans extracted the minerals for more than two hundred years. The work was astounding. Enormous quantities of lead and silver were extracted from an area of between fifteen and seventeen kilometres, to be transported to Rome via ports on the Bay of Biscay." Manuel Laborde relates the name 'Peñas de Aya' to the presence of iron deposits, because there are also mines of this metal in other Basque places with the names *Aya, Ayala, Araya o Ayabarrena*, and because very near to the Peñas, in the Aguiña pass, there is a 'cromlech', an Iron Age funeral circle. The Sanskrit word, *ayas* or overwhelming, describes it well.

The biologist Javier Peralta made a study of the area around the Peñas de Aya, which is of particular botanical interest as a result of the soil and its immediate proximity to the sea. "The climate is typical oceanic with heavy rainfall that can exceed 2,300 mm a year. In accordance with the climate, the vegetation is Atlantic. A large proportion of the area is moorland, and small springs emerge from its interior. A yellowish-green moss called 'esfagno', typical of peat bogs, lies around the stems of the heather and furze. The fact that

A reaper sharpens his scythe in the traditional fashion. Mountain meadows and fern-covered hillsides are common here.

the ground is always wet impedes any dead vegetation from decomposing, resulting in a jet-black organic soil in the peat bogs. The cracks in the rocks provide refuge for *petrocoptis pyrenaica*, which, with its white flower and green leaves, decorate the crag in the spring."

Following the line of the border with France, at the most northerly point of Navarre, the reddish crest of the Larrún Mountain rises, formed from conglomerate and sandstone. To its right we find Ibantelli, on the northern slope of which lies the protected area of Labiaga, which covers a relatively small area of a little more than one hectare but is nevertheless of great geological interest. The reserve was created to protect the black slate deposits and the fossil flora of the Carboniferous period. It is three hundred and fifty million years old. In the past, these carbon deposits were mined on a small scale.

THE FOUNDRIES

The Iron and Steel industry, which was developed early on and widely done throughout the north of Navarre, occupies a privileged position in the Cinco Villas. Here the Iron Age commenced around the year 600 BC. Evidence of the mines and foundries remains, and some legends talk of the *jentillak*, primitive pagan settlers who worked the metal in the mountains.

From the XIIth century on, there is much documentation on the subject. The foundries (*olak*) were workshops where iron oxide was mixed with charcoal to convert it into free metal. They did not blend the metal, but reduced the oxide and cast the slag. The ironmasters (*olagizonak*) set up their trade in the mountains near a small iron mine at the entrance to a wood in order to collect timber to make into charcoal. These did not last long; when the mineral or charcoal sources became scarce the equipment was moved to another spot. In this way, immense quantities of wood were consumed. The deforestation of the area dates back to the Middle Ages.

In the middle of the XVth century, the foundries descended from the mountains to the banks of the rivers. The waterwheel became the driving force behind all industrial activity, as Vidal Pérez de Villarreal describes: "A waterwheel worked the ironmaster's hammer which beat the spongy iron from the furnace to remove the unreduced slag or oxide and concentrate the lumps into a compact mass called *agoe*. The foundries, situated on the rivers, used the hydraulic power to move the ram onto the anvil and to operate the blowers. The furnace was the centre of it all; from this came the forged prod-

[PREVIOUS PAGE] *In the centre of the Old Part of Lesaka stands the triangular-shaped main square, presided over by the Town Hall. The tower of the Zabaleta family can be seen behind.*

ucts, and the art and skill of the ironmasters was clear to see."

The ironmaster, dressed in an ankle-length tunic and wearing a special scarf on his head, was both feared and respected. On occasion, he was seen as a magician, most probably because he manipulated three powerful elements: fire, air and water. The work in the forges was hard, with a ten or twelve-hour working day for only eight to ten months of the year, when the water supply was guaranteed. However, the ironmasters had more money than the farmers did. There would only be four workers at each forge, but other jobs were created around it: mining the minerals, cutting firewood, preparing the charcoal and transporting the different products on mules or ox carts, or by river on barges. Almost all the foundries in Navarre belonged to the town halls and were put up for tender every four years. The tenant committed himself to employing people from the village and exploiting the communal woods in a rational manner. Intervention by the Kings in the work of the foundries was constant due to the direct profits they gained from them and on account of the implications of iron and steel products as far as war and external trade were concerned.

The foundries of Navarre reached their high point in the XVIth and XVIIth centuries, as a result of new ventures in America. At the end of the XVIIIth century, interest in these establishments was revived due to the war, and thirty still remained. In 1847, the remaining nineteen foundries produced 12,329 metric quintals (1 quintal = 100 kg) of soft iron. The largest number of foundries was always found in the small towns of Bera y Lesaka, where the highest output was obtained, and where the iron and steel tradition still continues today with a casting and rolling industry. In the XVth century, there were up to eight forges in Bera. The ruins of the Berrizáun forge are still to be seen in Igantzi, and in Etxalar the ivy-covered walls, arches and furnaces remain. The home of the *olajaun* forge owner, the Araníbar *caserío* (Basque farmhouse), of ashlar construction, can be seen in Arantza.

The ironmasters have been associated with art and music throughout European history because their work, accompanied by the soft sound of flowing water and the rhythm of the hammers in the background, forms a well-defined melody, although without words. The folklorist Padre Donostia published an ironmasters' tune in his *Cancionero Vasco* that was sung when the workers changed shifts. In Lesaka, a percussion instrument has been preserved, called *tobera* (nozzle) like the tube of the foundry bellows, or *palanka* like the steel bar used to play it. The rhythmic peal starts *piano* and *moderatto*, increasing in speed in a crescendo until the end, which is announced by two beats with the drumstick. The metallic sound of the *tobera* is usually accompanied by verses in Basque to serenade

The Bidasoa flows gently under the bridge at Sunbilla.

the bride and bridegroom or married couples who are on bad terms, or sung when newly-made cider is first tasted.

BIDASOA SALMON

The river Bidasoa, into which the waters from the streams and brooks of the Cinco Villas flows, is unique. It is 69 kilometres long. At its headwaters it is called the Baztán, after the valley in which it rises, and it keeps this name through the Bertizarana valley until it converges with the river Ezcurra at the Arrizurraga gorge, where (now adolescent) it decides to change its name. This capricious river permits itself even more fancies: it forms the border with France from Endarlaza on leaving Navarre, and near its mouth it houses the Island of the Pheasants, *La Isla de los Faisanes*, which is Spanish for half the year and French for the other half.

The river has inspired artists. Many studies have been made of the 'Escuela de Paisajistas del Bidasoa' (Bidasoa School of landscape artists), impressionists who are interested in capturing "this light that is not to be seen in any other place, this light that caresses and envelops the contours of all things in a sleepy gentleness", according to José de Arteche. Javier Zubiaur, who has come across painters along the entire course of the river, assures us that what unites them is the Bidasoa itself and not the way of painting it. He adds: "The natural attraction is bestowed by the river and its innumerable tributaries; the whitewashed farms scattered over the mountainside; the variety of tones and shades of the woodland on the heights; the diversity of crops on the lowlands; the footpaths, bridges and canals near the villages; and its hamlets, with their clean tidy houses huddled together around the church as if defending their privacy."

But there is also the Bidasoa of writers. Pierre Loti, commanding officer of the Coastguards, made it the scene of this novel, *Ramuntxo*: "The water of the Bidasoa is like a still, flat mirror, more luminous than the sky, and reflects and inverts the constellations. The clear sweet night in this little corner of the world where the smugglers go silently about their work..."

In *La Leyenda de Jaun de Alzate*, Pío Baroja's desire was to sing the praise of the area in its primitive, natural state, and he converted the Bidasoa into a character: "I am a small but charming river, more famous than many big rivers. Strabon, Ptolemy and Pliny have all spoken of me. Within me lies some of the severity of Navarre, some of the softness of Gipuzkoa and a little of the grace of France. I gather the songs of my streams. I have miraculous sources. I pass through wide sunny valleys and narrow ravines. I reflect the green mountainsides, the noble houses and *chozas* (shacks) on my banks. In the winter I bellow like a bull and rush in furious foamy waves;

The reddish summit of Mount Larraun rises above the scattered caseríos (farmhouses) near Bera.

in summer I have calm green pools. At nightfall my surface turns blue and thousands of stars sleep in my depths."

As a result of its anarchical temperament, Baroja assures us, with acid humour, that the Bidasoa "will one day form an independent Republic: no flies, no monks, no Customs officers." But before saying this, he shows the following sentiment in the prologue of *Jaun de Alzate*, "It is true that our corner of the Bidasoa does not possess a brilliant culture or a splendid history: there are no great mountains or valleys or magnificent cities; but not for this do the nightingales stop singing in the branches of the trees on a summer's night,

nor do the larks in the meadows on sunny mornings. For us, the devotees of this land, the realm of the Bidasoa is a gentle, sweet, well-known song, always old and always new. This fickle, changeable climate is in harmony with the tone of our spirit; its versatility gratifies and distracts, and we far prefer it to the pompous immobility of other lands and other climates."

The Bidasoa gave its name to a narrow-gauge railway, which originated as a mining train, and prolonged its life another half century transporting passengers and goods. The last journey was made on 31st December 1956. After being reconditioned, the old track has become one of the most attractive tourist routes in Navarre and illustrates the traditional economy of the zone: pastures, fields of maize and vegetables, chestnut groves and apple orchards. It is a journey through an authentic botanical garden, with dozens

of species of trees, rich alder groves, and even a dense wood of bamboo, while a carpet of grass covers the old stony surface of the railway track. The origins of the old train in the mining industry are to be seen along the embankment in the traces of water mixed with reddish soil, the ruins of the foundries, and in a splendid place name *Burdinzelaieta*, which evokes the idea of rich meadows. The Bidasoa is harnessed for electricity, and at the hydroelectric stations one can appreciate the careful design of the small dams, staggered to allow the salmon and trout to pass upstream. River, train and salmon are linked by a much-repeated anecdote in the area: it is said that the workers who built the railway went on strike because they were so sick of eating salmon, an exquisite dish to be sure, but one which, when repeated time after time, they found abhorrent.

A small population of particularly protected salmon still swims up the Bidasoa each year. The salmon, *izoki* in Basque, is an extraordinarily large, strong fish that normally grows to a length of some 90cm. It is said to be 'anadromous', i,e. that it spends most of its life in the sea, but on reaching sexual maturity it makes the long journey to spawn in the same river in which it was born.

The Bidasoa salmon come from the western coasts of Greenland and the North Atlantic after having built up substantial fat reserves. The large salmon, which have spent up to three years in the sea and weigh between ten and fifteen kilos, are the first to arrive, in February. Fishermen call them *haunditakoak* (winter salmon). They are followed by the April fish, *apiril-arraiak*, which have spent a minimum of two winters in the sea and weigh between four and seven kilos. The last to arrive, from June onwards, are the small

'salmon trout', and are the most abundant of all. After a period of adaptation in the brackish water of the estuary, they swim upriver with the first freshets of autumn, energetically jumping up the dams. They overcome waterfalls, rapids and obstacles with astonishing agility, sometimes leaping more than three metres into the air, provided the water is deep enough. When they have reproduced, exhausted from the effort, the salmon allow themselves to be swept down river, but only five per cent reach saltwater again, most of them dying after running aground on the riverbank or from diseases they cannot fight for lack of defences. The Bidasoa fishermen call these flaccid, emaciated fish 'runts' or *izokizarrak*.

Salmon fishing in the Bidasoa has been of great importance throughout history, and it is widely documented in the chronicles of the area. Disputes between the inhabitants of Vera y Lesaca talk of more than 1,500 salmon being caught annually in the XVIIth century. At the beginning of this century several hundred fish were caught each year. One exceptional fish is remembered, which was caught in 1906 and weighed 19 kilos. Industrialisation and hydroelectric power stations have been determining factors in the fall in the number of fish caught. Hope has re-emerged in the form of a plan to clean up the rivers. Mature fish have been caught to reproduce in captivity and restock the river with fish. The young fish are released into the river after a period of one year in the breeding pools.

HERITAGE AND FOLKLORE

The *Cinco Villas* form part of Atlantic Navarre, bathed in the damp air that blows in from the sea, frequently bringing cloud and rain with it. This atmosphere is expressed in the scattered *caseríos* with their hay fields and traditional mixed farming methods. It is quite usual to find up to three different crops in one field: maize, turnips and beans. This type of production cannot be achieved without frequent fertilising, for which ferns are piled up into ricks (*metak* in Basque) and then used as a bed for the livestock, where it is converted into an unbeatable organic fertiliser. Lime, often supplied from the village of Arantza, is added to correct the acidity of the soil. Although lime is produced in many places, Arantza used to supply the whole area.

The construction of lime kilns, *kisulabeak*, escalated in the XVIIIth century when it was discovered that quicklime considerably increased production in fields fertilised with manure. The kilns that remain have a cylinder hearth with a domed cylindrical oven. They were built near patches of limestone rock, on a slope to facilitate access. There were both private and communal kilns. Groups of six to eight people worked in shifts to supply timber for fuel. The process of burning the lime began at low temperatures and then the temperature was gradually increased to around 1,000 degrees. After about five or six days the stones began to turn bright red, shrink in size and then turn into lime. A few days later the lime was cool enough to be removed from the kiln.

[OPPOSITE PAGE] *In the northern part of Navarre, near the Bay of Biscay, many old tracks, bridges and roads have been preserved.*

Large areas of the oak and beech woods that grew naturally, and at one time covered the landscape, still remain in the Cinco Villas. At the foot of the Larrún Mountain there is an interesting patch of acacias, and chestnut trees grow in abundance a little higher up the mountain.

The San Juan Xar nature reserve is to be found at Igantzi on the left bank of the river Latsa. It takes its name from the San Juan 'cave-hermitage' where a spring rises which is famous for curing skin complaints. The natural charm of the area combines with its botanical interest. The purpose of the reserve, which measures 2.8 hectares, is to protect the only hardwood hornbeam trees, *carpinus betulus*, in the Iberian Peninsula. The population of amphibians and reptiles includes newts, toads, frogs, small peat bog and rock lizards, water snakes and vipers.

Beautiful tracks and old roads have been preserved. One of them leads out of the neighbourhood of Altzate in Bera and crosses the Kaltzada Erreka stream twice before rising up towards the Usategieta pass. The village of Arantza has a well-maintained road system. Building it must have been very hard work: one side of the road was dug out of the mountain whilst the other was supported by 'road stones' which were sunk into the ground vertically so that the construction would last. The grass that has grown up between the stones serves to beautify a job well done.

The architectural heritage of the area is also worthy of note. The popular building style is attractive and balanced, the best examples dating back to between the XVIth and XVIIIth centuries in Etxalar, in the neighbourhood of Altzate in Bera and in the heart of Lesaka, where there are two unique houses, Alzatebaita and Txanpalenea, with their sumptuous projecting eaves carved from wood. Lesaka also has a late medieval tower that belonged to the aristocratic Zabaleta family and is an example of a Gothic style fortification. Locally it is referred to as 'Casherna', after the French *caserne*, a name it has had since the Napoleonic Wars.

The XVIth century churches at Bera and Lesaka both contain large altarpieces. Lesaka's altarpiece, which dates back to the middle of the XVIIIth century and was paid for by a legacy bequeathed in Guatemala by an *Indiano* (Spanish emigrant to Latin America who made his fortune there), portrays the Immaculate Conception in Rococo style, exquisitely carved in Madrid in 1754 by the famed Luis Salvador Carmona, who the 'Catálogo Monumental de Navarra' considers to be the greatest XVIIIth century Spanish sculptor.

Furthermore, the organs in the parish churches of Bera and Lesaka are listed as being 'of great interest'. The one at Lesaka, made in Zaragoza by Manuel Roqués in 1891, has 'truth and strength' in its reed stops and a flute of great quality. The organ at Bera was made in 1895 by the organ builder from Gipuzkoa, Aquilino Amezua, who installed instruments produced at his workshop in Germany, France, England and Cuba, and who wanted to locate one of his best works near the border. Amezua sought the ringing quality of the human voice and studied the throats of goats and rams. The organs at Arantza and Etxalar are also Romantic and 'of great interest', the latter having a curious piano-harp stop.

The most attractive piece of contemporary architecture is the Health Centre at Lesaka, which was finished in 1987 and designed by Manuel Iñiguez and Alberto Ustárroz. The building

Near the portico of the church at Etxalar there is a Baroque cross and a magnificent collection of funeral steles.

or the last verse of the ode, and on occasions he places the pairs in imaginary situations which they must dramatise. In recent years, young women have joined this fine profession, and have also beaten the men in some contests.

'OLENTZERO'

The *Olentzero* is a grotesque character, a charcoal burner by trade and a great eater and drinker, who is paraded through the streets of the towns and villages (accompanied by songs) on the evening of 24th December. His name has its variants. One of them, *Onenzaro*, appears to provide the key to the mystery that surrounds the character. It would appear to mean 'the era of what is good'. Without doubt he is laden with cultural symbolism. He is the pagan personification of the Winter Solstice, and according to the traditional songs he is also the ambassador who announces the news of the Birth of Christ on Christmas Eve. Some people connect him to the figures that recite the Liturgy during the last days of Advent. He is the symbol of the year that is ending, but above all, a solar symbol transmitting his strength to the yule log, *xubilaro*, that burns in the hearth.

He varies according to area. He may an insatiable glutton; an unintelligent blockhead; a fearsome figure, and even a protecting talisman.

It is in Cantabrian Navarre, in the valleys that border with Gipuzkoa and Laburdi, where the tradition of the *Olentzero* has been upheld. Lesaka, which has passed its ritual on to other places, claims to be the village where the figure of the Olentzero originated, and sings to him:

Olentzero, buru haundia,
entendimentuz jantzia,
bart arratsian edan omen du
hamar erruko zagia
Ai, urde tripaundia.
Ai, urde tripaundia.
Horra, horra gure Olentzero,
pipa hortzian duela,
eserita dago,
kapoitxua ere baitu
arraultzatxuakin,
bihar merendatzeko
botill-ardoakin
botill-ardoakin.

shows the same timeless features that make the centre of the village so exceptional. It is built in the 'casa-patio' style, i.e. with a central courtyard that provides ample light, plenty of space and a clear layout.

The Town Halls, some of them Baroque with a polychrome façade like the one in Bera, maintain the old multicoloured silk flags, which are ritually waved by the Mayor to a solemn tune, *ikurriña goratu*, before the Holy Sacrament at Corpus Christi and during the festival of the Patron Saint. There is a wide repertory of traditional dances: *zortziko, makil-dantzak, gizon-dantza, alki-dantza*. Two unique dances remain in Lesaka, one of them called *Tantirumairu*, is the inheritor of a 'Moors and Christians' festival that was celebrated up until the end of the XVIth century. The other is *Zubigainekoa*, performed by the *dantzariak* (folk dancers) every 7th July on the parapets of the bridge over the river Onín which separates the two neighbourhoods of the town, Legarrea and Piku Zelaia, enemies in days gone by, to reaffirm their reconciliation.

Far from disappearing, both interest in and the strength of the Basque oral expression of the *bertsolariak* have increased in recent years. The *bertsolariak* are popular poets who improvise long odes with beautiful images to precise metres, basing their songs on a series of traditional tunes or even on rock or pop hits. What was once a rural pastime is now an entertainment with a purified style well suited to commenting on diverse current events. The *bertsolari* may vie with his colleagues in improvising fourteen or more verses at one go. A presenter proposes the themes, and sometimes sets the rhyme

[Olentzero has a big head, but he has sense. Last night he drank a wineskin of ten 'arrobas' (one arroba is 28.5 pints). Oh, what a pot-bellied pig! Here is our Olentzero, with his pipe between his teeth. He is seated. He will also have capon and eggs with a bottle of wine for tea tomorrow.]

The tune that accompanies this verse was used by Ignacio Baleztena who set it to different words that became very popular and announce the San Fermín festival "Uno de enero, dos de febrero..." (First of January, Second of February...).

THE 'PALOMERAS' OF ETXALAR

Las palomas pasan
año tras año en el otoño
por encima de nuestros montes.
Llegan cuando las hojas
toman color de viejo caldero.
Nubes de palomas cruzan el cielo
como cendales de humo
que arrastra el viento.

[The pigeons pass over our mountains year after year in the Autumn. They arrive when the leaves are changing to the colour of an old cauldron. Clouds of pigeons cross the sky like veils of smoke drawn by the wind.]

These verses were written by Martín Indaburu, who was born in the Bizkarrondokoborda *caserío* at the foot of the Peña Plata, and form part of a Basque poem, *Haizegua*, loaded with lyricism and beautiful images that sing of free flight and the sadness of the passing pigeons trapped in the nets or shot down in the Usateguieta mountain pass.

In Etxalar there is documentary evidence of capturing pigeons in nets from the XIVth century onwards. The season runs from 1st October to 20th November. However, the weather is not suitable for shooting every day, and the best days, usually in the last two weeks of October, are those that start with clear skies at dawn and a northerly wind. Over the last twenty years the number of birds captured in this way is around 2,000. The first birds are usually sold live to be used as decoys to lure others. The majority are eaten, and are more desirable than those birds that have been shot!

The ornithologist Jesús Elósegui has accurately reflected the art and atmosphere of the *palomeras*.

"Legend has it that this hunt originated when a shepherd threw a light-coloured stone into the air to herd his sheep just as a flock of pigeons were flying over. The birds took the stone to be a goshawk and dived down for safety to avoid being attacked from below. Having repeated the experience, the shepherd saw the possibility of driving the flocks of pigeons towards a strategically placed net. Later, the stones were substituted by beech or alder wood paddles, similar to table-tennis bats, carved with an adze and an axe and then bleached with milk of lime.

The hunters, all from Etxalar, each wait in their respective positions. A shout announces the arrival of a flock of birds flying at medium height. They are woodpigeons, still a long way away in spite of having been spotted with the naked eye. The horn sounds from the stone tower hidden among the beech trees. There is silence. A *palomero*, up to now invisible, appears on the pulpit situated at the western end and throws a paddle towards the end of the valley, and then another and another. The effect is striking: the flock of pigeons dives down towards the ground at the same time as the *palomero*, shouting furiously, waves a long narrow white flag. The pigeons, having recovered from the shock, change direction and start to rise again on the opposite side. But, another surprise, a second *palomero* throws his white paddles down from the top of a camouflaged metal tower in amongst the trees. The pigeons, totally confused, seek refuge on the ground. A whistle blows softly. The pigeons rush along one of the rows formed by the beech trees, trying to find a way out of this fatal trap, but it is here where one of the almost invisible nets has been positioned and it falls down over them."

On arrival in Etxalar, the traveller will see a flour mill that is still in use; in the atrium of the church there is a museum of upright discoid slabs which were sculptured from the XVIth century onwards to preside over the tombs of the deceased; and one will perhaps recall Mérimée and Bizet's immortal gypsy, Carmen, who will give a Basque greeting: *Laguna, ene bihotzarena.* "Comrade of my heart. I am from Etxalar. I work in the factory to earn enough to return to Navarre, to be at my poor mother's side, who has only me and a small *baratzea*, an orchard with twenty cider apply trees, to support her."

According to linguists, *Ultzama* is the Celtic word for 'river', and in a different form of Basque it means 'valley'. Rainfall is high here, and when it blends with the sun that appears between the clouds, the people of the Ultzama valley, the *ultzamarras*, say that the *azeribodak*, or fox's wedding, is being celebrated. A pleasant expression, like the fields which are always green except when covered in snow. The intense process of human settlement in the valley has not prevented valuable areas of original plant life from remaining in the area.

ULTZAMA
Meadows and mountain farmhouses

[PREVIOUS PAGE] *An oak tree witnesses the joining of a wood and a meadow.*
[ABOVE] *The landscape in Ultzama and the adjacent valleys is the result of a growing trend towards cattle rearing.*

NATURAL LANDSCAPE: VELATE AND THE ORGI OAK GROVE

To the north lie gentle loamy limestone mountains, covered in woodland, where the Altantic/Mediterranean watershed is located. These common woodlands, Malain and Mortua, cover an area of 3,460 hectares. To the south, the land descends until it becomes a hilly plain.

Belate is a mountain pass, road, monastery and fortress. Following the construction of tunnels, the once tranquil pass, which lies at an altitude of 847 metres, has now become the starting point for pleasant walks or mountain hikes. Nearby stands the inn, the 'Venta Quemada', with Baztán ash trees lining the road overlooked by beeches. There are fenced fields and a plantation of Lawson cypresses, robust evergreens with elongated conical crowns, can be seen on the grassy hillside.

Close to the nearby Venta de Ultzama, a flat sandy track leads through the ferns to the Monastery-Hospital of Santa María de Belate. Long before the road from Pamplona to France was opened through the pass in the middle of the last century, a mediaeval road linked Bayonne and Pamplona. The remains of the road used by the pilgrims travelling to Santiago de Compostela are visible on Ermitakolepo hill together with the ruins of the XIIth century hermitage of Santiago. The monastery was established on this road and there is documentary evidence of it dating back to 1165.

In the XIVth century, the monastery, which originally came under the Bishop of Pamplona, was a split into two parts: one a monastery led by a prelate, and the other a convent, governed by a prioress. Later on, when the monks and nuns had left, a priory attached to the cathedral in Pamplona was established, with a dependent brotherhood made up of 200 members in the XVIth century when its decline began. The hospital left no-one unattended: the poor and the pilgrims who passed by in the summer were given cider and bread and then they went on their way, but in the winter some stayed for up to twenty days and there was always a bed, a fire, clothes, bread and tasty broth for them. Two women, "who spent their lives as enclosed nuns in seclusion", took care of the cleaning. In 1513, the monastery was sacked by the troops of the King of Navarre, Juan de Albret, when they retreated following their failed attempt to recover the Kingdom which had been conquered by the Castilians. It was also devastated by the French troops of the Convention in 1793. The church, which was restored a few

years ago, is a XIIIth century building with a simple façade bearing four archivolts and a fireplace with a surprisingly large chimney. A fair was held next to the building until the XVIIIth century, when it moved to the village of Lizaso.

The Monasterio de Belate is well-protected, lying deep in the valley where the source of the river Ultzama emerges. The stream rises above the woodland in the high meadows where rushes grow. The little river flows down the steep slopes in the shade of the beech trees in cascades and wells, splashing the heather and blueberry bushes. On approaching the monastery it flows between great blocks of red sandstone that emerge from a carpet of moss and ferns. On reaching the valley it becomes a river with a strong, regular flow, although on occasions has carried five times more water than usual, yet a rare drought dried it up completely in the last week of September 1955. Poplars, alders and willows escort it through the valley to which it has given its name, where it is also accompanied by oak groves and crab apple trees. Pines and a few oaks grow along its final stretch as it journeys on to meet the river Arga.

The Nobel Prize for Literature Laureate, Camilo José Cela, an admirer of what he considers to be "the sweet severe Navarrese landscape" dedicated this eulogy to the river: "The Ulzama is a vein of fertile water and tasty fishing; in the Ultzama the trout leaps, the barbel pecks, the eel lives and the lamprey slivers, the *madrilla* breeds

and, with skill, the tasty *chipa* can be fished." The head of the river is of great interest for its fauna, and here the Pyrenean newt is to be found in its most westerly habitat.

Many streams and brooks flow into the river, which forms an open landscape in the valley and traces a 'Y' shape with the river Arkil that is *ultzamarra* from beginning to end and flows through an alder grove in Eltzaburu, entering Lizaso from the right.

More than half the 96 square kilometres occupied by the municipality of Ultzama is covered by woodland. Beeches represent 60 per cent of trees in the area, and oaks 28 per cent. These two species mix together in the east on the isolated Arañotz-Epaizpuru mountain.

The oak grove 'Robledal de Orgi', which covers 87 hectares, is one of the few vestiges of the original ecosystem once found in the valleys of temperate Navarre. It is of considerable size and important, due to its position in the south of the valley between Olano y Gerendiain, and it also provides the landscape with a wide variety of colours according to the season. It is in a reasonable state of conservation despite the fact that in the past it was intensively exploited, felled, broken up and sold in the form of firewood, acorns and brushwood. It is a complex wood made up of pedunculate oaks of varying age and appearance and around fifty different species of trees, shrubs and creepers. The varied nature of the wood provides refuge for a wide range of fauna and produces fruits and seeds that feed the animals in the winter. There are hawthorn, elder and holly, and the ground is carpeted with moss and grass.

Orgi, a natural recreational area, also has more than forty species of birds, among which the typical woodland birds stand out: great tits, thrushes, nuthatches, treecreepers, woodpeckers, song thrushes or bullfinches, as well as birds of prey such as the tawny owl and sparrow hawk. The rare pygmy woodpecker (*dendrocopos minor*) is an ornithological treasure, called *okil txikia* in Basque; it is the smallest of the woodpeckers in Europe, the size of a sparrow, and spends most of its time fluttering around in the highest branches of the trees. It marks out its territory with a drumming sound between January and June. Amphibians have also found their home in the wet areas of the oak grove where newts, tree frogs, and toads are all common. Mammals of note are squirrels, dormice, beech martens, foxes, badgers, hares, hedgehogs and wild boars.

'EL BOCAGE', A HUMANISED LANDSCAPE

Ultzama is a livestock-farming valley, its climate well-suited to grazing land and ferns. Hayfields and forage crops occupy the flat land and the lower slopes, which are closed in by wire fencing, hedges or trees. In the same way as throughout the whole of temperate Navarre there are *caseríos* (farmhouses), although fewer in number than in the northern Atlantic valleys where it is not so cold as in Ultzama, whose rivers run to the Mediterranean. Scattered huts are to be found in the woods, but they are only used for storing hay and penning sheep for the night. The people live together in groups down in the valley, the villages being small with large houses. The soft landscape never loses its charm, even at night when tiny scattered lights can be seen flickering in the distance.

The mediaevalist Miguel Angel Ladero Quesada says that "a common feature of European landscapes, but above all in Atlantic areas, was the extent of the woodland, which in general did not begin to be taken over by ploughed land until the XIth century." The population was small and the dominant climate, cold and wet, made agriculture difficult. The permanence of the woods was also due to the fact that they were an integral part of the landscape and rural economy. The local diet was based on cereals supplemented with all types of vegetables, in particular turnips. The fruit trees, chestnuts, apple and pear trees fulfilled an important function as their products could be conserved and eaten later in the year. Perhaps the crops that were most lacking were those for fodder. Hay was used, of course, but alfalfa and clover had not been heard of, thus limiting indoor livestock production to a great extent. Equine and bovine stock was valuable, more for transport and haulage purposes than for meat, milk or manure. Cattle, horses and mules were a sign of wealth, to such an extent that in Basque, someone who owns livestock is called rich, *aberatsa*. Pigs were fed on the grazing land and ate the acorns and beechnuts in the woods more than any other animal. Hunting and fishing completed the food supply.

Both the population and the amount of ploughed land increased between the XIth and the XIIIth centuries. In all the Ultzama villages there are many plots of land called *labaki* o *berroa*, which means

exactly that, ploughing. During that period the landscape must have matured and taken on some of the basic features that still characterise it today. The tendency changed later as a result of natural disasters and epidemics. In the Navarre described in the XIVth century censuses a notable decrease in peasant homes can be observed, to such an extent that 60% of the depopulation prior to this century took place between 1348 and 1500. In the Middle Ages there were 21 villages in the Ultzama valley. Nowadays there are 14 municipal councils. The hamlets in the valley underwent a population boom in the XVIIIth century, at which time the majority of the houses that are still standing today were built.

The late XIXth and early XXth century geographers, Madoz and Altadill, present a more diversified rural landscape than today's when referring to Ultzama and the neighbouring valleys. Livestock predominates, but there are fields of wheat, potatoes, vegetables and *menuciales*, which in mid-Navarre is the name given to fodder crops sown on fallow land, such as common vetch and lentil vetch.

In the 1960s expanding urban markets and changes in eating habits demanded an increase in meat and milk production. As stated in a town-planning pilot study by the architect Juan López Asensio, "the valleys of Atez, Basaburua, Imotz y Ultzama lost a quarter of their population in the 1960s. This migration is directly related to the trend towards specialisation in cattle farming. The traditional diversified economy, which required more manpower, has given way to livestock farming based on selected breeds. This generated mechanisation and land consolidation and contributed greatly to the migration of the population. People stopped leaving the area when industry was introduced into the Ultzama valley. Currently, due to the character of the inhabitants of these valleys, traditional life is valued, a fact that implies the adoption of modernity in harmony with the environment."

Following the recent division of land into plots, the need for which was unquestionable, there is a growing awareness of the importance of preserving natural hedgerows, not only to protect the rural landscape but also to maintain the balance of nature and to improve agricultural production.

These hedgerows are made up of lines of shrubs and brushwood that grow along the edges of roads, fields and woods. They are natural fences formed by maples, privets, willows, hawthorns, dogwoods and blackberries. When the hedges are abundant and link together a *bocage* is formed, an agricultural landscape of outstanding beauty, of enclosed fields.

The biologists Enrique Herranz and Jokin Larumbe have made a detailed study and assessment of the general movement throughout Europe towards maintaining and creating hedgerows. They make no pretence about the problems: between two and six per cent of land is lost, they hinder the entry of machinery into fields, they create added maintenance work, and some oversized hedgerows can favour frosts and harbour fungi, insects or other animals which harm agriculture. But all these negative aspects can be avoided with effective planning. There are also many advantages involved: they provide shelter for livestock from the wind, cold and sun, they retain and save water, they favour early plant development and production, erosion is avoided and various different products such as firewood, poles for gates and varied fruits for both animal and

A shepherd with a flock of lacha sheep, which give milk and a thick, coarse wool.

human consumption are obtained from them. "The ecological importance of the hedgerows is the most interesting aspect. Birds roost and nest in them and spike their prey on the thorns. At ground level they provide protection for insect-eating toads, spiders spin their webs between the leaves, and some hunted species breed in the hollows. All this wildlife concentrated in a small area is a factor that contributes to the balance of nature. The countryside of grazing land and fenced fields represents a tourist attraction for a varied cross-section of the public made up by naturalists, hunters and hikers."

Green lizards and hedgehogs are commonplace among the branches. Butcher-birds, yellowhammers and tree pipits can be seen in the clear skies over the meadows. When the autumn comes they are replaced by flocks of larks and song thrushes.

CIVIL ARCHITECTURE

"This house was built by Martín de Repiz and Engracia Etulain Echandia. Year 1777." This carved stone inscription can be seen on the lintel over a door in Alkotz. Similar legends are to be found on many facades.

Whilst in the Ribera area of Navarre the family was nuclear and inheritances were shared out equally between siblings, in mid-Navarre and the mountains there was a system of leaving everything to a sole heir, not necessarily the eldest but the one chosen by the testator. In a poor rural environment property could not be split up, and Navarrese Law sought its permanence. The House was what was most important —one House, undivided, lasting. Many farmhouses were named after the founder of the family or his profession and sometimes after the position of the house in the village. Many of these names, which have often appeared in censi since the XVIIth century, still remain today and the owner is often given the same name as his house.

The oak wood at Orgi is one of the very few original ecosystems at the top of valleys in the temperate zone of Navarre.

In 1929, Leoncio Urabayen, an early promoter of studies into humanistic geography, published a delightful book, *La casa navarra* ('The Navarrese house'), in which he studies the different types, the features of the construction such as roofs, walls or spaces, and the evolution of this style of civil architecture since the XIVth century. This is the period when the oldest examples he photographed were built (it appears that up until the XIIIth century houses were built from wood and were frequently destroyed by fire). The artistic appearance of some streets and squares in Navarre is the result of fine stone and woodwork, the ordered rhythm of spaces, be they doors, balconies, windows, porches or chimneys, and by the angle of inclination of the roofs.

There are many well-preserved large old houses in Ultzama. They are square or rectangular stone buildings that are always open and generally have a perpendicular ridge-roof and a balcony running along the whole length of the facade.

There are several stately houses in Eltso with coats of arms on their fronts. In Gerendiain there is a group of XVIIIth century farmhouses with large eaves. In Zenotz there is a mansion with a hipped roof and some other very fine examples with projecting stones on their doors, windows and corners. There are also some beautiful and well-preserved houses in Eltzaburu, and monumental examples in Arraitz.

Three groups of houses deserve special attention. Those that line the banks of a stream in Auza are a pretty sight. The view of the main street in Iraizotz is unforgettable, wide and quite steep with its fountain in the foreground and the sturdy XVIIIth century houses faced with large square-cut stones and big balconies that converge towards the church at the top. In Ilarregui, the houses are laid out forming an open square leading to the parish church; it is one of the best examples of XVIIIth century civil architecture in Navarre.

The great economic changes in recent years have brought about improvements in the condition of the houses and have also generated the construction of small estates of 'weekend houses' that are not, however, always in keeping with the traditional style of architecture.

An example of fine contemporary architecture is the Ultzama Golf Club, which was built on 60 hectares of communal grazing land belonging to Eltso and Gerendiain in 1966. It was designed by Fernando Redón and Javier Guibert. The clubhouse is situated on the southern side of the highest hill opposite a clearing on the edge of an oak wood. With the possibility of future extension in mind, the architects chose a 'meccano'—type structure made up of metal tubes with star-shaped capitals joined to pine beams. The ground plan forms a hexagonal network with a reticle of equilateral triangles. The roof forms a hexagonal pyramid. The sides of the roof adapt themselves to the hill and descend at an angle of 30º, coinciding with the slope of the land. The exterior walls are brick, and the inside walls are set at the top with glass to accentuate the feeling of a sheltered protected area. A covered south-facing terrace opens out onto the beautiful surrounding countryside. This private club has 1,400 members and has hosted both national and international championships and tournaments.

HOW PEOPLE HAVE LEFT THEIR MARK THROUGH THE CENTURIES

The Abauntz cave is located near Arraitz, at the Aritzarte crag above the narrow pass formed by the Zaldazain stream as it flows between two large rocks. The many excavations carried out here have revealed it as being one of the areas of Navarre with the widest range of prehistoric strata. It was occupied, with one or two periods of abandonment, from the end of the late Palaeolithic age (approximately 13850 BC), until 408 AD. It was first used as a more or less permanent shelter for hunters/gatherers. Burials were carried out here from the Eneolithic period (in around 2290 BC), and it was also used as a hiding place during times of instability under the Late Roman Empire.

Oral tradition has named this cave 'Lamizulo', and connects it with legends telling of *lamias*, mythological women with feet of geese who occupy their time washing clothes, carding wool and combing their long hair with a golden comb. Several inhabitants of Arraitz have told the archaeologist Pilar Utrilla that "Lamias lived in the cave in times gone by and used to ask the shepherds for milk. One day, a shepherd from the Sunbillenea famhouse mixed sheep droppings into the milk, and when the lamias noticed this they cast a spell on him: from that time on someone in his household would always have just one arm, or be lame or mad. The *lamias* chased the shepherd to the entrance to the village, but on hearing the church bells ran back to the cave." Others say that they gave or took away gold coins, depending on who you were, and that all this gold is buried in the foundations of the Sunbillenea farmhouse.

The Abauntz cave is not the only monument in Ultzama that dates back to prehistoric times. In Lizaso there is the grandiose Maxkar burial ground, sixty metres in diameter, and on the communal land of Mortua there are the Loiketa, Ganbeleta and Mugakosoro dolmens. Nearby is a Bronze Age sandstone mould, the only one in Navarre, used for making flat axes.

Legacies from prehistory also appear to be present in the gastronomy of the gastronomy, with *gaztanbera* (similar to junket), sheep's milk curdled in a birchwood receptacle called a *kaiku* which is shaped like a truncated cone with an oblique axis. The *kaiku* cannot be put on the fire, but the milk must reach a temperature of 38° in order to form curds when rennet is added. White-hot stones (*esne harriak*) are put into the milk to heat it, giving the junket a slightly burnt smell and taste, '*kiskalurrin*'. Ophite stones were once used in Ultzama, but they were later replaced with iron balls. The writer from Galicia, Alvaro Cunqueiro, writes in 'Viajes imaginarios y reales': "In the Basque Country I was once the owner of a serpentine stone, an ophite from a Pyrenean shepherd's hut that warned off the lightning on stormy days, and on calm days it was heated in the embers to boil the milk quickly, giving it a certain taste." And, as far as the *kaiku* is concerned, something similar must have been observed by the Greek geographer Strabo when, referring to this land and its people he wrote: "They use vessels carved out of wood."

There are documents referring to Ultzama that date back to the XIth century. In 1211 King Sancho el Fuerte readjusted land tax amongst the nobility through a law that distinguished between Ultzama Mayor and Menor. In 1350 the 'Libro de Monedage' makes a distinction between a valley of Ultzama located to the east, and another Val de Ultzama de Yuso. Until the middle of the XIXth century the Member of the *Cortes* (Parliament of Navarre) for the valley and the councillors from each of the villages were responsible for governing the area, and they met in Lizaso. Larraintzar is now the main locality of the valley.

The artistic and religious heritage of the valley is interesting.

Green meadows next to an oak forest. Ultzama has many areas called labaki or berroa, meaning 'ploughed land'.

The oldest church is in Urritzola and was built in the Gothic era. Its XIIIth century bell tower was built over the central span of the nave. In Auza, next to the north wall of the priest's house and the village hall, there is a set of Gothic paintings of the Virgin Mary which probably decorated the apse of a previous church built at the beginning of the XIIIth century. There are Roman or Medieval baptismal fonts in Iraizotz, Larraintzar, Suarbe and Urritzola; the one in Auza is Renaissance and is of singular interest for the decoration on its stand. Alkotz's Processional Cross is of embossed silver filigree that was made at the end of the XVth century. In terms of religious imagery there is also a collection with a notable Gothic figure of the Virgin and Child from the first half of the XIVth century that came from the demolished hermitage of Udoz. It is now kept in Lizaso. In Zenotz there is a Romanesque altarpiece. The rustic hermitage of Santa Lucía de Arañotz, situated near the top of the mountain on the edge of the wood, and much-visited on the occasion of the pilgrimage on the first Sunday in June, belongs to Iraizotz and Eltso.

The valley was the scene of battles during the XIXth century. Later, in the Royalist War which ended in 1823, the Royalists were defeated at Larraintzar by the Government troops commanded by Colonel Cruchaga. Some episodes of the Carlist Wars also took place in the area.

Due to its close proximity to Pamplona, Ultzama supplied the capital with wood and coal right up until this century. Local industry, which grew up around the natural resources available, is based on carpentry, construction materials and dairy products and at one time employed 45 per cent of the working population. A multinational recently closed its factory in Iraizotz, an event which raised serious questions about the economic future of the area.

The hotel and catering sector, with reputable restaurants and *sidrerías* (cider houses), is an attractive leisure option. There is also a permanent children's camp. Every year between August and October, each village celebrates its festivities with the *ingurutxo* dance.

Our journey ends in Eltzaburu, where the 'Yeguada de Ultzama' is located, a stud farm owned by the horse-breeding association, 'Sociedad de Fomento de la Cría Caballar'. Its 120 hectares of grazing land are used for breeding thoroughbred foals that start their race training as one-and-a-half year olds.

In northern countries, from Canada to Japan, there exists the widespread belief that, on the second day of February, the bear awakes from three months of hibernation and emerges from his den. It is a sign of a change of season and the beginning of another year. The bear and other animals are incorporated into the carnival pantomimes, the winter festival which portrays the eternal drama of the circular flow of time and a drowsy Nature which needs to be woken up by a noisy ritual. A time for purifying and cleansing in order to scare away all evil and burn everything old and worn out; a time when people dress up and conceal their faces with masks. But, while Carnivals today are done for fun or in rebellion against daily routine, in the past they were used to invoke magical powers.

CARNIVALS
IN DEPTH

[PREVIOUS PAGE] *Carnival is a pagan festival. Masks and costumes had a sacred, ritual origin.*
The Zanpantzar from the villages of Ituren and Zubieta preserve the atmosphere of ancient rites: enigmatic clothing, a marching step, and a metallic, harmonious and rhythmic sound.

SIGNIFICANCE AND NAMES OF THE FESTIVAL

Carnival is a very ancient farming festival which is linked, in the lunar calendar, to the celebration of the beginning of the year, just at the time when Nature is dormant. The waning moon in January signals the inactivity of the sap in the plants and this is the best time for pruning.

In classical Rome, *februaria* (purifying rites) were performed in which naked young people flogged passers by with strips of goat skin. They came after the *lupercalia* festivals, aimed at protecting the cattle, and the *saturnalia* festivals which, once the winter crops had been sown, meant a complete transgression from rules and conventions. The Spanish word for February, *febrero*, corresponds to the Basque *otsaila*, which can be translated as 'the cold month' but also as the 'month of the wolf."

The first full moon in Spring determines the date of the Christian Easter, and this is preceded by forty days of preparation or Lent, a time for giving up eating meat, and, just before Lent, Carnival time.

Manuel de Larramendi, author of the first grammar and dictionary of the Basque language in the middle of the XVIIIth century, indicates three words which have served to designate Carnival in this region: *zanpantzarrak, aratuzteak* and *iñauteriak*. The anthropologist Julio Caro Baroja related the first word, which is French in origin, to *Saint Pansart*, the carnival character of mediaeval times which he refers to in his work, *Rabelais*; Caro Baroja also believes that the second word (Shrovetide) aptly translates the idea of giving up meat, although he has doubts about the meaning of the most common word '*iñauteriak*', which for some could mean 'a time for fun' while for others it could represent 'a time for pruning'.

Caro Baroja indicates that 'in winter there are some explosive moments full of vitality which are loaded, however, with a sense of religion, and a certain Dionisian touch as far as everything burlesque and terrifying is concerned: the Carnival festivities. There has been too much speculation on the pre-Christian origins of the carnival, yet not enough has been said about how it contrasts with the Lenten period within the actual Christian way of life'. Carnival is a festival of lust which is in complete contrast to Lent.

The ethnographer Jose María Satrústegui is of the opinion that Carnival was originally the celebration of the beginning of another year with the arrival of Spring. There was a purifying rite to rid the old year of all its negative forces, and another propitiatory rite to ward off evil spirits and to ask for fertility for the future, the new year, whose birth was personified in figures or representations. The Church christianised that festival and its rites, opposed its pagan meaning and established a preparation for Easter with abstinence and fast.

Carnival was a time for eating and drinking copiously, a rare privilege for the lower classes in those times of hunger. Before the arrival of refrigerators, pigs were slaughtered during the coldest months of the year, beginning in November since, as the saying goes, 'the time of St Martin arrives for all pigs'. Cold conditions and salt were used to preserve a wide range of products, the sustenance of a villager's daily rations. The pigs were slaughtered one after the other in the various homes, working as a network of solidarity and exchanging 'presents' between families in order to guarantee the consumption of fresh bacon throughout the winter months.

The young people held *fiestas*, and, in order to spread the cost out, there were house to house collections or *puska* accompanied by music and songs. On occasions there was a fake robbery. A young lad dressed in fox skins (or simply a youngster not dressed up) took away eggs, bacon, garlic sausage or long pork sausages which the housewife had 'left' lying around in some visible spot. Nowadays collections are still made in the rural areas. The young people hold their dances and festivities in the remotest farm houses or *caseríos*, and now they are given money for the Carnival.

Juan Antonio Urbeltz, an expert in European symbology and folklore, emphasises the pagan idea of the Carnival. It is a time for pruning and purification. Pruning is carried out at a time when Nature appears to be inactive and dormant. The fancy dress, the mask, in the ancient classics is translated by the Latin word *larva* which is also used to designate insects. Within Carnival, there is a protective ritual to frighten off harmful animals and the door to door collection represents the payment of a tribute as protection against them. A tremendous noise must be made to frighten away all that is dormant and invisible and which could harm living creatures, and bonfires must be lit to burn everything harmful. The forty days which followed were to cleanse and purify. No meat was consumed, although not just any meat, but pork, which had been consumed in abundance during the winter months.

During Carnival in the cities, towns and villages the mask and fancy dress, of holy origin, now offer an opportunity to fool around, make jokes and make caricatures. It is a mockery of authority and of one's usual appearance, which is conditioned during the rest of the year by social conventions which stifle free expression, even when it comes to dress. There is a curious paradox here, since the only time when a person searches for and actually finds their true self is when the face is concealed by a mask.

The ioaldunak from Ituren wear a woollen garment on their backs and cover their heads with a cone-shaped ttuntturro crowned with cock feathers.

The *Zanpantzar* of Ituren and Zubieta retain the flavour of the real thing: enigmatic costumes, the right rhythm, a powerful metallic sound which has been described as the 'most harmonious cow bell ringing in the Pyrenees'.

This roving carnival has been established for the Monday and Tuesday after the last Sunday in January. It has been described as a 'good neighbour festival' between two nearby villages in the Ezkurra river basin. Ituren, with three districts, has the characteristics of a 'roadside village'. Zubieta, which covers a wider area, is derived from *Zubi*, a double arched bridge across the river.

There are all manner of floats and masks in this carnival, but the most eye-catching spectacle is the groups of *ioaldunak* which form two bands and ring their huge forty centimetre long cow bells, or *polunpak*. These bells are strapped around the waist and are rung in step, with a two-four time. The *ioaldunak* from each village can be differentiated by some detail of their costume. Those from Zubieta wear a white shirt, whilst those from Ituren wear a type of wool waistcoat or *espaldero* and their rhythm is slightly quicker than the former. Their costumes are noted for their white petticoats with lace bottoms, the horse-hair hyssop carried in the right hand and, on their heads, a *ttuntturro*, or fifty-five centimetre high, cardboard cone covered with cloth and crowned with cock feathers.

On Monday it is a sight to see those from Zubieta marching to Ituren and, on Tuesday, the other way round. They march along an old route, deep in concentration, their eyes cast to the ground. In the leafless wood, the rhythm of the powerful metallic percussion seems to wake up the sap, revitalise the meadows, frighten off the pests and fertilise the sown land.

The bear (*hartza*) is usually present in the Ituren and Zubieta processions. The most aggressive bear, one which escapes from his careless keepers and attacks strangers with particular fury, appears in the Arizkun Carnival in the Baztán valley. Here the procession represents a wedding and the traditional *sagardantza* dance is performed. A sweet melody accompanies the elegant movements of four young people wearing conical hats decorated with coloured ribbons, who offer and bargain over the apples they hold in their hands.

Without leaving Cantabrian Navarre, the Carnivals of the Bidasoa villages are a beautiful sight. The floats in Sunbilla, the beautiful costumes in Arantza and the amusing transvestism in Bera, where the *iñudek eta artzaiak* group appears with the girls dressed as shepherds and the boys as wet-nurses. In Lesaka, the *sakuzarrak* are grotesque masques which stumble along, their legs and bodies covered with sacks stuffed with hay, which end up being torn and destroyed by the children at the end of the festivities. Near the Urumea river, Arano and Goizueta retain the *zagidantza* dance, which is performed with a litre wineskin. The *Mozorrok*, dressed in white, are accompanied by the *Zomorrok*, very black-faced charcoal burners who chase the women to try and kiss them and blacken their faces.

Juan Garmendia Larrañaga has collected information on rural carnivals in Navarre and Francisco Javier Tiberio has studied in detail some which have been revived in the Barranca-Burunda corridor and in Ergoiena. There are thus those of Ihabar, centred on the figure of *Aitezarko*, and those of Arbizu which end up burning the *Aittun Aundia*, or big grandfather, and the *Amiñ ttikia*, or little grandmother. In the *Iyoteak* of Unanua, seven enigmatic *katolak* or iron masks appear; the *moxaurrak* dress up carrying small cowbells, little bells and long sticks cut from the hazelnut tree and which they use to whip any passer by in the street or any one appearing at a balcony or window. In Urdiain, *mantajunas* and *momuxarros* also pursue anyone who incites them with long sticks.

Alsasua-Altsasu has had its own Carnival since 1982, adding fresh elements to those which have been saved from oblivion. *Akerra*, a Billy goat personifying Lucifer, presides over the movements and the dances of the *momotxorros*, who have had new dance steps created for them. The fierce appearance of the *momotxorro* makes him imposing, although the character has become more moderate. A large basket placed over his head acts as a support for the horns, braids and horse manes covering his face, and a large sheepskin covers his back. From his shoulders, a bloody white cloth hangs before him. The *momotxorro* causes the cow bells tied around his waist to ring as he moves. He also carries a wooden pitchfork to harass those watching him pass by. At one particular point, the masks represent a scene of ploughing and sowing.

The Lanz Carnival, which Pio Caro Baroja made a film of in the sixties, was reproduced in prints by Jesus Lasterra, earning him a national prize. It is the most famous of all the carnivals in Navarre.

The village youths, or *txatxos*, dressed in skins and cloths, multicoloured hats and armed with brooms, shout violently and form a chaotic and picturesque procession around the main masks: the Fat Man, the Horse and the Giant.

Ziripot is a clumsy, fat figure covered with sacking stuffed with hay. He walks with difficulty and leans on a stick cut from a hazelnut tree to try and maintain his impossible balance. He falls to the ground time and time again, pushed by a nervous little horse or *Zaldiko*, which neighs and gets frightened by the masks. From time to time they manage to slow down his nervous trot, hold him still and some blacksmiths, armed with a fire in a small boiler, hammers and pliers, pretend to shoe him.

The central character, *Miel Otxin*, is a giant made of straw with his arms crossed and made by the young people using a simple beech branch structure. The powerful visual effect of height and rigidity is emphasised by a long conical hat, adorned with coloured papers, and a checked shirt which draws one's attention to the figure's grotesque mask. He is carried astride the shoulders of a lad who, being a good dancer, moves to the beat of the march and gives movement and life to the giant which moves about and turns around.

Miel Otxin represents a bandit, a highwayman who is executed at dusk by a rifle shot. The masquerade contains old pagan rites of collective safety and also symbolises the death and resurrection of the Carnival. The *txatxos* dance a cheerful but severe *zortziko* in a circle around the waste burning on the fire.

On the northern slopes of the Pyrenees, the festivals at Valcarlos-Luzaide bring the Navarre carnivals to a close with the *Fiesta de Volantes* or *Bolantak*, which has been held for several years now on Easter Sunday. This is the only time of year when you can see an elegant procession and enjoy a rich set of dances whose steps, choreography and costume are repeated in the folklore of the whole of Lower Navarre.

Miguel Angel Sagaseta has studied the ritual and the attraction of up to twenty-three different dances in which the *iauziak*, with a Renaissance and courtly air and interpreted by the *volantes*, are differentiated from the popular *kontradantzak* dances which are far more recent and are danced in pairs. One's attention is drawn to the fact that these traditional melodies are not interpreted by native instruments but by a small conventional wind and percussion orchestra. This is exceptional in folk art.

There are two processions, one in the morning and one in the evening. In the morning a courtesy call is made to the neighbouring locality of Arnegi and there is dancing in the square of Valcarlos at midday. In the afternoon a visit is made to the priest and a number of dances are performed in his garden; then the procession goes along the main street and stops at the *frontón* (pelota court) where the complete set of dances is performed and the game of the fox and the pot (*axe ta tupina* in Basque) is played.

As they pass through the streets two horsemen head the procession, wearing red trench coats, white shirt fronts and red berets with a tassel. They are followed by the *Zapurrak* with white leather aprons, axes over their shoulders, round caps and overgrown beards. Behind are two 'small giants' and another two *makilariak*, experts in spinning batons between their fingers, throwing them high into the air and deftly catching them. Then come the *gorriak*, carrying a wooden sword. Behind the *Bolantak*, of which there are many and of all ages, march the *banderariak*, carrying the *ikurriña* (Basque national flag) and the Valcarlos flag. The musicians bring up the rear of the procession and several couples of *dantzariak*, boys and girls. During their numerous jumps, the *volantes* cause little bells to jingle, and the long multi-coloured ribbons attached to their backs flow out behind them. Their shirts are decorated with broaches and little gold chains. Their trousers have gold stripes and red and yellow braids. Tassles hang from their red berets, adding to the effect of movement created by these gravity-defying dancers.

DANCING FOLLOWS A FULL STOMACH

"It is Shrovetide" they used to say. In the middle of the cold winter months they would put an end to the bad year with enormous meals in preparation for the hardships of Lent which would soon follow.

Javier Santxotena, a restaurant owner in the Baztán valley, has been able to compile the gastronomic tradition of the Carnival and,

like someone taking the old and the new from the food cupboard, he has brought it up to date.

There are a series of dishes which are still maintained. Tradition requires a good broth for starters, such as the *Baztanzopak* which is made by cooking sheep's head and offal, and a steer's leg with lots of vegetables. This is poured over slices of toasted bread and seasoned with saffron. *Txerriankak* (pigs ears and trotters), previously hardened in salt for three or four weeks, are cooked with vegetable stock in the Mountain region or with milk which has been slightly sweetened with sugar and cinnamon in the Ribera. Chicken with rice or gently roasted spare ribs give way to the deserts: rice puddings, fried custards or the popular *torrijas* which make an exquisite sweet from milk and bread leftovers.

The youths of Ituren and Zubieta have discovered new gastronomic pleasures. They club together to buy a calf which will provide plenty for all: a tasty broth for any spare moment; lunch with fillets of meat and potatoes; rice with sautéed kidneys and sweetmeats; liver in bread crumbs with onions, and a fraternal *guisote* (large stew).

Such a greasy meal needs a good wine to accompany it, either white or red. And the lads who do the *puska*, collecting from door to door, are offered biscuits and a small glass of aniseed liqueur. This drink is very traditional in the *caseríos*. The day the pig is slaughtered, at dawn, after sacrificing and searing the pig and just as they are taking out its liver, the housewife appears with a bottle of aniseed liqueur and a plate of biscuits.

PAMPLONA, AN URBAN CARNIVAL

Carnival is becoming more and more popular in the medium-sized towns and villages. The cool, damp climate and a monotonous calendar with no holidays explains the desire to meet up for fun, the urge to joke and the popular initiatives to liven up the streets and cheer up the people who are "too serious" and hard-working the rest of the year.

The groups which are most involved in traditional culture have had the good sense to fantasise to a large extent, to pay some

[LEFT] *The Carnival at Lanz, the subject of a film and reproduced in beautiful engravings, is the best-known of all those in Navarre thanks to its spectacular scenes.*
[RIGHT] *The txatxos of Lanz, dressed up in multi-coloured clothes and hats, make up a chaotic, picturesque cortège. Here they are shown dancing a zortziko.*

attention to the past, and gradually develop a festival full of different activities so that their fellow citizens may cheer up and enjoy things in their own way.

In Pamplona the Dance Group Federation '*Euskal Dantzarien Biltzarra*' started a carnival procession. The Association of Boilermakers '*Iruñeko Kauteroak*' later took charge. The activities increase every year and so does the number of people who dress up and participate.

The Pamplona Carnival has taken something from tradition: masques like the '*Oso Margarito*' (Margarito Bear), street bands like '*El Píspiri*' or news on the '*Giants of Fire*'. But far more has been invented in order to fill a Saturday to the full. The *quicios* are a ritual procession in the morning, a more relaxed and spontaneous parade in the afternoon, an open air dance in the evening and whatever each person wants to add. The Pamplona *Gaiteros* (bagpipe band) have composed a march for wind and percussion instruments, a dance for *Zaldikos* and a 'Canonical Dance' interpreted by the giants, *Don Lancelot, (*Mr Lancelot) and *Doña Graciosa de Arazuri (*Miss Gracious of Arazuri), illuminated by fireworks. Groups of *Zíngaros* (bohemians) and *Caldereros* (boiler makers) beat frying pans and metal objects. Musical bands push and maintain a fantastic set of beasts: serpents, bears, *mulasa* and *zaldikos*, and an amusing mob of water carriers, chimney cleaners, *rompecañas*, *botargas* (straw filled figure), boiler makers, stokers, fantasy masks and minstrels.

Other towns have 'reinvented' their carnivals. The *Cipoteros* of Tudela dance *jotas* in the company of the *Capirote*, a newly created masque. Estella has drawn from tradition to recreate the *Aldabika* bandit who is set loose for a few days in the company of the *palokis*, festive big-heads who are able to change into giants.

In his epic poem *Euskaldunak*, Nicolás Ormaetxea '*Orixe*' wrote that "we have our own Sinai here." In Aralar, a limestone mountain range honeycombed by hundreds of caves and chasms and covered with woods and pastures, an underground water reserve emerges in the form of beautiful springs. Sheepherding seasonal migrants (transhumants), attracted since Prehistoric times by the fine, abundant grass, left their mark in the form of the largest concentration of dolmens in Navarre. Christianity imposed its new form of worship and beliefs in the *Ara Coeli* of the Monte Excelso, a Sanctuary wrapped in mists and legends.

ARALAR
The Sacred Mountain

In 1995, on the fiftieth anniversary of taking over as the priest of the Sanctuary of Aralar, Inocencio Ayerbe reminisced on the major changes that had taken place over the years. The peak can now be reached by roads up both sides of the range. In the past, getting to the top of San Miguel was a prize for sweating climbers who reached it along bridle paths.

One day in September 1909 the writer Miguel de Unamuno did exactly that. Accompanied by three friends and guided by the messenger of the sanctuary, they made the ascent in two and a half hours. They had started from Uharte-Arakil after dark and walked "with the moonlight filtering through the beech trees over the rough track." Unamuno speaks of the guard dogs which 'welcomed' them with their fierce barking, and of Don Miguel, the chaplain who died recently, a zealous keeper of tradition who would not let the *Diputación* (regional administration) build a road so that the arduous route to the top would still make the pilgrimage a worthy one. Unamuno goes on to describe the countryside: "San Miguel de Excelsis, high up on a ridge, exposed to all the winds and all the suns. From time to time, when the fog lifted from the range, you can see the fields of the Barranca and the valleys of Araquil and the Burunda. On the other side you can see as far as Pamplona and opposite, the imposing plateau of the Andía and Urbasa ranges."

The rector of Salamanca University no doubt enjoyed the magnificent view from the bench cut out of the rock called *Putretoki*. Many people do the same today, and if the sky is clear they are impressed by the view of the rocky slopes and the deep valley cut by erosion over millions of years. If there is cloud cover over the hollow, you can see the spectacle of a bright sun bathing the peaks with light, making them look like islands floating in a sea of fog.

The Navarrese writer Manuel Iribarren, National Literature Prize winner, also contemplated the view. He describes an ascent from the other side, "starting from Lecumberri by a little-known route at the time, long and leafy. We set off early in fog and walked for the first few hours over slippery earth and rocks and between ferns. The tangled vegetation and the leafy trees emerged before us among the fog, which lingered lazily… We finally reached the top around noon, but could not see the sun. It was, however, triumphant, fantastic, above an ocean of gassy grey protuberances like wandering smoke, which covered and hid the deep valleys. The Lord must have seen something like it from the heights, according to Gustave Doré, in the first days of the Creation."

Aralar covers 208 square kilometres. Two-thirds of the area is in Navarre and the other third in neighbouring Gipuzkoa. The range rides over valleys: to the south is the corridor of the river Arakil, along the Roman road from Bordeaux to Astorga (the Province of León), and small villages grew up along the route and the river. The walled *bastidas* (fortified settlements) of Uharte-Arakil and

Etxarri-Aranaz emerged in the 14th century to defend these villages from the banditry that plagued them in the Early Middle Ages. To the north-west the range is crowned by the Irumugarrieta peak, overlooking the Valley of Araiz and the cwm of the Malloas from a height of 1,427 metres. Everyone now uses this name for the great rock wall, although tradition gave the term *(Malloak)* to the steep communal meadows where the *segalaris* (reapers) worked, sometimes tied to a rope so they could work on the slopes. They cut the grass with scythes and then slid it down in bundles to the isolated farmhouses *(caseríos)* on steel cables.

The topography of the Aralar range is complex. It has clear-cut limestone crests, especially at its extremities. In other parts of the range, where loam is found, it looks like a gently undulating plateau.

Precipitation is 1,700 millimetres per annum, which is quite high, although there are hardly any surface rivers or lakes, except the odd large pond. Aralar is a karstic area, full of valleys and chasms: its water is absorbed, runs along underground channels and reappears in springs on the edge of the range.

The beautiful source of the Aitzarreta, a cave which opens out in the impressive rock wall of Etzanza, flows irregularly according to the amount of seasonal rainfall. It is rushing and wild in winter but clear and tranquil in the summer. Another river, the Ercilla, also has its source nearby. Its flow is quite strong because it powered a flour mill for many years (the ruins can still be seen). This river disappears quite quickly, however, as if it regretted being born at all. It goes into a curve and disappears into the ground just eight hundred metres from its source. It surfaces again further down in the form of the river Larráun near the village of Iribas, where another tributary flows into it along the chasm of Lezegalde. Cavers talk of the special beauty of the cavern. The descent into it is vertical at first and then takes the form of a ramp, entering a large gallery with a thirty-metre deep lake which regulates the flow of the river Larráun.

Caves and chasms are found everywhere in the Aralar range. The deepest one (375 metres), on the slopes of Mount Aparein, is called *Ormazarreta*. Other deep caves of note are Vizcaíno (160 m), Beingo (97 m), Nilutz (130 m), and Artzematuta (200 m).

The heart of the Sierra, 'El Monte de Aralar', covers 2,190 hectares, of which 60 per cent is beech and 40 per cent pastureland. The villages which make up the 'Unión de Aralar' have the right (although not on an equal basis) to exploit this area. There are seven municipalities and nine village councils. It appears that the original pasture, water and wood use rights go back to the XIVth century: King Luis el Hutín granted these rights to Etxarri-Aranaz when he set up the *bastida* in 1312 and Carlos II extended them to Lakuntza in 1365, and later to the other villages.

On the Gipuzkoa side there is also common pastureland for grazing and forestry under a similar administration system, called the 'Unión de Enirio and Aralar'. This consists of 15 villages from the Gohierri area. The Navarrese and the inhabitants of Gipuzkoa, rivals in the exploitation of the mountain range, reached *concordias* (agreements) in 1519 which were not always respected later on. The borders were formally drawn up on 27th August 1857 on Mount Ureginaga, where the main boundary stone is located.

Some traditional activities of the area have fallen into disuse,

[PREVIOUS PAGE] *The Sanctuary of San Miguel seen from the summit of Artxueta. The rock face of San Donato-Beriain is seen in the background.*

The Dolmen of Albi. The Aralar mountain range has the highest concentration of megalithic monuments in Navarre: 44 dolmens and one menhir.

such as collecting snow to refrigerate food in the summer or the use of manure, fern and withered leaves as bedding for cattle. Neithere are firewood and timber much used so much in construction these days. The area covered by trees is 2,106 cubic meters, with 718 cubic metres for firewood. The right to free grazing for an unlimited period is very important, however, as is the right to build shacks, huts and sheep-folds.

Dense beech forest used to cover the entire Aralar range, although deforestation by human hand started a long time ago. However, some areas which were pastures, such as Albi and Mugardi, have recovered their ancient forest vegetation.

Oakwoods cover the bottom part of the range on both slopes. The beechwoods appear at an altitude of around 640 metres and go up as far as the rocky boulders of the summits.

In the leafy woodland the beech is the predominant variety, with some clearings present as a result of cattle farming. The *muxarra* (grey dormouse) is very common in the woods, it is found in the hollows of centuries-old tree trunks and is very noisy when it runs wild on summer nights. There are large areas of oak and chestnut trees in the range, and also wild pines, replanting of Japanese larch, and the odd mountain elm and service tree.

The Natural Reserve of *Putxerri* covers 83 hectares on the south slope of the range. Its special soil and climate accounts for the distinctive vegetation. The soil has evolved very little owing to the steep slope and the geology of the area's karstic fissures. Furthermore, the climate of the north slope of Putxerri is much cooler, damper and darker than the south slope, which is almost always without cloud cover and open to winds. The most notable feature of this Natural Reserve is the large number of yew trees, both young and old, in the beechwood. There are also copses of hazel-nut trees, service trees, lindens and maple trees, and in Spring there is a blaze of blossom from squill, ramson, anemone, and laurel.

The transition from tree-covered to clear ground is often marked by holly-trees and hawthorns. These act as a barrier, defining the woodland against the invasion of herbivores. The smell of hawthorns in flower is very strong in the month of May, and furze and heather are often found where cattle grazing is less prominent.

25th April (St. Mark's Day) is the traditional date on which the cattle start going up the mountains. Summer grazing continues until the first snowfalls in November. Pyrenean cattle can be found in the pastures, as are stallions and mares related to the Basque Pony and Navarrese *Jaca* breed. The sign of their village of origin is usually branded on their rump.

The green landscape is speckled with fair-faced *latxa* sheep, which produce more milk than meat and yield quite rough wool. They know the terrain well. They graze and sleep without a shepherd, who only gathers together to check the flock from time to time and during the milking season, which lasts from Spring to July. The numerous large shacks and a few half-ruined sheep pens leads one to think that there must have been more flocks in Aralar in the past, which is true but the average size of the flocks was smaller than it is now. The huts and sheep-cotes are usually surrounded by the ash-tree, traditionally very highly valued for a number of reasons: its wood (flexible and hard) which is ideal for tool handles, its firewood for charcoal-making, staffs, a good bean-detecting tool, and its foliage (good food for sheep and rams).

Some travellers/walkers buy the delicious sheep's-milk cheeses direct from the shepherds. When the cheese has matured, the Day of the Shepherd *(Artzai Eguna)* is held in Uharte-Arakil on the last day of August. It is an all-day festival, with the cheese-making process on display in the village square in the morning. Selected cheeses take part in the quality competition, and the best ones are sold in a live auction. In the afternoon, the Final of the Navarre Sheepdog Championship is held in the field of Geinbera.

For trekkers and skiers Aralar is a real paradise. It is easily accessible, and has varied scenery and shelters to spend the night protected from the rain, snow and the treacherous fogs of the range. The forest house and the shelter of Igaratza are meeting points for mountaineers who meet to scale the peaks of Txindoki, Balerdi, Irumugarrieta, Tuturre or Putxerri. There are two equally scenic routes to Artxueta via Burnigurutze, or alternatively starting out from Madoz through the bucolic valley of Ata. The Sanctuary is a rustic shelter and offers comfortable accommodation.

A PREHISTORIC PLACE

The geographer Alfredo Floristán describes Aralar as a "moutain shelter and grazing and livestock area, like a prehistoric island which has remained indifferent to historical circumstances at the border of the ancient Basques." Before him, the prehistorian and ethnologist José Miguel Barandiarán highlighted the close relationship in the Western Pyrenees between pasturelands and those of megalithic culture. The sheep and cattle raising population were undoubtedly mostly shepherds.

The Aralar range has the highest concentration of Megalithic monuments in Navarre: 44 dolmens and one menhir, plus the 17 in Gipuzkoa.

In his book *La Prehistoria de Navarra*, the historian and

con su Ymagen dela Virgen del sagrario de la Cathe-
ubo antiguamente en la obscuridad de su Capilla, de donde
fue colocado assi en esta Capilla maior, en el año 1765

archaeologist Juan Iturralde y Suit tells how Professor Francisco de Huarte "had the chance to see certain rocks, specifically dolmens, and a human jaw was found under one of them; some mountaineers from the area, who knew of its existence, called it 'trego-arriya'. He goes on to tell us of his decision to explore further, and expresses his delight at the discoveries he made during the winter of 1894: "These dolmens are hidden in dark woods, and I had the immense satisfaction of seeing the first dolmens discovered in Navarre: these were the places where those primitive races camped, fought and lived thousands of years ago and left us these barbaric and mysterious monuments ... they are made from limestone like the mountains from which they were cut... The entrance to all the dolmens I have discovered is on their eastern side."

Iturralde y Suit studied 13 dolmens in Aralar, several caves and also the *Erroldan-arriya* menhir on the top of Ata, where he observed its 'mysterious chiselled grooves' and their incredible age. He considered the popular belief that Roland (of the *Chanson de Roland)* had pulled up the stone to throw it a great distance but did not make it that far to be "anachronistic and exaggerated." Popular folk tales often associated these megaliths with the mythology of *'jentil-arriak'*, built by the nocturnal genie *Maide*, with the shepherds' custom of throwing stones at the dolmens of Obieneta and Ziñekogurutze, a ritual considered to be a kind of prayer.

Those initial explorations by Iturralde y Suit were followed by the studies of Ansoleaga, Aranzadi, Barandiarán and Elósegui. Twenty-six dolmens have been excavated in the part of the Aralar range belonging to Navarre. They are usually small, simple and blend in well with the countryside, and are nearly always found at altitudes over 700 metres.

The word *dolmen* comes from the Breton language and means 'stone table'. The dolmen belongs to the first phase of megalithism, which runs from the Calcolithic to the Bronze Age. They were most commonly found about 2000 years BC. They are common graves where the dead were buried together with utensils and offerings to the gods.

Dolmens can be found all along the Atlantic coast of Europe. Until very recently it was believed that they were a cultural practice 'imported' from the Middle East, although Carbon 14 tests have shown that the European ones are older than those of the Fertile Crescent. According to the prehistorian María Amor Beguiristain, "there is more emphasis now on the autochtonous nature of many prehistoric inventions, and there is a trend towards phenomena which bring cultures together." The dolmens of Aralar are not the tombs of shepherds who used to go up the mountain to let their sheep graze in summer, but are burial places for entire family groups, with a high proportion of females. The men and women of the 'Western Pyrenees' group were people whose facial features were similar to their present-day counterparts: large head, narrow jaw, medium height and bulging temples.

[TWO PREVIOUS PAGES] *The altarpiece of Aralar, a masterpiece of European Romanesque enamelwork. It was probably made in Pamplona at the end of the XIIth century.*

The names Aralarre and Araceli, the constant medieval references to the Sanctuary of 'Monte Excelso' and the survival of specific rituals to the present day, for example a barren women stepping on a brick or putting one's head into the hole of a chasm to pray (Barandiarán affirms that the Romans did this in ancient times) have led to conjecture as to whether there was a pagan temple up there: a Roman *ara votiva*, perhaps inherited from an indigenous form of worship.

In the IXth century Christianity started to become widespread in the area. The anthropologist Julio Caro Baroja tells us that "when there were still pagans in the north of the present-day territory of Navarre, the primitive Navarrese monarchy was already a Christian one, there is no doubt about that ... It also seems that there were two main figures of devotion in the distant past: Santa María and San Miguel." For the people of the time San Miguel inherited some of the attributes of Hermes or Mercury, a mediator between Heaven and Earth, someone adored in the mountains. The messenger of the Olympian gods has wings on his heels and head, while the archangel has them on his back. They both lead souls up to Heaven, and appear next to the devil, weighing them on Judgement Day. In the liturgy of the dead San Miguel is the 'flag carrier', or 'carrier of the sign'. The image of Excelsis shows the angel with the cross over his head, just like the one in the Romanesque capital at Berrioplano (near Pamplona). The effigy venerated today is the work of the Pamplona silversmith José de Yábar, who covered the old wood cutting with silver in 1756. Every Spring the figure is taken to towns and villages to bless the fields and fertilise them as it goes by (as popular belief goes) with rain.

Alcuin of York, an adviser to Charlemagne, was the first to preach the miracles of San Miguel, and in the Carolingian era (12th century) Francisco Iñiguez Almech refurbished the Pre-Romanesque remains he recognised in the lower part of the greater apse of the sanctuary.

Is this the oldest Christian place of worship in Navarre? According to available documents, this honour belongs to the hermitage of San Pedro de Usún (829). The first mention of San Miguel de Excelsis is not found until 1032. The church was consecrated in 1074 and a monastic community settled there. The brotherhood of San Miguel became famous in the XIIth century, and at that time the church was the most visited in Navarre, so much so that the monks built a chorus chapel in the centre of the nave which is still conserved to this day.

The basilica, at 1,235 metres above sea level and surrounded by spectacular scenery, is a striking building. Only the base and three horse-shoe windows in the central apse remain, plus the springs of a vault. The Romanesque building was small when it was consecrated, but was considerably extended in the first half of the XIIth century when the naves and the portico were built. Everything is austere: there are no sculptures, just smooth stones. There are no capitals, which are replaced by a simple impost from where the barrel vaults start. The interior is dark, and the little light there is passes through the small grated windows of the apses and the circular windowsof an octagonal dome.

first picks up a myth, then loads it with magic, and only at the end (and in recent times) does it acquire religious significance. This is not the only legend of Aralar. The first establishment of the Sanctuary is attributed to a poor woman in the XIIIth century who arrived at the mountain with the idea of building a church. She dragged wood and stones across a flat piece of land and, through God's grace, the materials appeared on high ground properly cut and in the right places. Another story in the 'Book of Miracles' attributes the foundation of the Sanctuary to the penitent horseman García Arnaut, who left his family and property to live among wolves, bears and other wild animals. He neither ate or drank, but his family sent him food which he shared with his only companions, the partridges.

The effigy of San Miguel visits over three hundred towns and villages. It also taken to visit sick people and bless crops. It is always accompanied by the April rains.

Many appealing legends are associated with the mountain range and Sanctuary. Nowadays they are all well-known, from the oldest through those added in the medieval period taken from the *Libro de los Milagros* ('Book of Miracles') of the XIIIth century, to the most recent.

The figure of the dragon or *'Herensuge'* seems archaic: it is a genie which lives underground and communicates with the outside world through the entries to certain chasms. It personifies the forces of Nature. Later on, the dragon is a terrible monster which feeds on human flesh and demands victims. Its rivals, which are usually a shepherd, a warrior or an anonymous young man, have to call on some magic trick to beat it. In the XVIIth century, —picking up the legend of the parricide of San Julián el Hospitalario, very well known throughout the Western world —the legendary figure of Teodosio de Goñi was created: the victim of the dragon is a noble gentleman who, dressed in a coarse cloak, gave penitence for the horrible crime of having killed his parents. He drags heavy chains along, the dragon appears and he prays "San Miguel, look after me"; a thunderclap breaks, the sky is rent and the archangel appears holding a cross over his head. A vicious battle is fought and the cross triumphs, the dragon dies and the chains are broken. The legend

THE ENAMELLED ALTAR-PIECE OF ARALAR

This altar-piece is the jewel of European Romanesque enamelwork and was probably made in Pamplona between 1175 and 1185 by a group of diverse artists, one of them an enameller from Limoges. Some specialists point out the range of colours in which the artists from Limoges were so expert, other see the Spanish influence of the Silos workshop.

The central part shows the Virgin Mary in a mystical garment, as the throne of Christ. Both are crowned. Some consider the star of Epiphany (under the letter A) to be the key to the general meaning of the altar-piece: it is a revelation of the Incarnation. The Tetramorphous is the symbolic representation of the evangelists.

The twelve plates of the series of arches are bordered by a frame of three blue shades. For medieval sculptors of religious images this was a way of symbolising the sky. Saint Peter can be seen at the top left. The Three Wise Men are shown at the bottom left , and to the right, an Annunciation. There is a row of 18 medallions with motifs taken from mythology and literature, and over the arches there are some embossed architectures —towers, capitals, niches— which could refer to heavenly Jerusalem.

This copper-enamelled jewel was stolen in October 1979 but almost all the panels were recovered in February 1981.

The small town of Ochagavía, the gateway to the largest forest in the Pyrenees, offers the double charm of its privileged location, at the confluence of two trout-filled rivers at the foot of the Muskilda hill, and its architecture, cleverly distributed along the two banks of the Anduña stream. Four bridges cross its fast, cold waters, which then run into the Zatoya stream, coming down from the vegetable growing area. They join in Ochagavía to create the Salazar river, the 'father' of an ancient community of pastoral origin. The University of the Salazar Valley, which entered history during the early mediaeval period and played a decisive role in the formation of the kingdom of Pamplona, is still alive and welcoming, determined to advance after suffering a deep crisis in its traditional economy.

OCHAGAVÍA
AND THE SALAZAR VALLEY

Ochagavía has always been the most populated town of the Salazar valley. It is the economic centre with fortnightly markets and cattle fairs which, up to well into the nineteenth century, were held in the Tapla pass, up on the Abodi mountain range. It was also a frontier and customs town until the European Union abolished the barriers. The Customs building at Pikatua now provides services for a cross-country skiing resort, and in the heart of the town there is a Nature Interpretation Centre. Winter sports and summer tourism enliven the bars and hotels.

Salazar has a harsh climate during the long winter, and this harshness increases from south to north to such an extent that the amount of rainfall in the mountains of Ochagavía is double that of the southern area. There are many icy mornings and frequent snowfalls. The great snowfall of 1432 is recorded in the 'Annals' of Padre Moret (a chronicler of the Kingdom of Navarre). It snowed incessantly for forty days, the towns and villages were isolated and food was scarce, to such an extent that the birds and even the bears and wolves, the most ferocious of beasts, let themselves be caught as if "tamed by hunger." There must have been many wolves in the Irati forest, and in the first third of the nineteenth century the sum of one hundred and twenty *reales* was paid for each wolf or she-wolf caught or killed, and half that sum for each wolf-cub. The valley's coat of arms depicts a black wolf with a silver lamb across its mouth. The very name of Ochagavía, of doubtful origin, has a definite prefix, *otsa,* a variant of the Basque word *otso,* or wolf.

This cold climate with frequent snowfalls explains the narrow sheltered streets which still conserve the beautiful boulder paving, and the type of dwellings, a prodigious blend of lime, stone and wood. The walls are thick and the facades have stone quoining. They are usually three storeys high: from the paved entrance hall there is access to the granaries, food store and tool room; on the next floor there is the kitchen, the living room and the bedrooms; and on the top floor the *sabaiao* (attic) is used as a drying and store room. Some large houses have keystone doors and coats of arms. On the whitewashed walls of others, the bright colours of the woodwork and the flowers stand out, and inside many of the houses old utensils are collected which could easily be used to form the basis of an ethnographic museum.

The roofs (gable or hip) are steeply pitched and are covered with flat tiles which replaced the traditional *oholak,* oak wood boards cut with an axe along the grain. Today this boarding can only be seen on the roof of the Parish Church tower. It was a waterproof and long lasting roof but was helpless in the face of fire. During the war against the Convention, on 17th October 1794 the retreating French looted the houses and the church and set fire to the town. One hundred and eighty-two houses were destroyed by the fire and many inhabitants, reduced to misery, were forced to beg from door to door in the other towns of the Salazar valley, where they were welcomed and supported. Two years later, many families still lived in huts scattered about the countryside and some of the houses remained without roofs. The Bishop of Pamplona gave his consent for the

[PREVIOUS PAGE] *A large grassy hillock in the Abodi range.*

sum of 161,430 *reales,* obtained from the sale of the church silver, to be used for the benefit of the town.

In Ochagavía, as in the rest of the Salazar valley, the houses have their own names which are often passed on from generation to generation. As Carlos Hernández states, "through their owners, the houses are individual subjects of the law who collect the profits shared between those who have a home open in the Valley for at least nine months a year, and in this way the Valley helps to physically maintain the houses, which is costly as a result of the valley's Alpine climate." The *salacencos* not only receive an annual share of the common property, in money or in kind, they also have the right to batches of firewood for their homes, and to acquire wood from the forests at a modest price in order to build their houses or agricultural buildings. Today some people are demanding that the way the money is distributed should be updated to give priority to community needs, assisting companies in their economic development, training, and improving welfare services. "The Entitlement is for life and must be enjoyed by men. If people continue to migrate from the valleys, the Entitlement will end up being pure history."

The festival of Saint John the Evangelist, which is still celebrated each year on 27th December, was, in the traditional culture of Ochagavía, the *Urruskide Eguna* ('Day for Dining Together'), an opportunity to get together and possibly even settle those quarrels which often arise in a small rural community. Days before, from the pulpit, the priest announced how the families were to pair off in order to eat together, mixing the rich with the poor. The custom declined when some people sent food to the houses of others but did not sit down at the same table. José María Iribarren, who has written about this now-extinct custom, compared it to a similar one in the neighbouring town of Almiradío de Navascués. There, on the Day for Dining Together, each person put the great iron key of the door to his home on a pile. The pairing was then decided by chance since an innocent hand took the keys from the pile, two by two.

Ochagavía lies on both sides of the Anduña river and has four districts. To the south, on the left of the river, there is th *Urrutia* quarter, which is Basque for 'far from the centre'. On the other bank lie the other three quarters: *Irigoien,* the highest and furthest east, *Iribarren,* the lowest and most western, and *Arasanatea,* or the Abbey, where the parish church is to be found. Two stone crosses mark out the village. At the entrance, next to the San Martín metal bridge over the Zatoya, there is a Plateresque cross from the first half of the XVIth century. Leaving the town and going towards Izalzu, at the fork with the road up to Muskilda, a cross bearing the Virgin and the Crucifixion was erected in 1975.

The Parish church stands above the village like a sturdy mass. The eight-sided prismatic tower accentuates the slope with its steep pyramidal spire. The church was the only building to resist the great fire of 1794, remaining as a solitary, scorched giant amongst the blackened walls and charred woodwork of the houses. The flames also destroyed two hermitages, and there is now little left of their stone walls: the hermitage of Santa Cruz, which was situated on the way up to Muskilda, and the hermitage of San Martín, located next to the road to Ezcároz, which the French had converted into a gunpowder store. It exploded when the fire reached it.

The cold climate and frequent snowfalls explain the sheltered narrowness of the streets of Ochagavía, where beautiful cobblestones are preserved.

Indeed, the church of Ochagavía had already been affected by fire in 1543. It was then reconstructed, giving it the appearance we see today. There are some remains of the Proto-Gothic church, built at the beginning of the XIIIth century, below the vestry and the doorway, part of the great Gothic church destroyed by the fire.

The real parish treasures are the three altarpieces of St. John the Evangelist, St. James and St. Catherine, and the choir stalls, carved by Miguel de Espinal, a maker of religious images, in his Pamplona workshop. The wood, lime for the altarpieces and oak for the thirteen ceremonial chairs, comes from the mountains of Ochagavía and Salazar. The work was finished in 1578 and was valued by the famous sculptor Jan de Anchieta, who considered it to be highly commendable. The Monumental Catalogue of Navarre indicates that the altarpiece of the high altar "is one of the best Renaissance works in Navarre and it also occupies an important place in the sculptures of the Spanish Renaissance as a whole." The altar front preserves the original colours given it by Martín de Zalba, a painter

from Pamplona, which are now shown in all their splendour after the restoration carried out in 1988, enabling one to appreciate the richness of the colours, the flakes, the hatching and pointing in gold, and the ivory incarnations.

MUSKILDA AND ITS TRUSTEESHIP

In other valleys in Navarre such as Lónguida and Izagaondoa there are places called 'Muskilda'. The term comes from the Basque *muskil*, meaning *morcueros* (stone piles related to religious traditions): dolmens, the ruins of ancient buildings, or stones taken from the fields.

Muskilda is a sacred mountain dressed with beeches in the *pako* (shade) of the north-facing slope. On the south-facing slopes, the remains of an oak wood are visible. A path goes along the summit to the pastures of Arpea and Abodi and then on to the Irati forest. From the heights there is a splendid view dominated by the Orhi, the highest peak in the Pyrenees range in Navarre (over 2000 meters), and, in the distance, the summits of the Roncal mountains adorn the sky, grey with bare rock and white with snow. The nearer scenery is a mosaic of farms surrounded by hedges and trees and dotted with huts.

There is a road, through Ollarzegiak and the beech woods of Ituzkia, which climbs up to the sanctuary, which stands at 1,020 meters above sea level and 225 meters above the Parish Church of Ochagavía. This historic path, almost two kilometres long, climbs up a slope strewn with memories. Half way along the route there are the ruins of the Santa Cruz hermitage. Then, on a small esplanade, the Gothic cross of Arrixuria. Further still, 'El Pilar', a stone prism built in 1654 and the 'Humilladero' or place with a cross/image. Finally, the buildings of the hospice and house of the hermit and, once over the 'El Cerrado' wall, the Romanesque hermitage dating from the second half of the XIIth century.

A XVth century wrought iron screen guards the presbytery and the lady chapel. The seated image of the Virgin of Muskilda is a late XIVth century sculpture. According to a Baroque legend, undocumented until 1755, it was a small cowherd who found the image at the foot of an oak tree, on seeing a bull that was escaping from the herd and was scratching in the earth. With successive disappearances and mysterious journeys from the Parish Church to the summit of the mountain, and by freeing the jailed cowherd, who everyone suspected of stealing the effigy, the Virgin Mary made it known that she wished to be worshipped on the summit. The cowherd became a hermit and his little donkey, with no guide whatsoever, made many journeys to the far away quarries of Mendi Itxusia, constantly bringing stones to construct the hermitage.

The small town of Ochagavía is owner and proprietor of the lands and buildings of Muskilda, which the council has administered with a civil board of administration, stubbornly defending its autonomy in the face of the pretensions of the hierarchy of the Church. The historian Jimeno Jurío has studied the various lawsuits and litigations, which came to a head in the year 1666. They were times of economic growth and the Bishop wanted to supervise the accounts. The board of governors opposed this and ignored a summons from the vicar-general, resulting in the excommunication

of those affected. In the middle of the XVIIth century the inhabitants of Ochagavía witnessed the cruel mediaeval rite of a candle extinguished and trampled on the ground, and for three consecutive Sundays they listened to the terrifying edict read at mass: "Accursed be the food you eat, the drink you drink and the air you breathe. Accursed be the earth you tread and the bed you sleep in. The sky shall rain nothing but fire and stone on you. You shall not enjoy the fruit of your work, nor find anyone to help you in your hour of need. Whenever you are judged you will be condemned. Let the curse of God be brought upon you and let the Holy Angels desert you. Let the demons be with you day and night. Let the earth swallow you up alive, so that you may go to Hell in body and in soul, and no memory of you remain amongst men."

THE DANCES OF MUSKILDA

The dances of Our Lady of Muskilda are linked to the trusteeship of the hermitage. They are performed on 8th September, both at the hermitage and in the town, and are exciting because of the solemnity of the ritual, the colours of the clothing, the vigour of the dancers and the force their music acquires, which is interpreted with the harmonious richness of the Navarrese *gaita* (pipe) and the rhythm of the castanets, drum and sticks.

It is a complex *suite* which, through the ages, has gathered together a range of choreographies and instruments. The oldest appear to be the four rhythms beat with sticks called Emperador, Cachucha, Danza and Modorro, three of which are composed of

just six notes, with scales of six and which perhaps date back to mediaeval times. The cycle is completed with a dance/game of neckscarves that starts and ends with two high quality musical pieces: a *Pasacalles* and a *Jota*. These dances were documented for the first time in 1666, although folklore experts have found symbols and ancestral elements which remind us of the agricultural work of the hoe, the strong and brave group of people who had to defend the villages from potential invaders, and even the mythological key of time in the two-faced mask of the chief of the group, 'El Bobo' (the fool), similar to the god Janus who, with his two faces, is capable of observing the past and the future at the same time.

What is to most admirable is the vitality of this gold-mine of traditional culture with which the *Ochagavianos* identify themselves.

A panorama of Pyrenean summits. Woods and meadows seen from the Lázar pass, where the valleys of Roncal and Salazár join.

There is no house in the town which has not formed part of the team of nine dancers, which also began a children's' dance group in 1974.

THE UNIVERSITY OF THE SALAZAR VALLEY

Sahats is the Basque name for willow, a tree which is to be found in abundance on the river banks. An extensive willow plantation *Zaraitzu*, appears to have given the valley and the river Salazar their name and perhaps even a wider area, the land of *Sarazaso*. This is

Dancers in honour of Our Lady of Muskilda. In the centre, the Bobo with its two-fronted mask. Records of these dances go back to 1666.

because the *saracenses* probably occupied the whole of the river basin, which extends far beyond the present Salazar valley, and even the more eastern valleys of Roncal and Ansó, and as far as the territory of Soule or Zuberoa on the northern (French) side of the Pyrenees.

The medievalist Martín Duque, who has studied the origins and historic evolution of the Salazar Valley, indicates that our earliest knowledge goes back to the VIIth century, when a Basque tribe dedicated to grazing settled in the area and was Christianised early on. That community, with a strong communal sense and their common property well defined, soon organised themselves into Councils which held open meetings of the inhabitants, summoned by the ringing the bell after high mass each Sunday. This custom has lasted in some settlements such as Sarriés or Ibilcieta right up to this century. The mediaeval councils had a democratic organisation, as far as was feasible in a hierarchic and unequal society. The historian Jimeno Jurío has gathered information which leads us to think that in the Middle Ages there were more serfs, undernourished victims of the continual plagues who were deprived of their rights than free men, who were farmers and nobles.

The contribution of the *saracenses* to the nascent kingdom of Pamplona and its declaration of independence against the Moslems of Cordoba was vital. The need for winter pastures for the cattle in the Bardenas (south of Navarre) forced them to set up relations and agreements and to marry into the *Banu Qasi* of the region around

[OVERLEAF] *The hermitage of the Virgen de las Nieves in the heart of the Irati forest. Two streams, the Urtxuria and the Urbeltza, join here to form the Irati river.*

Tudela. When the valley was incorporated into the kingdom of Pamplona at the end of the IXth century, it lost its political autonomy and formed first a 'tenure' and then, from the XIIIth century onwards, an *almiradío* or *bailío* of the Sangüesa district, although it preserved its peculiar administrative system. Only one mayor presided over the common neighbourhood assembly of the whole valley. At the end of the XIth century the *Junta General* (General Assembly)was created which met at the St Cecilia hermitage in Ibilcieta or in the village hall at Ezcároz, and it operated for centuries as a limited Council with representatives delegated from each locality.

It was not until the XIth century that the limits of jurisdiction of each town and those of the 'University' of the Valley were differentiated. Municipal jurisdiction was determined on the basis of the Parish demarcations established to collect tithes. In order to carry out tax assessment and collection, in the XIVth century the three 'quiñones' or territorial divisions were created, and the valley is still divided in this way: the *quiñón* of Aldegaña (Ochagavía), which is solely for this town, that of Errartea, which includes Esparza, Ezcároz and Jaurrieta, and that of Atabea, which includes the eleven remaining villages: Gallués , Güesa, Ibilcieta, Iciz, Igal, Izal, Izalzu, Oroz, Ripalda, Sarries, and Uscarrés. It was in the XIXth century that the Salazar valley was divided into municipalities.

In our times, as Martín Duque writes, "The General Assembly of the Valley of Salazar is no mere commission delegated by the Councils or the inhabitants to correctly administer common property. It is still the representative body of the Valley, as an institution of public entitlement, and is the direct and uninterrupted successor of the primitive community of the *saracenses*." Today the Assembly administers 14,463 hectares of common fields and mountains. It consists of eighteen members, with six elected from each *quiñón*, and gets together in Ezcároz as an Ordinary Meeting in the last fortnight of each quarter. It is presided by the Principal Mayor, a post which rotates between the three *quiñones* following a traditional order.

ECONOMY AND CULTURAL PATRIMONY

The climate and the altitude are the reason why Salazar has always been a cattle valley, although the number of livestock is gradually decreasing. One town alone, Ochagavía, had 50,000 head of sheep in the middle of the XIXth century; today, adding all the municipal property registers together, there are not even half that figure. As well as sheep, almost all the inhabitants took care to breed pigs in the mountains. In the southern settlements there were smallholder productions of cereals and grapevines but these were not sufficient to satisfy internal consumption. The cultivation of selected seed potato had some very good years from 1927 onwards around Jaurrieta. The exploitation of wood in the forests, for ships for the Navy and the construction of buildings, grew in importance from the XVIIIth century onwards, when some *salacencos* became intrepid navigators on the *almadías* (rafts) along the difficult routes through the gorges of Arbayún and Lumbier.

Emigration has been going on for a long time and many *salacencos* left the valley to try their luck in America. Not all of them

The mediaeval bridge at Ochagavía over the river Anduña. The house on the other side has a steep gable and hipped roof.

were as successful as Diego de Artieda y Chirino, who founded the New Kingdom of Navarre and the city of Esparza in Central America in 1578, so Salazar is still remembered in Costa Rica.

Industrialisation has not reached this valley, where the population is ageing and is on the decline. Tourism brings hopes of a revitalisation: the natural patrimony, especially the Irati forest, with its magnificent beech woods and fir plantations (see separate chapter), hunting or fishing for trout in the crystalline waters, folklore, gastronomy, and the artistic beauty of the buildings are all good reasons to visit the area.

Each town is well worth a visit. There are many well-preserved places to discover, with paved streets, stately homes, medieval bridges and palaces, hermitages lost in the mountains, Romanesque and Gothic churches, the inheritors of ancient monasteries like those at Igal or Izizuloa, furnished with Mannerist, Renaissance or Baroque altar pieces. On special festival days, such as in Jaurrieta, it is still possible to see girls wearing traditional costumes as they sing and dance the *Axuri Beltza* melody. And on Christmas Eve, in Esparza,

the children's choirs still sing the verses of the *Eguberri*, and, in Ochagavía, the pleasing Basque-Latin carol *Verbum caro factum est Maria beti Birjinik*.

The younger generation has rediscovered the 'lost link' of the Basque language, which, in this century, has produced writers from Salazar such as Ciriaco and Federico Garralda. When the native language was in difficulty, Arturo Campión, a writer from Pamplona, went to Salazar and in his book 'Fantasy and Reality' he shows himself to be fascinated by the "grandiose and severe scenery of the Sierra de Abodi and its black, wooded foothills and the Orhi summit with its shining snow against the stormy horizon." Campión affirms that he heard the story of Garchot in the town. 'The Bard of Izalzu' who sacrificed his son Mikelot by suffocating him with balls of mud so that those who wanted to make him sing in a foreign language could not hear his beautiful voice. The songwriter and singer Benito Lertxundi mentions the story in a beautiful ballad he sings in the Basque language: *Txori kantazale ederra, nun ote haiz kantatzen? Harrien negarra haizeak darama Saraitzuko ibarretan barna* (Beautiful singing bird, where will you be singing now? The wind spreads the wailing of the stones across the valley of Salazar).

The road anxiously searches out the shelter of the deep gorges, fleeing from the rocky areas, the gloomy sierras, and the savage mountains. Of all the valleys in the Navarre mountains, the Roncal valley is the purest of them all; the only one to conserve a fighting spirit", wrote the novelist Félix Urabayen. The rugged scenery offers a variety of vegetation, passing from Mediterranean forest to the pasture lands high up in the mountains. This area, which is transverse to the Pyrenean axis, is inhabited by a community of people of markedly different characteristics, evident in their singular administrative regime, fine quality apparel and rich dialect, in which the Roncalese are called *Kalesak*.

RONCAL
The valley and the mountains

The easternmost valley of the Pyrenees in Navarre can only be considered an Alpine valley at Belagoa, its upper end, which has been carved by glaciers. The snow and mist last the whole summer in the Larra area. To the south, however, the sunny gateway to this woodland and cattle area has long been dominated by 'bread-making crops, fields of cereal, and other crops and where vines were cultivated right up to the XVIIth century. There is a difference in altitude of over eighteen hundred meters between the highest part, located at 2,434 meters on the 'Mesa de los Tres Reyes', and the lowest, deep down in the Burgui Gorge. With regard to Burgui, as it is the southernmost town, the inhabitants of the other six towns generally call it the *ribera* or "on the river plain." This is no exaggeration if the climate and altitude are taken into consideration. The geographer Casas Torres considers the Roncal to be a "typical Mediterranean valley, although in the highlands", and, according to Floristán, it is a "sub-alpine valley on the Mediterranean slopes of the Pyrenees."

It appears that the name Roncal has something to do with the configuration of the valley, which runs transversal to the geological structures. *Erronkari*, as the Basque term for the valley indicates, is related to the idea of a string, gorge or cliff. The Esca river flows along the folds of rock, sometimes through narrow passes where the shadow of the night appears hours earlier than in the rest of the valley, and other times in more open spaces, but always flanked by slopes covered with pine and fir-trees and crowned by rocks with cascading brooks.

Eighteen kilometres separate Burgui from Isaba. The road and river run almost parallel, and the vegetation changes gradually, dark masses of conifers alternating with meadows dotted with gorse. The setting widens before the gigantic and white mass of Ezkaurre. Between this rocky spot and the one at Ardibideginea, are the 'Ateas', a gateway created by the old cattle movements. It was first transformed into a farming and forest path and then, in 1920, into a road, opening up a tourist route of remarkable charm. The groups of red pine give way to beech woods at the foot of the great mountains, which encircle the Belagoa valley. Initially the road only reached the Arrako hermitage, from where one had to continue on foot or on horseback to France through the Arrakogoiti pass, following, like the shepherds, the old 'wool route', of which the 'Arrako' and 'Juan Pito' inns are a reminder. The road then climbs up rocky escarpments towards the passes and the fine pastures of the upper mountain, before going in between the rough rocks of Larra. There the black pines, a relic of the Tertiary Age, emphasise the desolate aspect of an impressive, abrupt and inhospitable landscape, presided over by a massif with some majestic summits: Anie, Ukerdi, Budoguía and the Mesa de los Tres Reyes.

Larra and Belagoa, in the north-eastern corner, are home to the highest peaks Navarre and signal the beginning of the high Pyrenees. Further west, there is no true Alpine level. This explains its

[PREVIOUS PAGE] *Belagoa is where the high Pyrenees begin, in an eastward direction.*

Burgui is the southernmost town in the Roncal valley. Its houses are clustered in the centre, and the streets go down from the church to the banks of the river Esca.

extraordinary ecological importance, as Jesús Elósegui, a biologist, mentions: "Larra and its surroundings mark the vital limit for some communities and many species of fauna and flora. Some botanical studies have described various species and sub-species totally new to science that live in the heart of Larra. As zoological singularities, we should point out: the Ptarmigan, white-headed blackbird, and capercaillie amongst the birds and the Pyrenean mountain goat, stoat, marmot, bear and vole amongst the mammals, which have all found their western limit here in the Pyrenees."

A good part of the surface area of Larra, (23.5 square kilometres) belonging to the Roncal valley, is protected and has been declared a Nature Reserve. This impressive limestone massif has been deeply and extensively moulded by rain, snow and ice. The exterior shows a tortured relief of ridges, chasms, depressions and blind Karstic valleys. The calcareous material, which extends upwards for more than two thousand metres, is pierced with cavities, halls, and a complex system of galleries of which over 125 kilometres have been mapped, containing several lakes and five great rivers. The San Martin chasm and the BU-56 are reference points for international speleology, and are explored each year, a depth of 1,388 meters having been reached there. Of the six hundred or more chasms in the sector, seven are more than six hundred metres deep. In the Larra Nature Reserve the central area, Ukerdi, occupying 322 hectares, is an integral reserve and enjoys special protection.

On the southern border of the Larra Nature Reserve, there is another integral reserve, Aztaparreta, which is considered to be one of the last virgin woods of Navarre. It occupies 100 hectares on the steep northern slopes of the Txamantxoia mountain. According to the scientists, Montserrat, Villar, Bunce and Elena, "Azta-parreta is today the most beautiful and well conserved example of beech woods and fir plantations in the entire western Pyrenees." It is difficult to reach and this explains the limited signs of human intervention in this area of intense vegetable biodiversity. The black pines, firs, beeches, sorb and mountain elms are accompanied by a rich undergrowth. The heavy rainfall favours the extension of lichens and mosses, amongst which small amphibians such as the sala-mander are to be found.

The steep slopes of Lakartxela, Lapakiza and Txamatxoia, the Larrondo summit, the Lapazarra crest, the Great Lákora Pass, the watercourse of Añabarkandía, the mountain floor of Zampori, Eskilarra and La Contienda, are covered in fine pastures. The much coveted richness of these high-level pastures explains the existence of a 'Facería' (peace agreement) between neighbouring French and Spanish valleys and a hitherto unheard of ceremony which has been repeated every year since the XIVth century.

The tribute of the three cows

The writer, Rafael Gambra, writes that "when, after the victory of Poitiers, the Franks managed to expel the Arab armies from Gaul, the inhabitants of the Pyrenees used to place various boundary stones dedicated to Saint Martín at the dividing passes, so that his patronage should free them from such terrible visitors", adding, "the most famous of these Stones of Saint Martín is to be found in the high and desolate Ernaz pass." The Stone of Saint Martín was substituted in 1856, on the occasion of the Limit Treaty, for a com-mon frontier stone numbered 262.

Regardless of whether it is a splendid hot day or there is a damp humid mist, every 13th of July thousands of people meet at this spot, next to the Arlás peak (also known as 'La Contienda') to witness the fulfilment of a mediaeval commitment. The so-called 'Tribute of the Three Cows' is, according to Fayrén, who has studied the interna-tional Pyrenean peace agreements, "a partial compensation for the use of the pastures and waters of Leja and Ernaz for twenty eight days a year", but the legend and the story have made it exceptional.

The rite is carried out with meticulous exactness. Everybody meets next to the boundary stone, each person in his own territo-ry. On the one side, the mayors of the Roncal valley, wearing traditional apparel of a hat, long, black, cloth cloak called an 'ongarina', walloon and short breeches, and, on the other side, those from the villages of Baretous who appear in their Sunday best, displaying a French Republican tricolour sash across their chests. The Mayor of Isaba, who presides the act, asks the Baretonese three times whether they are willing to pay, as in previous years, the tribute of the three cows, which must be "two years old, and of the same teeth, skin and horns", with no defects or wounds. Those ques-tioned respond affirmatively another three times. One of the French aldermen places his right hand on the boundary stone and, alter-nately, each person from each side places his hand on top. The Mayor of Isaba places his hand on last of all and pronounces the solemn wish: "pax avant, pax avant, pax avant" which is repeated by the rest. The veterinarian from Isaba checks the cows, which are

accepted: two of them always go to Isaba, and the other one goes alternately to either Garde, Urzainqui or Uztarroz. The receipt is handed over, the four guards to witness the *facería* are named, they take an oath and anyone who has anything to say is invited to step forward. The meeting is closed by standing up and signing the act. Lunch is then offered 'House of the Valley', the Roncalese bring-ing roast lamb and the Baretonese liqueurs and coffee.

Conflicts over pastures and springs, which occurred right across the Pyrenees, were resolved first of all by good neighbourly, oral com-mitments, or later on by drawing up a letter of peace. Disagreements were almost always due to a lack of clear boundaries or vagueness about the rights of each party.

The historian Florencio Idoate found references to the Erlanz pastures as early as the XIIIth century. There is a legendary tradi-tion which speaks of discussions, quarrels, death and revenge, complicated by personal quarrels amongst the shepherds which led to war between the valleys. It is certain that there were acts of violence and that, to end them, Roncalese and Baretonese referred the matter for the decision of the Mayor of Ansó, Sancho García, and five other neighbours who adjudicated pastures and springs and determined boundaries, regulated the use of the *facería*. In 1375 he dictated a sentence which included in its clauses the handing over of three cows at the Saint Martín stone each year.

In the choir of the parish church of Isaba, there are some XVIIth century choir stalls with seats of honour and decorated boards. The representations of dances and agricultural work are worthy of note, and, in particular, a staging of the Tribute of the Three Cows.

A cattle-rearing and woodland valley

The Roncalese have been shepherds since prehistoric times. Early on, they burned and cut the woodlands to encourage cattle farm-ing, rearing breeds of sheep, cows and horses which are still present today. They were obliged to move their herds to lower lands in the winter, since the snow made it impossible to pasture in the high-lands. Along the 'Cañada Real' (Royal cattle or sheep track) of the Roncal valley, which began on the flatlands of Belagoa and, after travelling a distance of 100 kilometres, ended in the Bardenas Reales (south of Navarre), there are numerous dolmens and cromlechs which suggest the movement of cattle in ancient times. From the Middle Ages there is a record of the entitlement of the Roncal valley to feed and make cattle pens and huts in the Bardenas. The cows from Roncal were also moved to the Landes of Aquitaine, as recorded in XVIth century documents. The by-laws of the Valley demand that the cattle routes should always remain free and unploughed. The fact that they had to be moved, in long, hard jour-neys has contributed to the select cattle breed.

Sheep have always had priority in the valley. Since the first reliable census carried out in 1634, an approximate figure of 100,000 heads has always been maintained over the centuries. Nowadays, this has been reduced to a quarter of the figure.

The cattle are no longer milked in the 'muideras' or huts high up in the mountain passes. The *Rasa* sheep, whose milk was used for preparing the Roncal cheese, have been largely replaced by the

Lacha sheep of other valleys, which today supply the majority of the milk to the cheese-making farms. A specific Designation of Origin protects Roncal cheese, a regional speciality. Industrial production has replaced farmhouse production but uses traditional knowledge to make "a firm cheese of a yellowish-white colour with its own special aroma and slightly spicy taste."

The Roncal Valley exported 70,000 kilos of wool to France along the 'Wool Route' in the middle of the XIXth century. The medium quality wool of the *rasa* sheep was appreciated for making mattresses. Nevertheless, the mills of the valley are now only of interest to etnographers. The women and also some shepherds knew how to weave and dye with 'capeche' extract, a pulse from which the colouring was taken. Wool was used to manufacture blankets, cloths called 'mancales' used to cover the bread during the rising and preparation stages, and, on their feet, 'peducos' (shoes of thick cloth), and 'peales', which were used to adapt one's feet to clogs.

The herds of cows and horses which do not need to migrate are maintained. Brown-Alpine and Pyrenean cows remain in the stables during the winter, eating the fodder gathered in the meadows at harvest time. The 'Burguete' breed mares stay out in the open almost all year round, and are only stabled when it snows.

The woodlands are another important source of income. Whilst the Roncal valley occupies 3.9 per cent of the surface area of Navarre, it contains 6.1 per cent of the woodlands and produces 5.6 per cent of the region's timber. The wooded area of the valley accounts for 17,764 hectares, with a clear predominance of conifers over deciduous trees. Up to the XVIIIth century a balance was maintained between the wood, pastures and agriculture, although this period marked the start of an intensive exploitation of the woods for use in the construction of the Imperial Canal of Aragon and for the shipyards of the Spanish Navy. From that time onwards, a large percentage of the population was involved in wood-cutting, transporting it by means of the *Almadía* or raft. The woodland resources have enabled good community services to be constructed, noticeably in the network of roads and paths, or in the solid town halls. The sawmills and wood loading points form part of the Roncal landscape.

The woodland is full of surprises. The Basari ravine, near Burgui, is home to a natural wood where the southernmost firs in Navarre grow. In Garde there is a singular tree which is protected as a natural monument: It is a 19-meter high walnut tree which gave a harvest of 13 sacks of nuts in 1970.

Crops have always been of slight importance, although at the end of the last century ploughed land took up four times the space it now occupies. It now accounts for just three per cent of agricultural land, at the bottom of the valley for producing fodder, cereals and potatoes. Some cultivated land on the sides of the mountains, has been abandoned. Next to the Zuberoa hermitage, located in Garde right under Mount Calveira, it is possible to contemplate a wide area covered by huts (*bordas*), which were used as stables for cows and sheep, grain and fodder storage places, and temporary

[PREVIOUS PAGE] *Livestock goes up to the high pastures of Roncal in summer, where the fog clings to the mountain passes.*

A stone hut in the Belagua valley.

dwellings. The old threshing floors and ploughing equipment remain, and even the old wooden threshing machines with stone teeth, a reminder of the time when people threshed out in the fields.

Many huts in the Roncal valley have changed their use. They have now been renovated for use as a second home or rural hostal. The hotel industry has grown and diversified. Winter sports and the cross-country ski slopes at Contienda, Ferial, Bortuzko and Eskilzarr attract thousands of people during the winter season. Tourism is a solid prospect for the future, given the natural, scenic and sporting value of the valley, and the historical heritage which surrounds it.

THE ASSOCIATION OF MUNICIPALITIES OF THE RONCAL VALLEY

The people of Roncal live in seven villages along the banks of the rivers Esca, Uztárroz, Gardalar and Biniés, which irrigate small market gardens for domestic cultivation. During the middle of the XIXth century, Pascual Madoz noted that all the towns in the valley, except Garde, which is the most eastern one, are to be found on the circumference of the Santa Bárbara Mountain, which extends its spurs towards them.

Burgui, which conserves its mediaeval bridge, also had a strategic castle to defend the valley and the Burdaspal monastery, which was visited by Saint Eulogio of Cordoba during the IXth century.

When the caliph from Cordoba Abd-al-Rhaman III directed an expedition to punish the kingdom of Pamplona in 994 there were skirmishes on the routes leading to Roncal. A legend recounts that the men of Roncal defeated "the king of Cordoba called Abderramen at the place of Olast", near Burgui, and that they took him prisoner in his own barracks at Yesa. Whilst the men discussed the prisoner's fate on the bridge over the river Aragón, a Roncalese woman got ahead and cut off his head with a dagger. For this reason the valley's coat of arms has shows a bridge with the bloody head of a Moorish king on it. Two more quarters were added to this one, and another with hills comprising the old coats of arms, a greyhound and a castle, was granted in 1797 as a mark of loyalty and strength, after the war of the Convention.

Roncal, a frontier land with France and Aragón, has had key strategic importance in some decisive episodes of history, such as the time of the conquest of the Kingdom by the Castilians at the beginning of the XIth century. Moreover, the first guerrilla bands fighting for the 'Independence' in Navarre sprang up here at the beginning of 1809.

Roncal constitutes a political/administrative unit which was already officially recognised in the XIth century by documents which do not refer to the Valley as a geographical space, but as an organisation. The Community itself receives privileges and signs pacts and agreements. By the year 1290 this Community was perfectly defined and formed by eight settlements, which were reduced to the seven present ones when 'Navarzato' disappeared. Various secessionist attempts by Burgui, Isaba and Garde demonstrated, throughout history, the unity of the people of the valley. The General Assembly, whose existence was first documented in the XVth century, personifies and represents the political and administrative unit. The Valley has its own 'war leader', negotiates payments to the Treasury, has the power to make rules, and has issued a series of Ordinances.

Juan Cruz Alli, a lawyer who has studied the institutions and the peculiar administrative system of the Roncal, affirms that "the Valley of the Roncal, its commonwealth regime, the local exploitations, and the strict pasture use régime are not understandable if not based on a society supported by a certain physical environment, with an economic structure based on cattle raising. The search for a balance between cattle raising, as the principal activity of the population, and agriculture, which is necessary for sustenance, will be the central theme for all the regulations adopted in the Valley. It is evident that the traditional institutions are really a result of the requirements determined by the physical environment, subsistence and the economy rather than a demonstration of the peoples' spirit."

King Charles III granted the inhabitants of the valley the collective privilege of nobility in the year 1412. The Ordinances defended an endogenous, closed system for economic reasons. They protected the family patrimonies of each town and, in the event of inevitable ruin they made provisions for appraising and acquiring property in order to keep it in the community. The Ordinances also established difficult conditions for granting residence, as well as demanding a long stay in the valley, they required pure blood and nobility. If you were not a "neighbour" but simply an "inhabitant" this meant that you did not belong to the community, which gave rise to a group of outsiders. According to the historian Floristán Imízcoz, "the inhabitants depended on the benevolence of their neighbours to be able to enjoy community privileges, which were meanly limited by the 'neighbours'. They could not take part with voice and vote in municipal assemblies. The only place where they were recognised was in church, although they had to sit in the back rows of pews. In the Roncal and Aézcoa valleys, they even dressed differently.

The association of municipalities which today constitutes the Roncal Valley is not the result of grouping together pre-existing municipalities, but the opposite. The whole valley was just one Community, University or Council. The General Assembly still has its own functions, although it has gradually transferred functions and powers (which were well defined in 1846) to the seven municipalities: Burgui, Garde, Isaba, Roncal, Urzainqui, Uztarroz and Vidángoz.

The 'House of the Valley' is located in the town of Roncal. The Assembly meetings and wood auctions are held here. The House keeps the records of the Valley, a collection of antique and luxury traditional apparel, and a gallery of five portraits of famous people from Roncal: two men of arms, an entrepreneur, a missionary and a famous tenor.

Typical dress is severe for the men, aristocratic for the women, and different for unmarried and married people and valley aldermen. With regard to male attire, worthy of note are the short breeches adjusted below the knee with a red tie, short cloth jacket, waistcoat, narrow woollen sash, linen shirt and felt hat. As for the Roncalese women, we can highlight the two long ankle length skirts, of a purplish blue colour, the inside one pleated and the top one folded upwards to show off the 'aldar', a bright red lining; jacket and bodice with blue brocade trimmed in gold or silver; long linen blouse; adorning necklace, and a jewel, *bitxi*, which hangs from the neck on a black tape; hair in two long plaits hanging down the back and twisted together with *zintamuxko* (a black ribbon). For church, a thin flannel 'mantilla' is worn.

The first in the gallery of famous Roncalese is a military man of the Renaissance period, a *condotiero* or leader of mercenary soldiers who acted with governmental authorisation in the Corsican campaign. Pedro Navarro, Conde de Oliveto, also has a monument dedicated to him in Garde, where he was probably born around 1460. He had a reputation for besieging fortified towns and fortresses, was a recognised strategist in the siege of towns, and was skilled in the art of handling gunpowder mines. He never fought for the sake of it but only when the possibilities of success were in his favour. Condemned to death, he was saved from the disgrace of the scaffold in the public square thanks to the governor of the fortress-prison where he was held. The governor ordered him to be killed by suffocation in the bed in his prison cell.

The second is the Jesuit, Cipriano Barace, an explorer of Bolivia, where he introduced cows and horses and cotton. The founder of 15 new towns, directed works as an architect, practised surgery and medicine, taught music and songs which he himself had composed with a drum and *vihuela* or early guitar, and wrote a catechism in the Moja tongue. He was born in Isaba in 1641 and died violently at the age of 61 under the arrows and clubs of the Baures indians, the object of his mission.

Pedro Vicente Gambra, the third famous son of the valley, is also discussed in this book on the section on rafts in the chapter entitled 'Gorges'. Born in the Age of Enlightenment, Gambra was, above all, an enterprising and ingenious man who devised and constructed at his own expense the weirs and locks to facilitate the transport of wood down river. He was also a captain during the war against the *autxas*, a name given to the French by the people in the valley.

The fourth portrait of the House of the Valley represents a

warrior from Urzainqui, Gregorio Cruchaga, a deputy of Espoz y Mina during the French wars.

As for the fifth portrait, it portrays a world famous opera singer who never forgot his Roncalese origin either in life or death.

JULIÁN GAYARRE

In a house he had built on the land of his parents' home in his birthplace, Roncal, a foundation-museum conserves the memory of Julián Gayarre, the famous tenor who was exalted by the the critics of the XIXth century, one in which the voices of Mario de Candia, Enrico Tamberlik and Angelo Masini all flourished. The first-named unselfishly instilled in Gayarre all his stage art and, above all, his expression and diction. Massini, who was Verdi's favoured tenor, was a rival for

A sunset of landscape and life. The tomb of Julián Gayarre, sculpted by Mariano Benlliure in marble and bronze. is silhouetted against the setting sun.

man of liberal ideology who enjoyed bullfights, the arts and a good coffee. He said little, but he was sincere and did not hide his opinions. He never managed to speak fluent Italian; he spoke Spanish with a mixture of Navarrese argot and he could also speak Basque: in the museum there is a letter in Roncalese *uskara* written in his own hand to his aunt Juana. He was never ashamed of his humble origins and loved his land and people, to whom he was both generous and unassuming. Every summer he spent a few weeks in his house in Roncal and he enjoyed being present at the Tribute of the Three Cows, paying lavish attention to his fellow countrymen and visiting the hermitage of San Sebastián of Navarzato, a martyr to whom his mother dedicated him at his baptism. With the confessed regret that he could not leave a recording of his voice, Gayarre sung for the

Gayarre; he had more *fiato* and voice, although the man from Roncal had better quality and expression of feeling.

His physical appearance was ordinary and his height was below average, but he became transformed as he sung. He had very broad shoulders, great lung capacity, a thick muscular neck and a normal larynx, which is conserved in the museum. He improved on nature through hard work, and his voice was noted for the beauty of the timbre, great balance, extension and force, which he achieved through a technique learned at the music school of Pórpora with Master Lamperti.

Gayarre triumphed on the principal stages of Europe and America. He achieved world recognition in the Scala de Milán on the 2nd of January 1876, with Donizetti's 'The Favourite' (also his favourite work). Later on, after perfecting his French diction, he crowned his career on the 7th April 1886 in the Paris Opera with 'The African Woman' by Meyerbeer; the Parisian press then called him "the top tenor."

In his repertoire there are 53 Italian, French, Spanish, Russian and German operas. He introduced the new opera by Wagner into Spain, and the composer called him the best singer he had ever had for his '*Lohengrin*'.

Gayarre, like the majority of his Roncalese neighbours, was a

last time in the Teatro Real of Madrid on the 8th December 1889. He sung a wrong note and fell into a deep depression. Influenza followed by a lung infection caused his death. It was snowing in Madrid on 2nd January 1890, but the people came out onto the streets to take their final leave of the tenor.

In accordance with his wishes, the remains of Julián Gayarre rest in the cementary of Roncal. His mausoleum, carved by Mariano Benlliure in marble and bronze, represents an allegory crowned by the winged genius of fame over the tomb.

The Roncalese musical patrimony has much wealth. Its folklore conserves the dances of the *ttun ttun*, Spanish and Basque dances, and some beautiful cradle songs such as *Margu lili artean*. We must also not forget the collection of XVIIIth century organs: the one at Uztárroz is of great interest, with recordings which imitate birds, and the *gaita* (pipes). But the most interesting one is the one at Isaba, much admired by concert players for the quality of its sound, its small pipes, and its beautiful Baroque frame. Other notable organs are found at Burgui, the Monasterio de Leyre, and the one built by Diego de Amezua at Vidángoz, although they are in very poor condition. It is surprising to learn that some distant hermitages in the mountains, such as Idoia or Zuberora, have Baroque organs which still conserve their frames.

The word *foz* (gorge) is inherited from the Romance language of Navarre, a language which fell into disuse at the beginning of modern times. It is used to designate a narrow ravine carved in limestone by a river. Gorges offer the special beauty of their rugged escarpments, where birds nest amongst the rocks. In the past, only the *almadieros* (rafters) dared to navigate these difficult passages, braving the *mayencas* (rapids).

THE GORGES

Wildlife and scenery

In his work entitled *Vocabulario Navarro* (A Vocabulary of Navarre), José María Iribarren indicates that "a gorge is a deep, narrow valley with a river flowing between high cliffs." There is another typically Navarrese word to describe the same thing: *poche* or even occasionally: *pocha*, meaning a narrow passage between two high walls. There are the gorges of Arbayún, Benasa, Burgui, Gaztelu, Iñarbe, Lumbier, Mintxate, Ugarra and Ugarrón. And, whenever we talk of a *poche*, we are reminded of the one at Txintxurrenea.

Geology has taught us that the pattern of our rivers was completed at the end of the Tertiary age, after the Pyrenees were formed. The gorges were then tenaciously carved out by a few rivers carrying large volumes of water down steep slopes. There was more erosion on the river beds than on the slopes and, for this reason, whilst the walls appear to be almost vertical, the beds are generally deep. Here the waters sometimes form stagnant pools whilst at other times the flow is swift and rapids are formed.

The rugged masses of rock, with abundant fissures, cavities and ledges are home to the great birds of prey. The bearded vulture nests on the crags and flies over these steep cliffs, and one of the largest colonies of griffon-vultures in the entire Iberian Peninsula is to be found here.

The vegetation hanging from the rock faces and growing on the slopes or colonising the lowlands is very varied, a mixture of Cantabrian, Alpine and, in particular, Mediterranean climates.

The wealth of fauna and flora is assured by the variety of climates and micro-climates, and also by the fact that these areas are impenetrable and inaccessible. The depths of the forests act as a refuge for mammals of many sizes. Otters bathe in the clear waters together with fish, while amphibians and reptiles sun themselves on the stones.

There is also considerable seasonal variation. In winter, the Wall Creeper, with its crimson-coloured wings and oscillating flight, abandons its Pyrenean breeding ground and descends to the gorges. In April the Alpine Swift arrives from Africa, performing acrobatic flights in the gorges in an attempt to capture white vulture feathers for its nest, which it will leave in September.

There are several rivers in Navarre which flow through defiles between the crags: the Urederra between Améscoa and the Allín Valley, the Arakil in Oskía, or the Larraun between the crags known as *dos hermanas* ('two sisters'). The real gorge territory, however, is to be found near Sangüesa, in the Pyrenean foothills drained by the Esca and Irati rivers, and the rivers and streams that flow into them: Urrobi, Areta, Salazar and Benasa.

There is nothing like aerial photography or climbing the nearby summits to obtain a magnificent panoramic view. Some bold people wait for the rivers to flow less quickly and use inflatable

[PREVIOUS PAGE] *The river Salazar enters the Arbayún gorge, which stretches for six miles and has a surprising variety of micro-climates inside it.*
[ABOVE] *The exit of the Lumbier gorge, where the remains of a bridge can be seen. Legend has it that this bridge, like many others, was built by the Devil.*

launches to navigate the interior of the gorges. There are also paths which enable a respectful walker to go deep inside the gorges to contemplate and admire the view.

The gorges are sanctuaries of Nature and should be considered as such by all visitors. The majority of them are Nature Reserves.

ARBAYÚN, A SYMBOL OF NATURE

The Arbayún gorge is one of the best-known and most photographed areas in Navarre, and was also one of the first to be declared a protected area. The Nature Reserve, occupying an area of 1,164 hectares, is also a Special Protection Area for Birds.

This six kilometre long, 385 meter deep canyon with an average distance of 550 meters between its rock faces, was cut by the Salazar river. In the middle of the XIXth century the *Diccionario* of the Academy of History described the place as a "river which forces its way into a narrow opening between two very high cliffs…and its course between them is called the *foz de Arbaion* (Arbayún gorge) which is densely populated with oaks and evergreen oaks. Horses pass between these crags, although the path is very rough and dangerous. Some very deep caves are to be found there, and everything contributes to make it a formidable place."

The Gorge has some good observation points from the road which ascends to the TV booster station of Arangoiti in the Leire mountain range, or from the viewpoint near the Iso mountain pass. Very near this viewpoint, going down to Bigüézal, there is a wide path which extends some six hundred metres along the right side of the gorge, enabling one to appreciate the varied micro-climates, the lushness of the vegetation and the spectacle of the birds of prey in flight or landing on caves and ledges.

The best way to see Arbayún, however, is along another path which begins at the Usún bridge, and follows the left bank along a somewhat dizzying route, involving stepping across gaps in the rock, and which penetrates for over three kilometres into the heart of the gorge. The route was made during the first third of this century to pipe water supply to the town of Lumbier. The inhabitants of Lumbier paid the people of Bigüézal twenty five thousand pesetas at the time for harnessing the water from a spring, and the stone cutters had to hang in the air to cut the gap in the rock. The narrow path, not recommended for faint-hearted tourists, passes between evergreen oaks, maple trees, hazelnut trees, yew trees, linden trees, beeches and a dense foliage of boxwood mixed with strawberry trees, holly, viburnum, and turpentine trees. Straight ahead stands the overhanging rock of *Peña Cornota* (Cornota cliff) and the limestone walls of the *Torazonillo* and the *Cenillico*, wild spots where now only a few goats venture. However, for decades they were frequented by tough men who had to devise a way of using ropes, pulleys and pegs to transport the slag and charcoal they made there. Many years later, natural reforestation has completely covered the scars left by the charcoal mining industry.

According to the biologist, José Ignacio Urmeneta, "in remote times, these gorges were probably a desolate, lifeless place of rocks and water. But the constant and unequal erosion of the stone created cracks, openings and ledges which would have been colonised by lichen and plants…and a great variety of fauna. The continual supply of organic material led to the formation of a shallow surface layer and today the gorge reveals a luxuriant layer of vegetation.

Although the area has a generally humid but Mediterranean climate, the interior of the gorge offers some surprisingly different climates due to the varied orientation of the walls. The diversity of the tree cover reflects this mosaic of climates, which is most visible in Autumn, when the dominant dark green background of evergreen oaks is splashed with the reddish hues of the maple leaves and the old gold of the beech leaves. By the river bank, with its torrential waters, there is a narrow stretch where ashes, willows and osiers grow. The ledges, edges and cracks in the cliffs are a habitat for some interesting flora.

There is a wealth of flora, but there is even more fauna. And this is particularly true of bird life: many prominent species of birds are present due to the extraordinary shelter offered by the cornices, cracks and holes in the fourteen kilometres of rocky cliffs. The vulture feeding areas are of particular interest. The colony of common vultures (*gyps fulvus*), with more than 140 pairs, is the largest colony in Navarre and one of the largest in the Iberian Peninsula. The gorge is inhabited by the bearded vulture *(gypaetus barbatus)* and there are also colonies or nesting pairs of honey buzzards, black kites, Egyptian vultures, booted eagles, golden eagles, Montagu's harriers, hen harriers, goshawks, peregrine falcons, buzzards and eagle owls. Species of doves also breed there and rock martins build their earthen cup nests.

The flight of a great bird of prey is an admirable spectacle and has been well described by José Ignacio Urmeneta, a fascinated observer of this harmonious association of rock, water and life which is Arbayún: "After the sun's rays have begun to heat up the eastern projections of the gorge, a light breeze gently moves the leaves of the kermes oaks, raised up to the high cliffs. This is the sign he has been waiting for. Extending his wings to reveal a wingspan of almost three meters, the vulture gently takes off from his rocky cornice and hovers in the air….a few minutes' gliding take him to the precise spot, which he had already sensed, where the first heat bubble of the day has just appeared. Comfortably installed in the invisible lift, his only concern now is to take care to maintain a sharp turn in order to gradually spiral up over the limestone rock faces. A short time later, more than a thousand meters of air separate him vertically from the rocky area where the colony nests…".

Arbayún is part of the otter's territory, a species with very limited resources. Martens, genets, badgers and foxes install their dens in the cracks in the walls. Hunting is forbidden in the reserve although until a short time ago wild boar hunts were traditional and numerous.

Leaving the gorge, the hermitage of Saint Peter of Usún stands in a spot of singular beauty on the left bank of the Salazar river. This hermitage was once a monastery and is the oldest documented building in Navarre. It was consecrated on 28th October 829 by Bishop Opilano. The present temple was built at a later date, although it does preserve in its walls the old pre-Romanesque bonding in the shape of a spigot, which could date back to the IXth century together with a beautiful monogram of Christ. The people of Romanzado gather there on pilgrimage on the first day of May.

Downstream from Nagore, the Urrobi river runs through a kilo-metre long narrow spot at the *Poche de Txintxurrenea*, where the rock walls are fifty meters high and end in the south in the conical mono-lith of *Neskaundi*, an eroded outcrop that acts as a look-out post. The name describes the spot well, since *Txintxumear* or *Txintxurrinea* means precisely a 'narrow pass'. The river and road run along the nar-row gorge, fighting over the space available. Dense woodlands of kermes oak totally cover the hill slopes and the evergreen oak goes right down to the banks of the river; there are clusters of beech trees, maple trees and gall oaks and a few Scots pines dotted about. The inaccessibility of the area favours the conservation of its vegetation and explains why a rare breed of woodpecker, the black, makes its nest there. It has a powerful beak which it uses to perforate the wood to find insect larva. When winter is over, it is given away by the noise of its forceful drumming and the characteristic "cri-cri-cri" of its song. The walls of the *poche*, which abound with caves and cor-nices, are home to four species of diurnal birds of prey: the Egypt-ian vulture, peregrine falcon, golden eagle and griffon-vulture. The agile squirrels, which are the trapeze artists of the woods, climb, jump and chase each other across the tree tops during the mating season. The Txintxurrenea Nature Reserve extends over an area of 71 hectares.

The Iñarbe and Gaztelu gorges, carved by the Irati river, are affected, together with the *poche*, by the Itoiz man-made reservoir. The first gorge occupies an area of 289 hectares of cliffs and woods between Oroz Betelu and Artozqui. The holm oak wood located on the limestone escarpments is of excellent quality and the entrance to the gorge is dominated by a Pyrenean oak woodland. The scenery denotes a change from the humid woods to the mountainous ker-mes oak woods, and different types of oaks, beeches, pine trees and evergreen oaks are evident. The rock area is home to more than twelve pairs of griffon-vultures and, during winter, the rare wall creeper comes to visit; lightweight, with crimson coloured wings and a hes-itant flight, it seems more like a butterfly than a bird. The Gaztelu gorge, in the municipalities of Usoz and Osa, occupies an area of 103 hectares in a defile with Mediterranean fauna and vegetation. The eagle owl is at its northern limit here. Many more familiar little birds also breed here: the wren (*txepetxa* in Basque) which sings a tuneful song all year round, the *txinbo*, a wonderful nest builder with its shiny black hood, and the jay, which crosses the ravine in clumsy flight, beating its wings irregularly. There are also many reptiles: the green lizard, the asp viper and the 'ladder snake' (*Elaphe scalaris*).

In the Arce and Lónguida valleys, which have experienced a ma-jor loss of population through the century, a tree and a shrub have been catalogued as natural monuments due to their longevity and astonishing appearance: the gall oak of Rala and the juniper of the Equiza farmhouse are found, as well as the *poche* and the two previ-ously mentioned gorges. In the desolate Arce valley, right in the open countryside, there is a striking Romanesque building: the small church of the *Purísima Concepción* (the Virgin Mary). The building is of har-monious proportions and the sculptures have a serene beauty.

The Areta river gives shelter to otters and Pyrenean muskrats as it carves a way for itself between Urraul and the Romanzado to form the Ugarrón gorge. This natural enclave of 104 hectares is of par-ticular interest for its bushy vegetation, with boxwood, kermes oak, privet, virburnum, mountain jasmine, turpentine and laburnicus. A path bordering the left cliff allows one to appreciate the wildness of the scenery. Ugarrón and Ugarra are the names of two estates belonging to the Forestry Heritage of Navarre. These two place names correspond to ruins. At Ugarra the abandoned hermitage of Saint Steven still remains. It dates back to the XIth century and has now been converted into a cattle fodder store. The hidden gorge of Ugarra was carved by a river which is now a dry stream for most of the year. Choughs breed in the cracks in the cliff where rock martins flutter. The gorge is surrounded by a dense wood of ker-mes and gall oaks, and is a refuge for wild boars, badgers and foxes. Four dolmens have been discovered between the two nearby gorges.

Near the Ugarrón gorge and close to the village of Epároz, there is a charming spot which is well worth a visit: the *Basílica de Santa Fe de Baratzagaitz,* a spiritual centre and, in its time, the town hall of the Urraul Alto Valley. In the XVIIth century a rough and asym-metric cloister was added to the proto-Gothic church, and its privacy and shade made it a breeding place for the owl. The ensemble of the buildings, carefully restored, is completed by a XVth century granary. The *Santa Fe* dedication is linked to the strong influence that the sanctuary of Conques exercised in southern Europe: the Bishop of Pamplona, Pedro de Roda, donated this basilica to the Aveyron monastery where he had been educated. Baratzagaitz was under the influence of the Benedictines, but it does not appear to have reached the status of monastery.

In the *Almiradío*, between Aspurz and Navascués, at the foot of the Illón range, the Benasa stream forms a winding ravine and offers an attractive walk under the cliffs along a pleasant path which goes through a mixed wood: there are fir trees and Scots pines (Alpine), beech trees (Atlantic coast), and kermes oak (Mediterranean). The route is inaccessible when the waters flow fast and it is precisely this difficulty of access that has favoured the conservation of the wood. The Benasa gorge is inhabited by the golden eagle and the short-toed eagle, and the bearded vulture flies overhead. The *Moro* cave can be safely visited. It extends horizontally for almost 900 meters and was a shelter for humans in prehistoric times. The Nature Reserve occupies a surface area of 153 hectares.

The Mintxate stream rises in the sub-alpine pastures of the Roncal Pyrenees, at the foot of Baratzea and Otsogorrigaine. It is a typical mountain river, and does not travel far. In its flat stretch it floods the meadows, and out of the muddy land grow rare and attractive flowers in Spring. Just before flowing into the Ustárroz river, as it crosses a marmoreal limestone, it forms the Mintxate gorge, a deep ravine revealing a folded geological structure. The rushing waters tumble over the great blocks of stone which have small Pyrenean plants and shrubs growing in the cracks between them.

The canyon carved by the river Esca between the La Peña and Illón mountain ranges constitutes the gorge of Burgui. Limestone rocks and dolomites form an impressive setting of vertical cliffs which break up into rock deposits, partially hiding layers of marl and sand-stone on the gentle slopes. This colossal gorge is the entrance to

[OPPOSITE] *Tawny vultures on a rocky outcrop. The gorges in the foothills of the Pyrenees hold many nests of birds of prey.*

the Roncal valley, on the present boundary of Navarre and Aragon. The Nature Reserve occupies an area of 155 hectares. In the area there is an oak wood with clusters of lime, maple, wych elm, rowan, hazel nut and ash trees. In this gorge, the kermes oak grove adapts to the mountain and is enriched with viburnum, strawberry and yew trees. This narrow pass has been declared a Special Protection Area for birds and forms part of the catalogue of important areas drawn up by the Spanish Ornithology Society. The wildlife living in the rocks is varied and numerous. The colony of griffon-vultures, which reaches 135 pairs, is the second largest in Navarre and one of the largest in Europe. Also nesting here are four pairs of Egyptian vultures, three pairs of golden eagles, two pairs of peregrine falcons, one pair of eagle owls and one pair of bearded vultures. There is a colony of choughs and in summer a pair of Alpine Swifts arrive. The woods give shelter to martens, roe deer and wild boars. From Burgui or Salvatierra de Esca there is an easy route up to the hermitage of the *Virgen de la Peña*. It is not a good idea to go up without a sandwich in your pocket, but it unthinkable to go up without binoculars. There are few observatories of birds of prey of this calibre.

To pleasantly discover just what a gorge is, the Lumbier gorge, carved by the Irati river in the foothills of the Sierra of Leire, has many attractions and is very accessible. The Nature Reserve extends over an area of 40 hectares and is just 1 kilometre long. One can take advantage of the wide path left by the old *Irati* railway to go through the reserve and savour all its charms. At the beginning and end of the gorge the river flows through a deep, narrow gap but, once inside, it opens up into a wide space between the rocky walls with a 130 meter drop in level. Griffon-vultures fly overhead and are always easy to watch since they form a colony of 188 pairs. Otters inhabit the river and a small dam can be seen through which the rafters used to pass and, on the banks, there is a narrow wood with white poplars, willows and alder trees. At the gorge exit the remains of a bridge are to be found which, as the legend goes, was the work of the devil. It has just one arch, was built in the XVIth century and was demolished in 1812.

Opposite the Lumbier gorge, excavations have brought to light the Roman 'villa' of Liédena, dating from the Late Roman Empire. It was a big rural country estate which was almost completely self-sufficient according to the archaeologist Blas Taracena. The history of the *villa* is complex, with periods when it was abandoned, reconstructed, extended and fortified. It may have finally been violently destroyed since marks of a fire have been found. The building was formed by a peristyle or central courtyard around which the rooms and offices were organised; it also had a pond, wine press, oil press and hot springs. The mosaics, with complicated geometric patterns, and which paved the courtyard, rooms and a gallery, are conserved in the Museum of Navarre.

Rafts

The gorges of Arbayún, Lumbier and Burgui were the dangerous scene for the transportation of wood by rafts or *almadías*. The *almadieros* or rafters, those skilled and daring freshwater navigators, descended the Esca, Salazar, Irati and Aragón rivers with the wood

A five-section almadía going down the river Esca. The oars are handled by punteros and coderos, some of them wearing the traditional woollen jacket.

cut from the fir, pine, and beech trees of the Pyrenees. Timber could be transported in this way as far as Tudela or Zaragoza on the banks of the Ebro river, or even to Tortosa near the Mediterranean Sea, with a heavy load for the construction of buildings, high-masted barques and also such important public works as the Imperial Canal of Aragón.

The word *almadía* is of Arab origin. Ethnographers, historians, writers, photographers and film directors have all described this activity, which was also practised in other wood-cutting areas although it had its own particular characteristics here. For the Navarrese who practised it regularly from the XVth century onwards, and most notably during the second half of the XVIIIth century, this occupation ended in the year 1952 when the great dam was built for the Yesa reservoir. However, it had already suffered fierce competition for several years from lorries which did not have to wait for the high water season to transport the wood. The daily wage of a rafter was similar to that of a farm hand, but the desire for adventure and an interest in travel attracted young people to a job which, in the end, was considered to be hard, inhumane and something to be abolished.

In the Roncal woodland and the Irati forest the trees were felled between May and August and the trunks were pulled by horses or oxen along paths or pools to the *ataderos* or places for tying up the trunks, the river 'ports' where the rafts were assembled.

The slightly trapezoidal sections were prepared by placing the thin part of the trunk in front and grouping together ten to fifteen trunks per section. Pines and firs were the most common types of wood. Sometimes one beech trunk would be intermingled with three of pine, but beech wood was never put by itself since, due to its density, it could scarcely float. A tip was carved at each end in the form of a quadrangular pyramid (*la escarba*) and a hole was made through which a cross bar would be placed (*el barre*) to link together all the trunks of the section by means of hazel-nut sticks. The width of the section depended on the rafting route: in the Roncal valley it could be four metres wide, but in the Salazar valley it could not be wider than 3.2 metres as it had to pass through the narrow defile formed by the Arabyún gorge. The sections of wood were described according to their length: *docenes* of 4.8 metres, *catorcenes* of 5.6 metres, *secenes* of 6.2 metres and *aguilones* or larger posts.

The different sections were tied together by oak or birch fibre and, once three, four or five sections had been assembled, the wood had to be soaked. In the first section, termed *tramo de punta* or tip section, there were two pinewood oars which were some five meters long.

The *punteros* or leading rafters and the *codero* (person at the back of the raft who steered with a large oar) needed great skill and good understanding to pilot the raft, negotiate rocks, clear the ramp-like gates in the dams to prevent it from folding up like a book, direct the embarkation through the bridge arches and approach moorings without crashing into them. The occupation was risky and the turbulent waters did take some lives.

In the second chapter of his novel *La última cigüeña* ('The Last Stork'), set in the Roncal valley, the Navarrese writer Felix Urabayen describes the travelling adventures of the rafters: "Life in the entire Roncal valley is so rough that the rafters, champions of the axe, have to maintain an eternal crusade against the waters, which rebel under their command... the human race navigates on these fragile logs, ... art borders on the epic as they avoid with serene alacrity an infinite number of loose rocks, which can scarcely be seen above the water. When the rock succeeds in halting the rafts, these people from the Roncal valley use a somewhat savage procedure. They jump straight into the water without bothering to take their clothes off; they recover the section divided by the blow and pressing this original lever into the river bed, they push with their shoulders, the only motor which does not fail...".

The *almadiera* or period of log transportation would begin in December and continue until May or June. It took six days to get from the Pyrenees to Zaragoza, if there were no setbacks due to too much water or a lack of current. The rafters took three days to walk back home, sometimes carrying an oar over their shoulder. The rafters wore the same typical working clothes as their neighbours: sandals on their feet and a goat skin jacket to protect them from the cold. The following verses are taken from the repertory of *jotas* or local songs:

> They say that the rafters
> have their life hanging by a thread,
> if this is so, let it hang,
> my husband is a rafter

> Artajona for wine;
> Baztán for meadows;
> Tudela for olive groves;
> Roncal for rafters.

> How unfortunate are we,
> from the Roncal valley!
> If you don't want to be a shepherd,
> Pick up an oar and an axe.

Florencio Idoate has studied the rafting traffic since the XIVth century, and emphasises that it is the story of 'continual disputes and differences' since the municipalities and feudal estates attempted to collect taxes and levies as the rafts went under the bridges or through the 'gates' built in the dams. Common Law made freedom of navigation along the rivers a principle, but there were times when, during the itinerary from the Roncal valley to Tudela, the rafters were obliged to pay out more than thirty taxes and duties which they either paid in cash or by leaving a *fusta* or rafting trunk at each toll. Any recourse to the Courts was of no great help until the abolition of the feudal estates in the XIXth century. The rafters were occasionally harassed and attacked so they learned to defend themselves.

In the General Archives of Navarre, the oldest document referring to the *almadías* dates back to 1343 and mentions the collection of passage dues in Sangüesa. At the end of the XIVth century, the rafting traffic increased and large quantities of timber were transported from the port of Santacara, on the river Aragon, to Tafalla and Olite for the building work on the palaces of King Carlos III ('el Noble').

History preserves the name of Pedro Vicente Gambra, the XVIIIth century entrepreneur from Roncal who carried out daring plans to channel the Esca river. In just one year, 1774, his foremen brought down 24,256 trunks. Gambra guaranteed the safe and prompt arrival of the wood for the works of the Imperial Canal of Aragon, directed by Pignatelli. In 1788 the minister Conde Floridablanca wrote about Gambra, considering him 'a recommendable vassal, useful for his Valley, the Kingdom and the State'.

During the XIXth century the extent of rafting was determined by the ups and downs of the successive periods of war and peace. Businessmen constructed mechanical sawmills along the banks of the rivers. After the Civil War, specifically during the nineteen forties, there was a fleeting revival of the rafting trade due to the lack of fuel.

Each year, on the Sunday nearest to the first of May, the emotion of this ancient occupation can still be relived in the *Día del Almadiero* ('Rafters' Day'), or *Almadieroren Egura* in Basque. This is held in Burgui, the village in the Roncal valley which had the largest number of rafters. The last generation of rafters taught the trade to their grandchildren. In the *atadero* at Olegía, four kilometres upstream from the village, two or three *almadías* are built every year and these descend the Esca river. Depending on the rate of flow of the water it takes between one to one and a half hours to make the trip, and the day ends after the dam next to the mediaeval bridge is crossed.

*A*ndía, means 'big' in Basque. This name, which now only applies to the eastern third of the massif, was used in the beginning to refer to the whole of the great plateau, including Urbasa in the centre and continuing west into the province of Álava, with the name of *Encía*. Urbasa and Andía have "always been" the common land of all the Navarrese, as is repeated from the XVIth Century onwards, firstly by the Regional Assembly of Navarre and then by the Government of Navarre. However, this condition of 'common in its original form' is debatable. Yanguas y Miranda, a nineteenth-century historian and lawyer, considered that in the Early Middle Ages the only people to be called *navarros* (Navarrese) were those who inhabited the 'navas', i.e. the valleys close to these mountain ranges from which, according to some, the very name of Navarre is derived.

ANDÍA AND URBASA
Common land of the Navarrese

The geographer Alfredo Floristán explains that "for many centuries the people from Navarre have considered Urbasa and Andía to be *sierras* (mountain ranges), but they are in fact softly undulating high plateaux stretching from east to west, they are *mesetas* with raised limestone edges." With reference to Urbasa, the 1903 Countryside Planning Project offered a graphic image: "it is like a back tooth, with the edges higher than the centre."

The magnificent ensemble covers over 21,000 hectares, with an average height of one thousand meters. The northern edge, which is higher and drops more steeply towards the valley, offers continuous rocky crests. To the south, the less prominent perimeter is bedecked with entrances to formidable gorges.

The *sierras* act as a natural frontier. Geology has brought 40 million-year-old marine sediments into contact with other, more recent, continental and lake sediments. In this western part of Navarre, the Mountains are separated from the Central Zone through a climatic barrier (cloudy and wet in the North and progressively drier and sunnier towards the Central Zone) as any traveller will notice. A road runs along the Zumbelz fault, limiting the two ranges. At one bend there is a noticeable change from Atlantic to Mediterranean, with holly oaks replacing beech groves. In the same municipality, the olive, which cannot be grown in the North, appears a short distance away in the South.

Andía and Urbasa are often cloaked in stagnant mists and stormy clouds which give off abundant rain and mist. Snow can cover the ground for twenty to thirty days a year. The rains are intense from December to May and dew is common in autumn, turning to frost in the colder months. Mist is frequent from October to January, but it can also appear in Summer when breezes are plentiful and low clouds cling to the woods at dusk.

Rainwater and melted snow have gradually modelled a somewhat chaotic relief on the limestone material, with depressions, sinks, grooves and potholes. Erosion has dissolved the rocks, forming a Karst. There are no rivers or surface streams. It is only after a storm that some depressions become short-lived pools, and fleeting and beautiful waterfalls leap over the ravine edges, such as the one which hurls itself down from Arteta in the shape of a horse's tail. Most of the water, however, filters through the rock and is stored. Floristán describes two topical and common images which try to explain this phenomenon: "Urbasa and Andía are like two gigantic sponges absorbing rainwater and snow which then ooze out at the edges. The surface of the ranges is like two large sugar lumps which have been dissolved irregularly and, deep down, have many subterranean reservoirs that feed the springs and river sources on the edge."

In the *sierras* there are numerous grottoes, caves and potholes. Some three hundred have been catalogued. The most noteworthy are the Mugalez and Fonfría potholes in Andía, with a drop of 185 meters, the Roble pothole, with a stream in its galleries, and the Itxitxoa, of archaeological interest. In Urbasa the Tximua pot-

[PREVIOUS PAGE] Rainwater and snow have modelled the limestone of the area into a rather chaotic relief, covered by vegetation.

hole (175 meters deep) has a large cave with a lake of crystal-clear water; there are also the tourist attractions of the cave "of arms", which was an weapons store in the Carlist wars, and the one called "the Christian cave" with lakes and stalactites.

RIVER SOURCES

The exact translation of Urbasa is 'wood of waters'. According to Luciano Lapuente, a historian and ethnologist, "it has many fresh springs, but few flow strongly." They do, however, have some beautiful names, such as Itziar, which sounds like a character out of a myth, Andasarri, Lezarogi or Urkimaku, which refer to stones and vegetables. The 'fountain of the lentils' is located on the edge of the Améscoa range, where there are numerous lentil-shaped fossils. In the heart of the range the 'spring of the mosquitoes' is to be found. But the most romantic spring of them all is Bassaunziturri, where roe deer jumped about not so long ago.

When the rivers spring up from between the rocks or gush forth from the spongy aquifers, the Navarrese call these damp and shady springs *nacederos* ('birthplaces of rivers').

The source of the Urederra river in Baquedano is a nature reserve covering 119 hectares. The icy, crystalline and 'beautiful water' (*ur ederra*) cascades down over an impressive circle of rocks. The water gushes forth at two places separated by a few dozen meters, and the outflow is impressive at the end of winter. This delightful spot can be reached along shady paths lined by yews, ashes, maple trees, linden trees, oaks and stately beeches. Where the path widens, the marks of the charcoal burners are still to be found on the blackened earth. This fast, clear brook is home to the grey badger, the greedy night hunter who is betrayed by his footprints and face-mask, and the aquatic blackbird, a little bird with a chocolate coloured uniform and a white bib, which flies quickly at water level and dives down to catch molluscs and small fish. The river erosion upstream, deepening its bed, has managed, through the fall of the rocky outcrop, to sculpture a sack-bottom effect. This should be observed from the dizzy heights of 'El Balcón de Pilatos' (Pilate's Balcony). Egyptian vultures, known here as *saizuriak* (white vultures) can be seen hovering elegantly overhead, proudly lending themselves to the bloodless hunting of our binoculars, whilst the gabble of crows resounds above the chaos.

The deep Erbioz gorge, where golden eagles can be seen flying above it, is an overgrown spot. Holly oaks are plentiful amongst the abrupt rocky surface. Some of the larger ones give shade to the source of the Riezu river (the origin of the Ubagua rive) with its crystal-clear water where trout are to be found. Opposite, hidden by a tangled thicket, is the entrance to the Katazulo cave, a legendary place. The nascent brook leaps over the weirs of the old mills and greets the hermitage of San Blas, where Fray José Martínez, the leader of all the hermits in the Kingdom, lived at the beginning of the XVIIIth Century.

Arteta is another river source. Waters from the Goñi valley rush down a narrow gorge, forming staggered cascades, wells and chutes, and then join up with the waters from the spring that has supplied Pamplona for the last century. It is surprising to see how it wells up immediately after the snow melts in Spring and intense rain. The place is visited by day trippers and students who gather information in a special Study Centre about the hidden behaviour of the underground waters. The song of blackbirds and finches can be heard amidst the noise of the surging water. This spot is also the scene of nocturnal excursions by foxes. Their courtship takes place on cold, December nights, filling the darkness with howls and cries. Two months later, when the lactation period is over, the howls of the vixen recommence as she insistently calls the male, who is away hunting for rodents for her babies.

The flat land of Urbasa, where livestock grazes on green pastures dotted with heather, juniper and hawthorn.

THE MARK OF MAN

The abundance of caves, the density of the woods, the rich meadows and the possibilities for hunting and fishing possibilities all explain the early human presence in the area.

From 1968 onwards Emilio Redondo, a tireless researcher, managed to locate up to twenty stone workplaces in Urbasa. He found a Palaeolithic bifacial piece dating back some hundred thousand years next to the Aranzaduia pond, the oldest Palaeolithic piece discovered in Navarre. Redondo's house in Zudaire is a firstclass paleontologic and prehistoric museum where he has collected forty thousand pieces, some of which are spectacular and of great interest. His best findings are now in the Museum of Navarre. The numerous Lower and Middle Paleolithic settlements at several locations along and across Urbasa all belong to the same, continuous form of human inhabitation, always out in the open. There is a central area of settlement in the heart of the range, in Aranzaduia, the springs of Aziarri and Andasarri, and at Regajo de los Yesos. It appears that supplies of raw material were obtained from the Otxaportillo area, where there is an extensive natural outcrop of flint.

There is a fascinating walk along the route of Urbasa's thirteen dolmens. The highest concentration of dolmens is to be found between the Bardoiza forest house and the Baquedano pass. The excavation of these dolmens was begun in the summer of 1921 by Telesforo de Aranzadi, José Miguel de Barandiarán and Enrique Eguren. At Zurgaina they found evidence of up to 18 burials. The discovery included human remains, bone necklace beads, flint knives and arrow tips, bronze punches, rough red pottery and animal bones. In the Andía sector, between 1951 and 1954, in the Arteta and Goñi district, four dolmens were identified with great tumulus of up to 18 meters in diameter which have not yet been excavated.

According to Luciano Lapuente, "when agriculture was introduced, the men who roamed the mountains and lived in caves gradually settled in the adjacent valleys where, thanks to their primary occupation right (*eskubide*) and after cutting down the woods, they gradually became owners of the cultivated lands. They built their homes beside the cultivated land and used boundary stones to mark out their plots. Grouped in small nuclei, these communities had the right to work the nearby hills, being governed by a *batzarre*, an open assembly of all the inhabitants, a prelude to the councils which still persist today. Those shepherds and stockbreeders spent many days following the herds, the reflection of their wealth, and they threshed out paths leading to the summits, linking mountain passes and sheepfolds and weaving an embryonic network of communications." Large stretches of the old roads are still conserved today.

At Urbasa's southern pass, at the entrance to the Améscoas region, there is a gorge. On a rocky projection, the remains of an old bastion are to be found, which was perhaps a Celtic hill fort, called Amescoazarra. The walls, foundations and remains of buildings are visible. This is "a place on a steep cliff, whose inhabitants are called *naverri*, that is, Navarrese" according to the late medieval chronicle of the Institución Príncipe de Viana. It is a wild spot and it is one of the places where the legendary García Ximénez, Lord of Abárzuza y Améscoa, might have been proclaimed the first King of Navarre.

Regardless of whether you approach Urbasa from Estella or from the Barranca-Burunda corridor, it is always necessary to ascend a mountain pass in order to get to the *sierras*. The old horseshoe paths which leave from each village also finish in a 'pass'.

The hermitage at San Adrián de Lizarraga, watchman for storms. Opposite, the 'keel' of Irubain, which marks the end of the San Donato-Beriain range.

This obstacle to communications meant that there was little transit for centuries. Moreover, the Urbasa range, bordering with Álava, served as a hiding place for outlaws and criminals. In the XIVth and XVth centuries, due to lineage disputes and neighbourhood rivalries, the area was full of bandits and thieves.

Until 1695, when the territory of the Marquis of Andía was created, the civil jurisdiction for Urbasa was unclear. It now comes under the municipality of Yerri.

At the end of the XVIIth century a palace was built to provide shelter to travellers and defence against villains. This is the explanation some people give on the origin of the building that was built on the huge plateau as a landmark. But the real reason does not appear to be so democratic or utilitarian. It is really to do with the stately desires of the Marquises of Andía, the Remírez de Baquedano family, who were authorised at the time to build a house and jail to deal with thieves, guard prisoners and administer justice. No-one from the Baquedano family lived in the palace, but their stone coat of arms was put on the facade as evidence of their nobility and privileges. Democratisation came with time, and the palace later served as an inn for shepherds, wood-cutters and travellers.

The Urbasa Palace is a four-winged building forming a rectangle, with squat towers at each corner. An elegant stone arcade leads to the vestibule and the great courtyard. Seven ivy covered balconies give the façade a note of elegance. In the chapel there is an engraving of the 'Santo Cristo de las Agonías', the work of Jacobo Buonavita, which was brought from Naples. This chapel takes the place of a hermitage which was in Andía until 1705, next to the Icomar pond. In 1594, King Philip II ordered a chapel to be erected in the 'royal mountains of Urbasa and Andía' in order to hold masses for shepherds.

Some history-laden hermitages preside over the edges of the *sierras*. At a picturesque spot high up on Andía stands the Santísima Trinidad (Holy Trinity) hermitage, belonging to Iturgoyen. It is a late Romanesque building in which the old medieval altar stone was used for the new altar. This is a large, one-piece stone. At the top of Beriain, San Donato is the highest hermitage in Navarre, at exactly 1494 meters above sea level. On Urbasa stands the San Adrián de Lizarraga hermitage, to guard against storms, and that of Santa Marina, situated between two huts. It belongs to Bacaicoa and Iturmendi and is visited during festive pilgrimages, when the *Zortziko* dance is performed. In the afternoon, on the way down, the pilgrims stop at the Dantzalarre meadow, on the dividing line between the two municipalities, to take their leave with one last dance.

During the first Carlist war, Urbasa was the scene of fighting. On the 21st of April 1835, the army of Valdés camped in extensive pasture lands around the inn. His rival, Zumalacárregui, had been harassing the rearguard long into the night. It was very cold and sleet fell constantly. Afraid that his men would die of cold and hunger, Valdés gave the order to carry on marching, But his thirty battalions could do nothing against the strategy of the few Carlists who were hounding them. When the army stopped and showed sufficient force, the guerrillas retired. The march was delayed, and no sooner did it recommence then Zumalacárregui's men audaciously reappeared, blocking off the routes down the mountain passes and inflicting severe losses on the enemy, despite the fact their cartridges were rationed. The battle was unequal from the outset, but 5,000 Carlist volunteers managed to defeat an army of 25,000. The Christians fled in a disorderly fashion, leaving 800 dead, 300 injured and 1,000 prisoners in the campsite. Two days later, at his headquarters, the Carlist general received the commissioner to his Majesty the King of England, Lord Elliot, and they signed the release of the captured soldiers.

Miguel de Unamuno mentioned this place and incident in his book entitled 'Through the lands of Portugal and Spain'. He refers to the "imposing meseta of the Andía and Urbasa sierras, a theatre of battles. There Zumalacárregui forced General Valdés to withdraw. All he had to do was let him camp up on the mountain, whilst he waited for him in the mountain passes below. The wolf was on familiar ground."

COMMON LAND

Urbasa and Andía do not belong to any municipality. They formed part of the patrimony of the Kingdom of Navarre and then became

State property from 27th February 1987. They are now the property of the Navarre Government. All the people of Navarre have the right to enjoy these mountains, having free use of the pastures, water, fruits, wood, coal, bracken, dead leaves, manure and snow. Some people, living at a distance from the *sierras*, have been able to prove that this secular right is still in force, by requesting and obtaining firewood. There are limits, however. One is legal, since these products may only be used for one's own needs, never for commerce. Distance and transport are other practical limitations, since far more cattle come from the nearby valleys than from the more distant villages. Moreover, a change in life-style has meant that some typical practices from the past have now been forgotten. The winter snow, for example, was collected in gullies and ravines and caves and was then transported to the large cool storage places in the cities in order to mitigate the rigours of the summer heat. Refrigerators deal with this problem nowadays.

Woods and meadows, the main sources of wealth, have always complemented each other. Nowadays, as in the past, shepherds and lumbermen rival each other.

In Urbasa, the flat land, sloping slightly towards the south, occupies 113 square kilometres, three quarters of which are covered by beech trees. In the centre there are large plains called 'rasos' where cattle feed on green pastures dotted with heather, juniper and hawthorns. The Basque study of place-names reports on an ancient green landscape which still exists: *Elordia* is the hawthorn, and in *Aranzadi* sloe berries are plentiful as are birches in *Urkimaku*.

The richness of the forests requires careful control: marking out areas for reforestation, cutting and clearing the wood in an orderly manner, and marking out tree nursery areas.

Andía, covering some 47 square kilometres, is a mountain range which has been stripped of its vegetation. Over the centuries the natural vegetation has been attacked by excessive tree felling and grazing, but deforestation is also due to complex historical causes. Perhaps the original wood was less dense or had more clearings than that from Urbasa, and this favoured grazing in meadows with short, fine grass. Moreover, the farmers ploughing the fields must have noticed the conditions of the soil and climate. In this respect, Urbasa offers better soils, similar temperatures and higher rainfall.

Pedro Montserrat, from the Pyrenean Institute of Ecology, points out the exceptional richness of the grazing land of the area, formed over thousands of years and adapting and renewing itself to resist grazing by herbivores and the herds of omnivorous pigs which roam the land. To make the most of the land, the cows use the roughest land on the edges, whilst the sheep crop the richest and most productive of the clearings. "The dampness, the droplets or *Txirimiri* (drizzle) of the mist, the manuring and the tramping of the cattle explain the extraordinary process of adaptation of these pastures. The common use by different types of cattle, horses, sheep and pigs has caused the plants to evolve to resist the pressure and renew themselves quickly. In Urbasa some hitherto unheard of conditions within Europe can be found: exceptional turf and meadow ecotypes of great interest. The grass of these pastures, which halts erosion, could also be used for sports fields and lawns."

Urbasa and Andía are the southernmost mountains in Navarre which still have green pastures in summer. Herds of migrating cattle from the *Ribera* (south of Navarre) reached them along the Tauste and Valdorba cattle routes. On the edges of Andía, the ruins of the neighbouring huts of several villages of the Goñi valley can be seen. Near Munárriz there is an exceptional building which has been well preserved: a round cabin, with a cylindrical body and high, tapered chimney. It was not always necessary to look for shelter, however, because on some summer nights the shepherds slept in the open on a soft bed of *ilarraka* (padded heather).

The XVIth Century had long passed when, as Florencio Idoate tells us, Urbasa received between one hundred and one hundred and fifty thousand heads of migrating cattle each summer, and every Wednesday hundreds of shepherds assembled to exchange the 'abandoned' cattle of uncertain ownership. Some herds of shorn sheep still come, but the milk-producing *latxa* breed now prevails. These sheep give us the tasty shepherds' cheeses which can be bought in some *txabolas* (simple huts built from stone and limestone and sand mortar, covered with turf or tiles). These basic dwellings still have a *gaztandegi*, a ventilated room where the cheeses mature. Cheese specialists say that the limestone soils of the Urbasa and Andía pastures mean that the cheese is sweeter than that of neighbouring Aralar, where the soil is more acid. The job of paid shepherd was, and still is, arduous; to encourage it, in 1604 the Court of the Kingdom decided that the shepherd could also keep twenty sheep of his own amongst the master's sheep.

Pyrenean cows graze here, but it is the mountain pony which is best suited to this environment. The Navarrese pony is a small horse which is restrained, rustic and vigorous. These ponies have always attracted the attention of the vegetable growers from Valencia who come to buy them at the fairs of San Fermín and San Miguel in Pamplona.

The cattle herds are taken up to the mountains in Spring and are brought down in the Autumn. Luciano Lapuente has studied this calendar of cattle movements and suspects that in ancient times there was a ritual magic to it. "At the beginning of the century, in the Yerri valley a custom is still kept which involves starting the departure of the cows and ponies to the mountains by making them step over a small fire at the farmyard door made with olive branches blessed on Palm Sunday." The sheep remain in the mountains until October and are sometimes caught unawares by the first snowfall. This is never the case with the cows since, "when there's snow in the air, they spontaneously go down to their stables. Quite the opposite to the ponies who are indifferent to the thickest of storms and cling to the sierra." This situation puts the bravery of the livestock rearers to the test, as they are forced to pull the struggling mountain cattle down the hillsides through sleet and snow.

There is a place in Urbasa known as *Otxaportillo*, a name which evokes a cross-roads of wolves. Today there are no longer any wolves in Navarre. The last one was killed in 1962, precisely in this area, where bears resisted right up to the end of the last century. In the Tximua chasm, potholers found a well preserved bear femur and jaw. In Bardoiza, a rolling plain, there is a pond coveted by pigeon hunters, and it is easy to notice traces of foxes and hares and, at night, listen to owls. The wildlife of the two ranges totals some 140 different species, the majority of which are birds and mammals. There are fewer amphibians and reptiles. The bearded vulture has been seen to fly overhead inspecting the terrain, and otters have been seen swimming in the river Urederra.

The beech tree is the 'lady' of Urbasa. The damp winds off the Bay of Biscay blow it up the slopes from the Burunda, northwards. It prefers the dark soil of the edges to the sandy soil of the plains. The beech groves, accompanied by bracken, continue south, thanks to the mist. On the southern slopes in the Améscoas, however, the solemn and leafy oak triumphs.

In Navarre the 'Limitations' are those areas of royal or communal mountains whose use was reserved to specific communities. The Limitations of the Améscoas in the south-west of Urbasa are excellent examples. The upper and lower Améscoa valleys have the exclusive right, documented since the beginning of the XVth Century, to an area of 5,178 hectares, a model of rational planning. More than two thirds of the surface area is covered by beech groves and the rest is pasture land.

The Limitations are one of the oldest and most important *facerías* (common land shared by various villages) of Navarre. This part of Urbasa has always been persistently defended by the people from Améscoa, who moved Merino herds of sheep off their property. Joaquín Salcedo has studied the singular legal system governing the Limitations. Local government and administration is done through a Mountain Committee which meets at the town hall of Aristubelza several times a year. In January it examines the books, in April it goes over the list of cattle which will use the mountain, in September it prepares the budget for the following year and in November it carries out auctions. Regarding the forests, the Committee marks out the land to be reforested, orders the clearing of woodland and allocates tree nursery areas. The people from the neighbouring villages, according to the bylaws, have the right to bring their herd, sow and fence off a plot of land not greater than five 'robadas' (just under half a hectare), cut trees, and make firewood and charcoal.

The production of charcoal, carried out in many areas of Navarre, was particularly dominant here. The cut and dried wood was placed so that it formed a large cone, covered with fine earth and turf, *zotalak*, leaving a central chimney, *txondorra*, and some small holes on the side. The secret consisted in getting exactly the right point for the slow burning, with little oxygen, to last some twenty days. The charcoal was reduced to about a third of its weight and gave off a lot of heat. 'Cisco' was the popular name given to the smallest pieces of charcoal, made with small branches instead of trunks. In the foundries they were called *iduri*. The charcoal burners, *ikatskiñak*, used to work as a team, and remained in the warmest woods for up to six months a year. They had a curious set of instruments, one of the most important being the 'moon axe' (*Illargi aitzkora*) with a rounded blade to cut the wood; they used a mallet and a ladder to climb up to the top of the charcoal pile and wore special shoes to walk round on top without getting burnt. The life and work of the last Navarrese charcoal burner, Anastasio Ochoa, who lived in Zuñiga and died in 1989, was the central character in Montxo Armendariz's film 'Tasio'.

Pontius Pilate's Balcony. At the foot of this imposing circle of rocks the freezing and crystal-clear waters of the Urederra cascade over waterfalls.

Forest and resource planning affects all of Andía and Urbasa. An important precedent was the project drawn up in 1903. This was a sensible measure since, up to that time, the use of fire-wood and wood was chaotic. With a licence issued by the mayor of any village in Navarre, any inhabitant could cut any amount as many times as needed. This meant that clearings in the middle of the low, branchy woodland became larger.

Excursions, mountain sports and tourism are the most recent and beneficial developments. Pressure from tourism is considerable.

The Urbasa range has conditions found nowhere else in Europe: extraordinary grass, and meadow ecotypes of great interest.

On some days in July and August over 13,000 visitors seek the cool shade of the beech trees. The Government of Navarre considers Andía and Urbasa as a single area that could become a Natural Park, where the ordered use and enjoyment of the mountain landscape would be compatible with the conservation of the Environment.

The desire to compete in strength and skill during the working day, to challenge friends when it comes to rest or play, and the great attraction of betting, led to the creation and development of popular rural sports and games (*herri kirolak* in Basque). These factors eventually raised them to the level of spectacle while preserving their original characteristics. The media (particularly TV) and the popularity of the best-known rural sportsmen have meant that betting on tree-cutting, stone-lifting and *pelota* (the most representative Basque ball game) have become enormously popular. Navarre has over five hundred *frontones* (courts where *pelota* is played), many of them used intensively.

ANCIENT SPORTS

Everyone is good at something, and strength, skill and agility have always been virtues to be admired. This is even more the case in closed societies where the population is dispersed and has a limited choice when it comes to leisure activities. *Bertsolariak* (Basque popular poets) have sung the praises of the most famous local sportsmen through the ages.

The autarchic rural economy and the efforts of the inhabitants of each *caserío* (Basque farmhouse) to feed their families meant hard, constant and diversified work. Daily life provided opportunities to train in these sports, and on certain dates there was even a chance to give an exhibition. Authocthonous sports emerged, the only rules being existing customs and norms, which have been formalised in recent years. Certain sports, only played in a particular area, extended to whole regions or, as happened with *pelota*, Basque emigrants took it to America, the Philippines, China and Australia. The Confederation of Basque Games and Sports was established as recently as 1980.

Betting on these games and sports has always been popular. Sometimes the bet is placed at the time of the event, or days and even months before it takes place. On other occasions bets are cleverly made depending on how the competition or match is going, through bookies who shout the odds as they change. This passion for betting dates back a long way. Juan Ignacio Izueta, a compiler of dances and customs, describes how villagers in the XVIIIth and XIXth centuries, even those who did not own their *caserío* but were tenants, bet thou-

The aizkolari stands on the young beech trunk with his feet very close together, stands erect and starts to hack away at the wood with accurate strokes that cause chips to fly off.

sands of ounces of gold on the matches and competitions. They carried the money in secret pockets and when they ran out of cash they bet their livestock, homes and even jackets and belts. Izueta tells us that "In the square at Hernani, in a game of *pelota* between four men from Gipuzkoa and four from Navarre, beds covered with the players' clothes and mattresses stood in the street until the end of the match, and each item had a value assigned to it by the local people.

[PREVIOUS PAGE] *Mikel Saralegui lifts a 250 kg. stone. The trial involves making the maximum number of lifts in a certain time.*

They say that this match was played around the year 1720." In a well-known bet on a tree-cutting competition on April 26th 1955 in the Bullring at San Sebastián between two of the best axemen of the time ('Luxia' from Gipuzkoa and 'Latasa' from Navarre), bets of 500,000 pesetas were placed on each competitor.

The 'Atlas Etnográfico de Vasconia' (Ethnographic Atlas of the Basque Country) has a large section describing hundreds of traditional children's' games. These games clearly distinguished between boys and girls and depended very much on the seasons because they were played in the open air. No toys were involved because for many generations children learned from their elders without knowing that some games like *tres en raya* (hopscotch) existed in Roman times, or others such as *tabas* (tiddlywinks) were played throughout the world. In many group games played in the streets and squares the children simply imitated the behaviour of adults, because adults are also playful.

Throwing the bar (*palanka*) was possibly the most popular game in Navarre in the past, and was one which generated large bets. In his youth Julián Gayarre, the famous tenor from Roncal, was a great *palankari* who won many competitions. This sport reached its peak towards the end of the XVIIIth century but disappeared following the exodus from the countryside to the towns. In the 1940s an attempt was made to revive it by organising competitions and even giving it official status as an athletics event. It is sometimes played in local pilgrimages or festivities in the Valdorba area (centre of Navarre). The bar can be thrown from the chest, through the legs, or by turning round. The winner is the one who can throw it farthest. The bar, made from burnished iron or steel, is shaped like a javelin with a conical design. When it falls to earth the thickest part hits the ground first. The smallest bars, from the Upper Urraul valley, are seventy centimetres long and have a diameter of three centimetres.

During Lent a game called *atxikan* was played in the village of Urdiain. It is a lively game (similar to baseball) and was played between teams of four men and women. José María Satrústegui has documented the technique and rules of this game. Others such as *perratxe* or *vilorta* (similar to golf) or *anikote* (similar to cricket) have disappeared.

Exhibition with a spherical stone. This variety (barrijasotzea) is the hardest and most demanding among traditional sports.

Soka-tira is a local version of the ancient and universal sport of tug-of-war, with two teams of eight players of equivalent weight. The rope is held in both hands and the last player in each team passes it over his (or her) shoulder and ties a knot. An area two metres wide is marked out on the grass or court, which the teams may not step out of. There is another two-and-a-half metre long 'dragging' area marked on the ground and on the rope, and a red ribbon is placed in the exact centre. Contests are usually two pulls, and the teams change sides to keep things fair. If a draw occurs the winner is the team which takes the shortest time to drag its opponents over the centreline.

There has always been great interest in long-distance running (similar to fell running). The traditional *korrikalari* (runner) was also called *andarín* (fast walker) because, as Rafael Aguirre Franco tells us, "Bets or challenges took place along paths or tracks. The distances were great and the athlete would walk fast rather than run. Apart from stamina, another quality came into play: orientation and knowledge of the course to find the shortest route. The course was not marked out exactly, just the starting and finishing points

were given and the *andarín* was free to choose short cuts. It was usually a contest between just two competitors who had previously placed a bet. Those *korrikalariak* did not have much in common with Olympic athletes. They wore trousers half way down their legs, wore *abarkas* (strong rubber-soled shoes) and carried a hazelnut stick in their hands."

The most glorious era of the Navarrese *andarín* was at the end of the XIXth and beginning of the XXth centuries. The valleys near the border with Gipuzkoa, Araitz and Larraun, provided the best-known runners. Francisco Echarri from the village of Arruitz, known as 'Naparzarra', ended his career in 1908 in the Tolosa-Pamplona-Tolosa race, a 124-kilometre battle won by the two Juanagorris (father and son), who took over the lead from each other in a series of relays.

Well-marked circuits and round bullrings are the scene of the exploits of the authentic *korrikalariak*, the predecessors of today's professional long distance runners. Juan Cruz Azpíroz (nicknamed 'Chiquito de Arruiz') was the best runner for over a decade. Nobody could rival him, so he used to give his opponents a head start or lay bets on himself in events in which he ran and cut tree trunks at the same time. The 'League of Lekunberri' was a difficult race over 6,040 metres, all uphill, from Lekunberri to the pass of Azpirotz. It was considered that a time under twenty

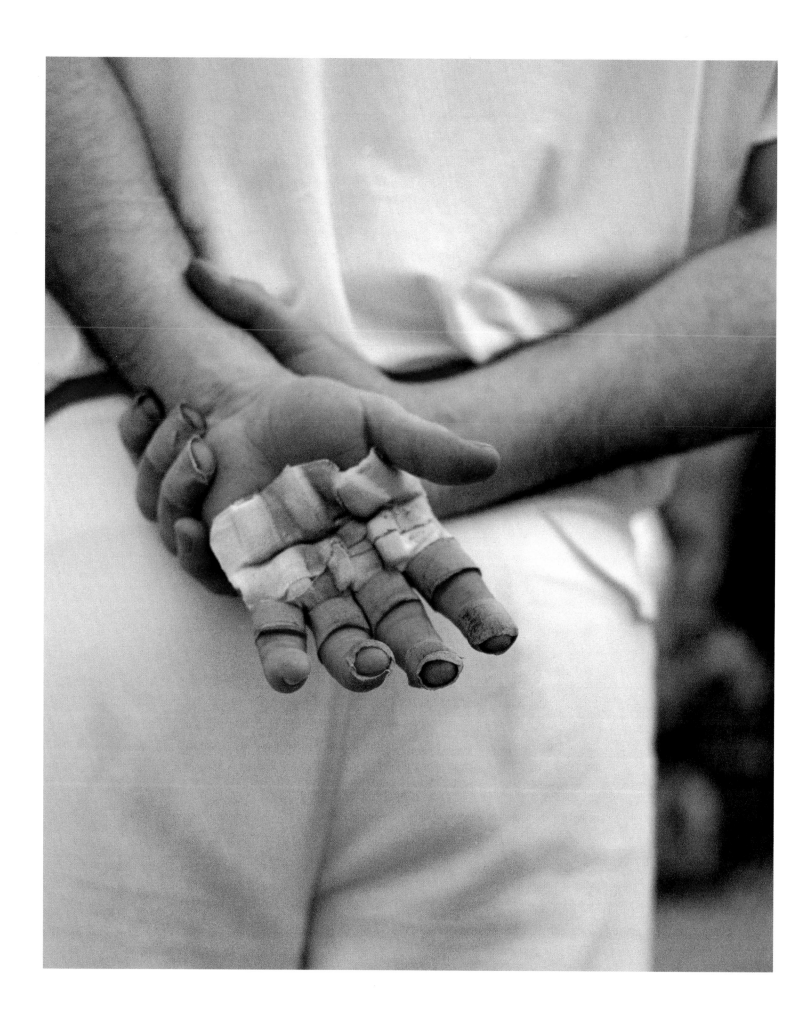

minutes was impossible, but on October 11th 1959 'Chiquito de Arruiz' broke the record with a time of 18 minutes, 57.6 seconds. Another famous *korrikalari* was Francisco Aldareguía, from the village of Aldatz.

There is a wide variety of rural games and sports, and these are often combined in series of five (*bost kirol*) or three (*hiru kirol*). The *Txingak* are two weights of 50 kilos that the athlete carries in each hand as he runs a distance in a certain time. The *segalari*, who trains by cutting the grass on the steep slopes machinery cannot reach, competes with his scythe in hard events in which the athletes perform, bent double at the waist, compressing their lungs and breathing with the torso at an angle. A Navarrese variation on this popular sport is called *arpanlariak*, where tree trunks are cut with a large saw handled by two people. The 'tronza' (or *arpana*) was not known in the woods until an Italian foreman, Aldo Moranti, introduced it to the workers of the Irati forest in 1860.

BETS ON AXEMEN, *AIZKOLARIAK*

In the Roman era the forests of the western Pyrenees were the site of an established timber industry. Like many industries, it went through periods of crisis and prosperity depending on the demand for houses and ships in the later stages of the Middle and Modern Ages.

The Basque names of the cutting instruments (axe, blade or scissors) all come from the word *aitz* (stone) and relate to prehistoric tools and occupations. The axe (*aizkora*) which the *aizkolari* uses is now made from steel and its design has evolved, taking much from the Australian axe.

The work of squads of woodcutters and charcoal gatherers gave rise to the bets made in forest clearings. The only witnesses were one's workmates, so they bet among themselves. There is documentary evidence of exhibitions in public squares dating from the XVIth century. The sport became more widespread in the XIXth century and the woodcutters would walk to the place where the challenge was to take place with their axes on their shoulders, after a few days of hard training accompanied by a ridiculously heavy diet!

The XXth century brought with it championships and a purer technique. Among Navarrese axe champions are Ezequiel Arano, Ramón Baleztena, Martín Garciarena, Miguel Berecoechea, Ramón Latasa, Patxi Astibia, Miguel Mindeguía and José María Mendizábal.

Green beechwood with no visible knots is used for the competitions, and the trunks are usually placed horizontally. Time comes into the calculation, but success usually has more to do with stamina than speed. Rhythm is very important, as is precision in the stroke of the axe and the ability to spread the effort, because the wood gets harder to cut as the core of the trunk is reached. The *aizkolari* stands up straight on top of the trunk with his feet close

together. When the referee signals the start of the competition he begins to strike with the axe and the wood chips start to fly. The effort is really exhausting. In the old days it was not unusual for one of the competitors to finish with his hands bleeding, the extreme case being that of Ignacio Saldías (nicknamed 'Naparra') from Urroz, who collapsed and died after a competition in Doneztebe one hot August day in 1933. Exhausting sessions of up to two hours have been known, although the time taken to finish is usually between 30 minutes and one hour.

The number of trunks to be cut varies and there are various kinds of competition: individual, pairs, relays, or the vertical cutting of trunks. The measurements of the trunks are based on their exterior circumference, not the diameter. These are usually determined according to traditional units: *onza* (inch), *oina* (foot), and *kana*. The wood is thus called *kanako* or *kanaerdiko* if it is of one or a half *kana*, and *oinbeteko* or *oinbiko* if it is of one or two feet. The most commonly used size of trunk is the *kanaerdiko*, with a circumference of 54 inches, equivalent to 1252 millimetres.

STONE-LIFTERS, *HARRIJASOTZAILEAK*

Two men from the village of Leitza (in the north of Navarre), Iñaki Perurena and Mikel Saralegui, have made this Basque sport popular in Europe, America and Asia through TV programmes and exhibitions. The *harrijasotzea* originated as a trial of strength between tough stone-cutters who lifted odd-shaped pieces of rock. Perurena reinvented and polished the technique to reach hitherto unsuspected records, always alone without rivals. In 1997 his pupil, Saralegui, achieved the prodigious feat of lifting a prism-shaped block weighing 326 kilos in 20 seconds.

Rafael Aguirre, a writer on Basque rural sports, says that "this is the oldest sport, but also the one with the shortest history. The strongman Arteondo reached his peak around 1925, taking stones to the village squares for exhibitions and marking the weights, shapes and dimensions. Until he appeared on the scene the events were neither programmed nor subject to regulations."

The granite stones have four shapes: cubes, cylinders, spheres and parallelepipeds. Their design improves with observation and experience to achieve easier handling and the optimum balance between weight and volume. The diet, training patterns and clothing of the stone-lifter have also evolved over the years.

The trial consists of making the highest possible number of lifts in a given period, which is divided into rounds. The lifters do not compete against each other simultaneously, but one after the other. The stone is lifted by a strong surge of the waist and arms, but for the lift to be valid the stone has to stay level with the shoulder. Finally, the lifter has to throw it down in front of his body. If it drops behind the lift is considered null and void.

Sportsmen who have practised different forms of *herri kirolak* insist that this is the hardest and most painful. Its fans agree with this when they see that it is possible to keep going in the other sports despite the fatigue and maintain a rhythm of strokes or steps, but the stone-lifter cannot afford the luxury of a single false move at any time, because the stone would fall to the ground.

*Pilotak ohore du euskal herrietan
zeren den ederrena joku guztietan*

[The game of *pelota* does honour to the Basque Country, because it is the most beautiful game of all].

This verse underlines the high regard in which *pelota* has been held for centuries. A document dated 1331 indicates that it was played in Pamplona at that time. Kings, nobles and commoners enjoyed the sport in galleries, courts and even in the streets, on account of its elegance, social nature and healthiness. Around 1540 a doctor prescribed it to a public official in the following terms: "Exercise on an empty stomach, play *pelota* for a short time until you start to perspire, and then play another game before supper." The clergy always provided its share of good players, and even the Bishop of Pamplona, Severo Andriani, was convinced of its value because, as he wrote in 1830, "the usefulness of the game of *pelota* is very clear: it is a local game, one which makes the members agile, requires skill, sets a good example, is interesting for spectators, and stimulates the imagination in an amazing manner."

In his novel 'Ramuntcho' published in 1897, the French sailor and academician Pierre Loti wrote one of the most beautiful and accurate descriptions of a game of *pelota*: "The *pelotaris* (players) have finally entered the court. They tie a glove to their wrist with a band and a wicker basket shaped like a large curved fingernail; they use this to throw the ball over and over again, a ball as hard as wood. They practice by testing the balls, then they choose the best ones. The spectators know the players well and follow everything very keenly. The match starts. The ball, thrown with all the players' strength, crashes loudly against the wall then bounces and flies through the air as fast as a bullet. Ramuntcho is playing out of his skin; he is at one of those moments when he feels full of strength and his body, lightened, gives full rein to his exuberant energy. The match is drawn. The 'crack' of the ball against the wall repeats itself, bouncing furiously each time it is struck. Sometimes the players catch it on the volley, hold it in the air, and then release it again. The spectators applaud and shout. The final point is for Ramuntcho. At that moment all the spectators flood onto the court, and coarse hands stretch out to shake his and congrat-

A guante Laxoa player in Oitz de Santesteban

ulate him from all sides. At this moment Ramuntcho is the real hero, a demi-God ..."

At the beginning of this century Rodney Gallop, a folklorist and lover of this land, wrote: "In each village, no matter how small it is, there are three things which give it character and charm. The first is the church; the second, the cemetery with its tombs weathering the elements and dark cypress trees; the third, the *frontón*."

Almost a century later, Gallop would be able to observe not only continuity, but also great improvement. Navarre has one *frontón* for every 1,000 inhabitants, and there are 505 in the census. Of these, 308 are open-air and 197 covered. Fifty-one are found in Pamplona alone. Valcarlos, a village with a population of 500, has four. The largest arenas are the 'Euskal Jai' in Huarte, which can hold 2,400 spectators, and the 'Labrit' in Pamplona, with capacity for 1,900. The *Pelota* Federation of Navarre has 5,200 registered players.

Gabriel Imbuluzqueta, a journalist who specialises in the sport, describes the situation as follows: "Navarre is nowadays an enormous playing field in which *pelota*, perhaps displaced by football, is the main sport. A few decades ago it was clearly the number one sport among children, adolescents and adults. It has lost its dominance but has not gone under, nor will the people of Navarre allow it to. For example, just look through the sports pages of the newspapers and the programmes of village festivities. Also, try and play a game in any *frontón* open to the public in Pamplona. It is not that easy, given the large number of players at any time. Equally high is the number of spectators who watch matches involving amateur or professional players."

The Pelota Federation of Navarre was founded in 1935 and has worked hard to promote the sport at amateur level through the organisation of school championships and competitions between villages. Some clubs have also made a decisive contribution through their training schools.

Navarre boasts the best record in hand *pelota* championships, the most important and hardest version of the game. Its main exponent is Julián Retegui from the village of Erasun, who remains active in his mid-forties and has reached the Finals for the last 23 years. Other notable *pelotaris* from Navarre are Ignacio Retegui, Julián Lajos, Ladis Galarza, Fernando Arreche, and the younger players Rubén Beloki and Patxi Eugui. The favourite version of the

The arpanlariak cut tree trunks with a large two-handed saw.

game among fans in Navarre is *remonte* (played with the wicker basket strapped to the wrist), which was born in the region and in which nobody has surpassed the great Jesús Abrego, from Arróniz, who covered the entire court and won in the most difficult combinations of pairs against threes. The professional version of *pala* (played with a wooden bat) is hardly played, although Oscar Insausti, from Pamplona, is the number one in this version, which is only played in long *frontones*.

The game, already documented in ancient times, developed towards the Mediaeval French *Jeu de Paume* which was played in southern Europe. It then took root and evolved in the western Pyrenees until it diversified over the years into the twenty-one varieties of Basque *pelota* that exist today.

In some village festivities it is still possible to see matches of the *largo* (long) version. This is the oldest form of the game, played on grass (*pilota soro*), where the court/pitch is divided into three areas called *escases*. There is no wall and the game is played with the hand. The 'service' is made from a stone square (*botillo*) where the ball is bounced and then served to the player who has to return it.

The version called *rebote* (bounce) is a variation on the long game. The court is divided by a line or 'rope' which separates the service and return areas. These two versions of the game are scored by games or *quinces* (fifteens), similar to tennis.

Gloves to protect the players' hands appeared later and are used in *rebote* and *pasaka*. Two pairs of players facing each other play in a covered court or *trinquete* which is divided into two by a net.

Since the XVIIIth various documents refer to walls, usually those of the churches, against which *pelota* is played: this was the start of the *al blé* (handball) version, the basis of the current game although the old name is no longer used. The *frontón* can also be a single vertical wall (*frontis*) or have one wall to the left and even a third wall to bounce the ball off. The horizontal plane is the *cancha* (court), where the ball first bounces, and the *contracancha*. A horizontal line is drawn on the wall called the *escás*. This line is covered with a piece of metal and a fault is called if the ball hits it.

The fronton is the scene of other popular versions of the game: *mano* (hand), *pala* (bat), and *cesta-punta*, in which the ball is held in the basket or *txistera* before the return of service, and *remonte*, where the ball is allowed to slip without holding it back.

Ricardo Ollaquindia, a compiler of historical and literary texts on the game, says that 'the game of *pelota* is linked to the history, folklore, culture, village festivities, and character of the people. It is a way of living together and competing against each other, a hard struggle followed by an embrace at the end, rest after exhaustion, an exhibition of strength and skill, a place to meet, an occasion to pray and swear, an excuse for challenges and bets.'

To finish, the most touching greeting between Basque speakers is the song from Lower Navarre (north of the Pyrenees) called *Agur Jaunak*, used by losing *pelota* players to ask for revenge, although without the slightest grudge.

Known in Basque as *Iruña,* the capital lies in the heart of Navarre, in a basin surrounded by mountains. From whatever perspective they consider it, the people of Navarre have always considered Pamplona to be 'the city', a 'good city', the 'ultimate city'. A series of municipalities make up a large residential, industrial and service area where over half of the population of Navarre lives. This city of a thousand facets offers good quality of life and stands out for its educational and health facilities, parks and open spaces. Pamplona's festivities, the *Sanfermines,* when the Running of the Bulls takes place, are famous the world over.

PAMPLONA

The City

THE PAMPLONA BASIN

Seen from the air, the Pamplona basin looks precisely that, a large bowl surrounded by moderately high mountains. The river Arga, which meanders lazily across the plain, has deposited sediments and eroded its course over seven million years, and in some places has lowered the altitude of the land some four hundred metres below its original level.

In contrast to the present situation of a large metropolitan area which is attempting to solve the challenges of water supply, waste disposal and transport, there is the background of the landscape and over two thousand years of history. The geographical limits of the *Cuenca* (basin) were defined in the Middle Ages in the *Fuero General* (General Charter), which mentioned mountain ranges and included a series of references to hermitages, castles, bridges and crossings which remain very familiar today.

The city and its outskirts make up an indivisible whole. The basin covers 466 square kilometres (4% of the territory of Navarre) and contains about one hundred municipalities of different sizes with a total population of 270,000, just over half the total population of the Community. The city of Pamplona covers only 23 square kilometres but has a population of around 170,000.

Located slightly north-east of the centre of the basin, the city is a focal point around which a series of concentric rings can be drawn from 'highly urbanised' to 'very natural'. These rings correspond to a triple vision of the basin: urban, rural and rugged.

The countryside reflects how the economy of the area has changed. Three thousand years ago hunters abounded in a forest of holm and gall oaks. The tree cover, broken only on some high plateaux where Iron Age settlements emerged, remained relatively unchanged until the Romans brought agriculture and the 'colonisation' of the land through small *fundi*, agricultural plots located at a suitable distance from each other and which are the origin of many of the country villages that survive to this day. Others emerged in the mediaeval era, when castles and churches were built, and the old Roman roads became important again with the advent of the Pilgrims' Way to Compostela.

In more recent times the concentration of arable land has meant that tracks, embankments, enclosing mud walls and hedges have disappeared, and the streaks of green along the courses of rivers and streams now stand out even more. The greatest impact on the countryside has been through public works that have left their mark on the landscape: large quarries, slag heaps from exhausted mines, factories, high buildings, railways and a system of motorways which surround and separate the city like a new defensive wall.

A delightful relic of the original forest which covered the plain is the oak grove of Zabalgaña, in the *Cendea de Olza*, where there are good examples of evergreen, gall and other oaks. This natural space, where dozens of bird species nest, is a Reserve which was a famous hunting ground for woodcocks and an abundant source of truffles in ages gone by.

The Aranguren range of hills, its steep slopes crowned by rocky heights, still has an excellent mixed forest on its shady side, with several large examples of beech, oak and pine. The undergrowth is rich, thickets and weeds abound, and the nearby cereal fields produce a barrier effect. In the Góngora area boars, foxes, genets, marten, badgers, squirrels and wildcats all find shelter. Above the rocks, about fifty vultures fly around and sleep there every night. It is a rich and wild wood, just ten miles from Pamplona.

A large geological fault in the limestone marks a cut-off point over the valley of Etxauri. In contrast to the cold of the heights, the grandiose rock wall acts as a sun screen and creates a micro-climate at its base which accounts for the enormous variety of crops, the valley's justly famous cherries, and the abundance of beautiful flowers (which thrive even in winter). Prehistoric shelters in the form of caves with paintings indicate that this area was inhabited from very early times and also bear witness to the great capacity for observation of Prehistoric Man. The rock face now attracts climbers who

have found as many as 329 routes to ascend it, all the while respecting the nesting habits of the birds there. A pathway along the top provides an opportunity for the less adventurous walker to observe the flight of a variety of species of vultures and eagles.

Just a stone's throw from the capital, the lake at Loza is a marshy space used by migrating birds as their last resting place before the long flight over the Pyrenees. On cold February nights it is an unforgettable experience to hear the honking of the flocks of large geese, which alight on the lake in their hundreds. The lake is not very deep and offers very good conditions for wildlife living on the bottom. The Ornithological Yearbook has documented the presence of 120 different species, among them a few at risk of extinction: the bittern and the spoonbill. Loza is an interesting place for certain amphibians such as the 'Dalmatina' frog, of which there is an isolated colony. It is also appreciated by botanists. Daffodils appear in February and March, and April and May is the time to watch the yellow irises and lilies as they bloom.

The agricultural scenery of the Pamplona basin has been decisively transformed in the second half of this century. According to studies by the geographer Ana Ugalde, the concentration of plots has affected two-thirds of the agricultural surface area. Farming, which employed half of the active population of the basin in 1950, only accounts for three per cent of jobs nowadays. It rains for an average of 150 days a year, with a total rainfall of over 800 litres per annum, so the area has always been a good granary, although improvements in efficiency have tripled yields since the middle of the century. The great diversity of the countryside in the past, made up of small plots of meadows, orchards, market gardens, vineyards and other minor crops, has given way to the relative monotony of large cereal fields which occupy three-quarters of the entire agricultural land area.

In the past the Basin was the breadbasket of the capital, a series of valleys and *cendeas* (municipal boroughs composed of several villages) where the sound of the big bell of Pamplona cathedral could be heard everywhere. The people of Pamplona called these honest, sober, astute and distrustful village folk *cuencos* (a play on words; 'cuenco' also means 'bowl'). The language spoken by these people is elegant and full of Basque expressions and sentence structures. They used to travel to Pamplona on Saturdays to go to market, laden with lambs, birds, eggs, fruit and vegetables. Their lifestyle disappeared among property developments and mechanisation, a rhythm of life which followed the seasons and their festivities (accompanied by the *gaita* —a kind of flute— and drum) with dancing in the vegetable patches, lovers exchanging sweet nothings and drinking the acidy white wine called *txakolí*.

Reminiscences, however, should not idealise the poverty, limited horizons and rigid control of society in the past. It is important, however, to conserve the natural and constructed heritage: Romanesque and Gothic churches, inns, farmhouses, palaces and fortified towers, mediaeval bridges, hermitages, mills, and the ruins of ghostly castles. The Pamplona basin has many examples of all these. It also has sheep-folds and tools from ancient trades. The excellent ethnographic museum at Arteta, in the Ollo valley, conserves elements of the traditional culture of the area.

Old farmland has been turned over to industrial estates, with the automotive sector nowadays being the main industry of the area. The electrical components sector is also important, followed by chemical products, food processing, and household appliances.

Municipal and district urban planning documents emphasise the importance of the physical environment, the framework in which society develops. Rural life as such has disappeared, but the relief and the countryside, whether natural or 'humanised', remains. As you walk down a street in Pamplona you can see rolling, tree-covered hills in the distance. A two-tiered 'crown' of nearby hills and distant mountains surrounds the city and its outskirts. The view of the basin from a high vantage point is a delight, rather like a scale model. There is a high (perhaps excessive) level of land occupation, the industrial sprawl is rather chaotic, other spaces and ancient farms have been abandoned, and there is too much noise: things have not been perfectly planned. The Old Part of Pamplona, however, has not changed its skyline; there are no ugly skyscrapers but an abundance of green spaces. The rivers flow clean, kites and eagles fly overhead, and the general chatter of birds can still be heard. It is a pleasant city to live in.

ANCIENT AND MEDIAEVAL PAMPLONA

Pamplona is a city of many names: Athanagia, Bambalona, Martua or Santsueña, names from Arab tongues, Renaissance myths and Baroque fantasies.

The old Basque term *ili* or *iri* (settlement) seems to be present in the official name of the city in both languages. The Romance (Spanish) name, Pamplona, comes from *Pompelon*, the city of Pompey, first mentioned by the Greek chronicler Strabo a few centuries before Christ. The Basque form, *Iruña*, appears on Roman coins, when the mint was called *Olcairun*.

Excavations in the Navarrería area of the city, led by María Angeles Mezquíriz, have revealed the origins of the ancient settlement. From the VIIth century BC an indigenous Gascon population occupied the raised plateau where the city stands today. The Roman General Pompey passed through and decided to spend the winter of 75-74 BC there with his army. The settlement finally covered 14 hectares had a population of 2,000 in the IInd century (its moment of splendour under the Romans). The present Dormitalería and Curia streets are oriented as the *cardo* and *decumanus*. The point where they cross, now in the atrium of the cathedral, was in the forum with a *macellum* or market. The way of life in the city, won over to Roman culture before Caesar conquered Gaul, was Italian, as shown by the discovery of ceramics and a *hipocausta* (Roman underfloor heating system). The town was damaged in a series of invasions and abandoned after being completely destroyed in a fire in 276. The area was later razed and built up again, but not on the basis of the layout of the old city.

The Visigoths, intruders and enemies, brought Christianity with them. In the third decade of the VIIth century a Frank or a monk composed a rather exaggerated song 'In praise of Pamplona'. The poet observed what can still be seen today: the mountains around the city, the river, the city walls and the flat plain to the north, full of flowers. He also saw what can no longer be seen:

"as many wells as days in the year", and some indigenous Gascons, "barbaric and enemy people" as far as he was concerned.

The Kingdom of Pamplona was formed in the cauldron of battles against the powerful Carolingians from the North and Arabs from the south. The oldest musical epithalamium in Europe was composed in the middle of the XIth century in honour of Leodegundia, daughter of the Asturian king Ordoño, who came to marry a prince from Pamplona. However, as the historian Jimeno Jurio points out, Pamplona was a theocratic domain run by the Bishop and the clergy until well into the XIVth century. The monarchs could not set up residence there, not even in the Royal Palace which Sancho *el Sabio* ('the Wise') started to build in the second half of the XIIth century.

Pamplona is often referred to in the plural ('las Pamplonas'). For more than three centuries three different boroughs, separated by walls, existed in the area previously occupied by a single city: Navarrería, San Cernín and San Nicolás. Three municipalities with their own communities, jurisdiction, Royal Charter and system of government. The burghers had exemptions and privileges which the others did not, although all the land was the property of the local Church.

The appointment of the French monk Pedro de Roda as Bishop in 1083 led to a major transformation of Pamplona. He began the construction of the great Romanesque cathedral and brought with him Franks to build inns, hospitals and shops to serve pilgrims on the way to Compostela.

The *navarros*, Basque speakers who worked as servants to the clergy, lived in the Navarrería. The Jewish quarter and the small (and short-lived) borough of San Miguel were also located within the Navarrería.

At the gates of the Navarrería, quite far from the walls, two paths went in different directions. The one to the right led westwards to Barañain, the other being the 'old route' to Azella. When buildings went up opposite each other the two routes became the main streets of the borough of San Cernin and the Población de San Nicolás, new 'cities' which developed according to a preconceived plan. San Cernin, shaped like a hexagon, was the largest and richest, most of its residents being Franks of diverse origin who spoke Occitan as their common language. Within the triangular Población de San Nicolás both the Navarrese and the Franks lived together, paying a levy to the Cathedral.

A moat separated the two walled areas. Between the new settlements and the Navarrería there was a gully and a 'No Man's Land', and a field where markets were held and construction prohibited.

From the outset the history of the three 'cities' was one of constant conflict, marked by social and economic inequality, the opposition of theocratic feudalism to the freedoms of the burghers, and confrontations supported by the armies of France and Castile.

[OPPOSITE] *The Old Part of Pamplona. In the foreground, the church and borough of San Cernín. In the background, the Cathedral and the borough of la Navarrería. There was an open space between the two mediaeval boroughs where markets were held. The City Hall was later built on this site, representing the union of the three boroughs of the city (plus San Nicolás).*

The battles were most vicious in the XIIIth century. Burnt stones on the pillars and Gothic arches of the San Nicolás church remind us of the first act in that tragedy. In 1222 the people of San Cernín invaded San Nicolás, pillaging houses and setting them on fire. Many people sought refuge in the church but the burghers cut their throats, even the youngest girls. The church and the entire area were razed to the ground.

Even more serious was the War of the Navarrería in 1276, with Pamplona split into two factions. Guilhem Anelier, on the side of the burghers, recorded what he saw and wrote a five thousand verse poem in Provençal about it. The poem abounds with images and movement, with enough material to write a full mediaeval war film script.

Disputes, mutual accusations, increasing hatreds, challenges, fortifications, catapults launching stones and fire, failed attempts at mediation, attacks with javelins and cross-bows, plots and spying, the sounds of pipers along battlements and alarm bells in bell-towers, pitched battles where "you could see blood run like wine along the canal", bandages and ointments to heal wounds, reinforcements, battering rams and catapults were the order of the day, until the leader García Almoravid fled without warning under cover of night and abandoned the people of the Navarrería to their fate. That war ended with the vengeance of Governor Beaumarchais and the massacre of an unprotected population at the hands of the soldiers. There were rapes, murders, pillage and fires, both in houses and in the Cathedral, where tombs were desecrated and the ruined cloister was turned into a stable. Everything was destroyed and there was

Pamplona still has four mediaeval bridges over the Arga. The most beautiful is La Magdalena, on the Pilgrims' Way to Compostela. Built on the Romanesque design of the bridge at Puente la Reina, it seems to be the heir to an old Roman bridge that was located here.

nowhere to shelter in the Navarrería ("on its ground you could cut grass and grow wheat"). Almost fifty years went by before permits to build were granted again, and the discredited Cathedral closed its doors to worship for over thirty years.

The rule of the clergy ended in 1319, by virtue of a concordat. The King assumed supreme power in the city and was named 'Lord of Jurisdiction' there. The conflicts did not end until Carlos III el Noble proclaimed the 'Privilege of the Union' on September 8th 1423. A single Pamplona was born, a municipality without dividing walls, with its present standard and coat of arms of a lion bordered with chains and a golden crown on its head. The City Hall was built on the old No Man's Land, and the present-day building stands on the same site. On July 21st 1512 Pamplona fell to the Duke of Alba and on that same day became the capital of Navarre and the seat of its power: the *Diputación del Reino* (Deputation of the Kingdom), the *Cortes* (Parliament) and the *Real Consejo* (Royal Council).

THE CATHEDRAL AND GOTHIC CHURCHES

The Cathedral is an emblem of the city. Its much-criticised façade, late Baroque rather than neo-classical, was considered ignominious by Victor Hugo and vulgar, dull and unwieldy by the novelist Pérez Galdós. At the end of the XVIIIth century the Chapter had the good sense to charge a famous and competent architect, Ventura Rodríguez, with the task of finding a solution in tune with the techniques and tastes of the time. The silhouette of the Cathedral towers, visible above the sturdy city walls, is the most typical view of Pamplona.

The site has been used as a place of worship since ancient times although various churches have been built in the same place. Christianity took over from a pagan cult with the arrival of the Visgoths. Remains of pre-Romanesque church sculptures from the Xth century have been uncovered here and also in another building that King Sancho el Mayor ordered built at the beginning of the XIth century.

From 1100 onwards, Bishop Pedro de Roda was the driving force behind the project for a grandiose Romanesque cathedral. The famous mason Maestro Esteban was involved in the work. There was no larger church along the entire Pilgrim's Way, except the

Cathedral at Compostela itself. Its cloister was destroyed in the war of the Navarrería, although nine beautiful capitals were rescued and now are on display in the Museo de Navarra. Also surviving from that period are the Chapel of San Jesucristo and the granary.

In February 1390 King Carlos III was crowned. A few months later, on July 1st the same year, the central part of the building collapsed. The building work for the present Gothic Cathedral started in 1394, was halted by the Civil War among the Navarrese, and finished seven years later. The monarch chose to be buried there, and his alabaster tomb (and that of his Queen, Leonor) stand in the Nave. The tomb, the work of Jehan Lome de Tournai, is the finest example of Gothic sculpture in Navarre.

The French Gothic Cathedral, stylish yet austere, has been returned to its ancient splendour after a major restoration completed in 1994 which set out to conserve its historical features, highlight its architecture and improve its usability. Darkened frescos, Renaissance stained glass windows and original woodwork were brought to life again. The floor was re-laid and the furniture recovered its previous beauty through careful cleaning and new lighting. There are many elements which draw the observer's attention, for example the Romanesque image of Santa María la Real, the

Gothic panels of the altar-piece of Caparroso, the Christ on the Cross (the work of Juan de Anchieta), the wrought iron grilles by Guillermo Ervenat and the choir pews, carved from English oak by Esteban de Obray.

The cloister, on which building work started in 1280, is a wonderful example of balanced beauty and harmonious rhythm and is clearly the most elegant part of the entire Cathedral. It is a delight to the senses. Birds sing and water trickles as the sunlight filters through the arches leading to the inner garden. When snow falls in winter the light is particularly appealing, highlighting the filigrees of the open-work windows with incredible precision, revealing the finely sculptured doors and reliefs, and the gracious icons of the keystones, where the winds and the work cycle of the agricultural year appear. The well-preserved Gothic paintings of the cathedral are now in the Museo de Navarra.

The Barbazana chapel, with its star-spangled dome, is reached through the cloister. It was used as accommodation for the clergy while they lived together under rules of obedience, and now houses the Diocesan Museum, rich in images and gold and silverwork. In the refectory, a large Gothic hall, there are heraldic symbols and an entire sculpted bestiary. The kitchen is next door, with

It is still possible to observe the old part of Pamplona from below the bells of the city's churches, a 'bell-tower view' as described by Angel María Pascual in his evocative prose of the 1940s: "We can see the city from these very bell-towers, bathed with gentle light, overlooking thousands of garrets and skylights, everything warm and delightful. The city changes, renews itself and dresses up according to each moment. The roof tiles, however, hardly ever change. From above, Pamplona has a yellowish colour, like the fallow land of the surrounding basin. Innumerable chimneys and skylights rise from the rooftops, even small, toy-like houses which never see the streets below nor are seen or suspected from down there. This is a humble, ancient and rural Pamplona, where a black cat runs at this very moment."

Of the old churches still in use, San Cernin (also known as San Saturnino) is the oldest, if we recall that its Gothic front was finished in 1297. Entry to the church is through an XVIIIth century outer porch which protects a bell-shaped front with a beautiful tympanum under a figure of Jesus Christ the Judge. Inside, the wooden floor catches the eye. It covers more than two hundred *fuesas* (ditches) where 22,800 parishioners have been buried since the XVth century, common people whose names appear in the Parish Register. Another surprising element is found above the chapel of Saint George: an enigmatic relief of a Knight from the Crusades who leaves his country and is blessed by the hand of God from a cloud in the sky.

The springs of the apse of San Nicolás are Romanesque from the end of the XIIth century, the lateral naves are Proto-Gothic and the main nave was covered in 1355. There was another (lower) roof prior to this because the church was originally consecrated in 1231. Thirteenth-century murals were revealed during the restoration work. The original floor was sixty-five metres lower, with family tombs built on it, as in the church of San Cernin.

In the Calle Ansoleaga of Pamplona there is a civil Gothic building which has returned to the function for which it was built: it houses the *Cámara de Comptos*, the Accounts Tribunal of Navarre. This institution is older than the Spanish Accounts Tribunal, and has preserved its extremely rich historical documentation, an endless source of information for researchers.

MODERN PAMPLONA

Following occupation by Castile in the 16th century, Pamplona took on the air of a military and market town, although without losing its ecclesiastical and agricultural atmosphere. It maintained this character until the arrival of industrialisation, around 1964.

Its castles became obsolete, although Pamplona became an impregnable fortress with the construction of the Citadel in 1571 and the walls of the unified city were strengthened in the Baroque period. Many buildings outside the walls were demolished for military reasons, and in some Romantic etchings the image of a magnificent fortress with its bulwarks and glacis still remains.

[OPPOSITE] *The most striking part of the Cathedral is its Cloister, a prodigy of balanced beauty and harmonious rhythm.*

Pamplona, 7th July. San Fermín, the Patron Saint, is fêted with flowers and sung jotas at a place linked to a local tradition: "El pocico" (the small well), where the first Christians of the city were baptised, just in front of the church of San Cernín.

a large, twenty-seven metre high chimney reminiscent of the one in the Papal Palace at Avignon. Access to the Rococo vestry is also through the cloister. Victor Hugo walked this way and later wrote: "Dante is in the cloister, Madame de Pompadour in the vestry."

The Cathedral of Santa María, in addition to being the place where Kings were crowned and the Parliament held its sessions on occasions, was the seat of the Deputation of the Kingdom and its Archives. Its Chapel of Music is still used. The present chapel was built in the XVIth century but can be traced back to the Middle Ages, making it the oldest musical institution in Navarre.

The towers of San Cernin and San Nicolás, which round off the Mediaeval profile of Pamplona, change colour according to the time of day and season. These two ogival churches, both recently restored, date back to the Romanesque period, together with other disappeared watchtowers and battlements. The church of San Nicolás has lost five towers but still preserves its cloistered surround.

Although a large part of the walls was knocked down from 1915 onwards, you can still stroll along the one and a half kilometres that remain and enjoy the view of the Pamplona basin. The walls are the collective memory of the city, and can also be a metaphor for a warm nest which houses the people and provides them with a pleasant space in which to carry out their complex relations. It also reflects a certain conservative mentality which enters into conflict with more progressive stances, different people and groups of socially excluded people. The chronicler José Antonio Iturri expressed this in a newspaper column: "These unfortunate people have neither past nor future. When they approach the city, the walls grow in size and the old skylights are filled with the menacing mouths of the cannon. The city's inhabitants remain silent, as if they could smell the danger, ready to bitterly defend something they are not really sure of."

Within the old walls, a street which is still called 'Nueva' (new), despite the fact that it is over four hundred years old, occupied the area previously filled by the moat separating the walls of the Burgo and the Población. The No Man's Land was covered with buildings and three squares which still remain: *Abajo* (in front of Santo Domingo), *Fruta*, now called 'Consistorial' (Town Hall Square), and *del Castillo*.

The Plaza del Castillo has been the largest public space in the city for the last five centuries. It has arches which were not designed at the beginning but which have been added over the years. It is in the form of a trapezoid but is perceived as square because the fronts of the building are not lined up straight. An XVIIth century document states that there were five squares in Pamplona at that time, and adds that "The most special of all is the Plaza del Castillo, no doubt because it was near the site of the old castle. It is square and very large. Some old houses give the square a pleasant atmosphere, and the bullfights held there are the best in Spain."

In his book *Pamplonario* Ignacio Aranaz sketched the heart of the city: "A square which is not a square, discreet and crossed by routes which lead to other corners of the city. The Plaza del Castillo is the centre, the place where people from outside Pamplona arrange to meet, somewhere everyone has to pass through at some time or other. It picks up the morning sun and moves it around the buildings until four o'clock in the afternoon. On its way it is accompanied by a 'chorus' of old people with their overcoats, *boinas* (Basque berets) and scarves. Mid-morning, the square has a provincial air, later in the day very special, with delightful twilights

The Plaza del Castillo is the largest public area in Pamplona. It is characterised by its trapezoidal shape and porches, a design which evolved without an original basic one.

reminiscent of painters, with a rose-red hint in the air. Important things happen in the Plaza del Castillo. All kinds of demonstrations are convened here, in a square which seems ready made for such events. On public holidays and when the weather is fine, having breakfast on the terrace of the Café Iruña is almost like being in San Sebastián."

The Enlightenment was a splendid period for Pamplona. The city had reached a population of fourteen thousand and was transformed from top to bottom. Nearly all the buildings were refurbished and Municipal regulations were drawn up so well that they served as a model for many other cities, Madrid among them. The great public building projects started during the reign of Carlos III de Borbón.

The inhabitants used to throw all kinds of rubbish, waste water and even dead animals into the old streets, which were either dusty or full of puddles but always dirty and smelly. The new system brought about a revolution, especially after the first streets were paved and drains installed in 1767.

Pedro García Merino's entertaining and well-documented work 'Obras y Servicios del viejo Pamplona' (Works and Services in Old Pamplona) describes the determination and financial effort made by a highly-indebted Council which nevertheless adopted a social and innovative system for obtaining funding: taxes on wine, gaming, bullfights and the length of building facades. New drainage was installed in only five years, a record considering the technical resources available at the time. Furthermore, the budget was only exceeded by five per cent, even taking into account that the cost rose by laying streets and pavements. The cobbles have lasted over two hundred years.

The architect Ventura Rodríguez designed the water supply project which was inaugurated in 1790. Bringing water from the spring at Subiza, 11 miles away, meant drilling tunnels through hard rock, ventilating these with deep shafts, installing 60,000 pipes, building bridges and (among other structures) the beautiful aqueduct at Noain with its 97 stone and brick arches. The city was enhanced by the fountains designed by Luis Paret and three of them are still working today in the Consejo, Navarrería and Recoletas squares. Of the colossal fountain of la Beneficencia, which used to stand in the Plaza del Castillo, there still remains one of the oldest and most beautiful statues of the city, the 'Mari Blanca'. Many recently married couples have their wedding photos taken in front of it in the Taconera gardens.

In the warlike XIXth century the Citadel, designed to defend the city against external enemies, became a threat to the citizens of Pamplona and a means of controlling them. The city walls of Pamplona converged on the pentagon-shaped fortress. Within the walls, however, between the Citadel and the first houses, there was a wide area called the Arenal, the Taconera gardens and the modern buildings of the Primer Ensanche. To the south, opposite the church of San Nicolás, the Paseo de Sarasate emerged, a promenade between the Old Part and the Segundo Ensanche (extension of the city centre).

Pamplona people often say that the Paseo de Sarasate is 'the living room of the city'. Old photographs show it as a place for strolling, with tramlines and thousands of lightbulbs for festivities. At the time it had *frontones* (where the Basque ball game of *pelota* is played), a bathing house and stables. Dutch elm disease killed off its strong elms and property speculation did the same to the standard height of the buildings along the promenade. What remains, however, is the excellent modern architecture of Joaquin Zarranz for the *Caja de Ahorros* (Savings Bank) and balconies and fronts from many different periods. At the east end of the promenade stands the Monument to the *Fueros* (chartered rights), erected in 1903 to proclaim the defence of the self-government of Navarre and its liberties and laws. "To the foreigner we will give him lodging, but we do not want to bear his yoke", says a text by Arturo Campión in Basque, although written using the Spanish alphabet.

Two rather old-fashioned representations of power are found at each end of the Paseo de Sarasate. The building that Julián Arteaga designed as the Courts, once these have been moved to a new building in the quarter of San Juan, will be refurbished and converted into the seat of the Parliament of Navarre. At the other end of the Paseo, the *Palacio de Navarra*, which people still call 'La Diputación', is the work of José de Nagusía. It is adorned with allegorical reliefs and sculptures by Fructuoso Orduna. Its main floor is "sumptuous, habitable, full of the dignity it holds" according to the Professor of Fine Arts, Pedro Manterola. The most notable features of the Palace are the collection of XVIIth century Flemish tapestries, a portrait of Fernando VII by Goya, a canvas by Elías Salaverría of San Francisco Javier, and murals by Gustavo de Maeztu depicting historic scenes. Within the grounds of the Palace, and fronted by a garden with an enormous redwood tree, are the Royal and General Archives of Navarre. There is a project to move the archives to the ancient *Palacio de los Reyes* (Palace of the Kings), a pro-Gothic building whose restoration has been commissioned to the prize-winning architect from Tudela, Rafael Moneo.

THE NEW CITY

The population of Pamplona reached 30,000 in 1910. At that time the city's growth was stunted by the walls around it. The First World War highlighted the defensive uselessness of the walls, and there was a celebration in 1915 to mark the "knocking down of the first stone." Three years later, however, not much work had been done. A demonstration was called to let the government in Madrid know what the vast majority of the citizens of Pamplona wanted.

In 1920 the building work for the Segundo Ensanche was authorised and set in motion. The project was designed by the municipal architect Serapio Esparza, who took his lead from the work of Ildefonso Cerdá in the *Eixample* of Barcelona. The Avenida Baja Navarra forms a diagonal axis and Avenida Carlos III is the central one, with a mesh of straight streets covering 96 blocks of buildings (with either interior patios or gardens) over an area of 89 hectares. Drawings and aerial photographs reveal the aim of giving continuity to the old city. The streets in the Ensanche extend in the same direction as those in the Navarrería. Part of the work involved the bold step of demolishing a theatre and a bull ring to open up the Plaza del Castillo and turn it into the place where the main avenue (Carlos III) started. The Plaza del Castillo and the Paseo de Sarasate thus became the centre of the city and the pivotal point of the two parts of the city, the Old and the New.

A city is defined by its architecture, and there are many striking examples in the Ensanche. The work of Víctor Eusa stands out, over five decades in which he evolved from expressionist and rationalist positions to a more classical or regional style. Schools and religious buildings abound in the urban scenery of Pamplona: the Seminary, the Casa de Misericordia, the church of la Milagrosa, or the schools of Escolapios, Maristas and Hijas de María Inmaculada. For Ignacio Linazasoro, "Eusa could be described as one of the most brilliant architects of the first third of the century, just on the basis of his religious buildings." Eusa's blocks of flats in the Plaza Príncipe de Viana or in the streets of Roncesvalles and García Castañón are also examples of utility, strength and design in which bricks and cement blend well together. Many people think that Eusa's best work is the Casino Eslava in the Plaza del Castillo. It was inaugurated in 1931 and still preserves almost all its original features to the present day.

Rafael Moneo has also left his mark on the Ensanche through buildings in the Calle Plazaola, the extension of the Plaza de Toros (bullring), and by solving traffic problems in a part of the city which many people cross by car or on foot: the Plaza de los Fueros, with its wide pavement and a garden separating pedestrians from the noisy and fast traffic.

In the suburb of San Juan the equally famous architect Oriol Bohigas was commissioned to breathe life back into a large space previously occupied by a metal company. The dual dihedral of the Plaza de Yamaguchi opens up like a large letter 'U' to the newest park in the city. Next to the Japanese garden with its geyser, waterfall, slopes and sand stands the Planetarium, where the galaxies shine in its dome by day and by night. The dome is 20 metres across and can show 9,000 stars, more than anyone on Earth is able to see by simply looking up to the night sky.

There are also interesting places to see in the popular suburbs. The initial phase of the Txantrea, a small garden city with two-storey houses opening out onto patios and market gardens, is well preserved. It also contains the most beautiful religious building of the last few years in Pamplona: the parish church of Santiago, with its bold concrete structure designed by Javier Guibert and Fernando Redón.

The two University campuses have developed quite close to each other. They cover a similar surface area but are designed to very different concepts. The private Universidad de Navarra has grown gradually on either side of the banks of the river Sadar and has a wide range of buildings designed by different architects. The Universidad Pública, on the other hand, was designed in one project and was built in a short time in a standardised manner. Its creator, the Navarrese architect Francisco Javier Sáez de Oiza, based his work on other European designs to make a departmental University. His starting point is a horizontal platform leading to a promenade linking the Vice-Chancellor's offices with the Library, with the different departments lining the promenade. The teaching and workshop buildings aim to represent the dual agricultural and industrial tradition of Navarre, joined by Culture as symbolised in the Library. It is very much a 'dry' style of architecture based on concrete and glass.

Pamplona is well-known for the quality of its Health Care services. There has been a public hospital for over a century on the present site of the old meadow of Irunlarrea. The surrounding walls have gone, and the pavilion-type structure of the hospitals enables visitors to walk and meet in pleasant gardens, taking some of the stress out of hospital visits and getting away from the characteristic smells of the long corridors of the clinics.

The ancient Hospital de la Misericordia, founded in the 16th century in the Old Part, now houses the Museo de Navarra in a building which was completely refurbished in 1986. Its collections are chronologically ordered from top to bottom, the lower floors containing archaeological materials. The most famous items in the museum are a Spanish-Arab small chest from the XIth century, a small ivory filigree, a major collection of Gothic murals and a superb portrait of the Marquis of San Adrian by Goya, a blend of naturalness and style. The top floor of the museum is a gallery of paintings and sculptures by contemporary artists from Navarre.

PARKS AND TREES

Pamplona is a green city, with four million square metres of parks and gardens and around 80,000 trees. These figures do not include new projects for ten-mile-long riverside parks along the Arga and Sadar rivers. There is a great variety of trees and vegetation, with some trees receiving special attention. For example, the annual pruning of each of the imposing white poplars in the Vuelta del Castillo takes four or five days. A pleasant stroll through the streets, avenues, squares and parks will allow the visitor to discover the city as a surprising botanical garden. The wide range of vegetation and the proximity of agricultural land around the city account for its rich birdlife (75 different species have been identified). They are visible by day and audible by night by their calls. On a winter's night you may be surprised to see the arrival of a flock of migrating wild ducks, which stop to rest in the heart of the city in the trees of the Plaza del Castillo.

There are many parks in Pamplona, but only two gardens: Taconera and Media Luna. They are formally designed gardens with ponds, roof gardens, climbing roses and flower-beds full of daffodils, tulips and delicate pansies and violets.

La Taconera is now a brighter, more floral place since the slow death of its old elms. It had lines of trees in the XVIIIth century

The Third Ensanche (urban expansion area) grew westwards in the form of the suburbs of Iturrama and San Juan, separated by Avenida Pio XII. The hill ranges of Alaiz and Errenegia, in the distance, mark the southern outer limits of the Pamplona basin.

but is basically a romantic garden with benches and little paths, tunnels of cypresses and labyrinths of yew trees. From the stones of the old gate of San Nicolás the observer's eye moves to the monument to Gayarre, described by Pedro Manterola as "a giant cream and meringue wedding cake on which the tenor stands", waiting to sing in 'The Pearl Fishers'. To the right of the statue there are discreet reminders of the Humanist Huarte de San Juan, a Renaissance predecessor of what is nowadays called 'careers guidance', and of the composer and music teacher Hilarión Eslava. To the left, there is a small zoo in the moat with deer and ducks, among other animals.

As pleasant (or perhaps more so) than the Taconera is the nearby *Bosquecillo* with its Indian chestnut trees where the leaves of the 'tree of St. Joseph' usher in the ever earlier arrival of Spring. Older people still remember some of the features of the Bosquecillo which have long since disappeared: a pond where swans and ducks used to swim, a dovecote, and the 'tree of the cuckoo' which the young Pío Baroja used to climb and dream in. They say that the aldermen handed over the keys of the surrendered city to the Duke of Alba at the foot of this tree. A hotel built in the 1960s broke the harmony of the place, which must have been admirable in previous centuries. The area now occupied by the statue to the writer Navarro Villoslada was also a pleasant open space. It used to be the fountain of San Antón, which flowed freely among bushy trees along a hollow reached by a zigzagging path.

The Media Luna garden joins up with the Fort of San Bartolomé, and offers a winding stroll along a small cliff overlooking the river Arga, with beautiful views to the east. In the distance, you can see the violet-white and rounded Mount Txurregi, the pyramid of Gaztelu and the opening of Oskía. To the left stand the sandstone walls of the Cathedral. Below lie the market gardens of the Magdalena, the stepping stones over the river, the ruins of the mill of Caparroso and the mediaeval bridge of the pilgrims. There is a roller-skating rink between plane trees and catalpas, a rose garden and a bar with a very popular terrace in summer. The four Rivers of Paradise are represented in the pond. Carp swim lazily and cut a red swathe through the still green water, which is only disturbed by the trickle of a fountain. A monument of classic columns houses a bronze statue to Sarasate, the famous violinist from Pamplona who was idolised by the music-lovers of the major European theatres.

SARASATE

Pablo Sarasate Navascués, born in Pamplona on 10th March 1844, is the best-known musician from Navarre. His scores are still interpreted by great virtuosi of the violin all over the world.

Sarasate, a Romantic author and great virtuoso of the French school (Saint-Saens, Lalo and Bruch composed works for him), was praised by Tchaikovsky, who, after meeting him, assured everyone that he was "a violinist in fashion, pleasant, elegant, and cultured."

The journalist Fernando Pérez Ollo has studied the biography and musical career of Sarasate in detail, and also the artist's relation to his native city.

The critics applauded his talent but condemned the thinness of his programmes. Sarasate's sound was clear and sharp, of exceptional tone and colour. His repertoire, however, did not seek great musical works, rather the chance for his performances to shine.

The pianist and composer Joaquín Larregla reminisced, forty years after Sarasate's death, that "Whoever heard him just once would later recognise, among all the violinists, the wide, fine and delightful tone of Sarasate. The bow he used seemed to have no end. The harmonious sounds were crystal clear, and the sound of those left-hand *pizzicatos* was really surprising. The notes were mathematically precise, whether played on one string or two. You almost wondered if you were hearing two violins."

The Czech musicologist Edouard Hanslick, Sarasate's fiercest critic, reproached him for the futility of his repertoire and even for his dubious musical taste, saying that he "confused grandeur with pomposity and delicacy with over-nicety."

Sarasate included one of his own pieces in all his performances. His repertoire of 54 compositions, which include sober and correct piano accompaniments and orchestrations, is designed so that the star can shine. Some of his encores still bring people to their feet today. Opus 20, (Bohemian Airs) is the most popular, and his Complete Works have been recorded on CD.

Sarasate lived in Pamplona for a very short time but loved his home city, and performed special concerts every year during *Sanfermines*. He never charged for them, brought scores to be premiered and worked with good musicians and conductors. Local public opinion on him was divided between enthusiasm and disdain. Pamplona City Council named him Honorary Citizen and named a promenade (Paseo de Sarasate) after him while he was still alive.

He died of emphysema in his home 'Villa Navarra' in Biarritz on September 20th 1908 and his body lies in a tomb in the cemetery of Pamplona. Both the Conservatory and the Orchestra of Pamplona bear his name.

Sarasate had two Stradivarius violins, which are kept in the Conservatory of Paris and the Teatro Real in Madrid. He bequeathed a 'Vuillaume' violin to Pamplona, together with a 'Gaud & Bernardel', a 'Bechstein' piano, musical scores, portraits and some personal belongings. There is a small Pablo Sarasate Museum in the neo-Gothic chapel of the Old Seminary of San Juan, inside the Municipal Archives (visits on weekday mornings).

SANFERMINES, THE FESTIVITY EXPLODES

Pamplona, siete de julio.
Cantan los mozos y
mozas.
Los de la Montaña en vasco,
los de la Ribera en jotas.

Iruñeko ferietan,
iragan Sanferminetan,
merkatu eder bat zautan
zaudelarik bi lerrotan.

The first stretch of the Encierro (Bull Run) in Santo Domingo. It is an initiation rite, proof of bravery and lack of moderation. The Bull Run holds its dangers, but they are relative. Thirteen people have died in the streets of Pamplona in the Encierro over the last century.

[Pamplona, seventh of July, sing the young men and women. Those of the north in Basque, those of the south sing *jotas*].

These folk verses show that Pamplona is also the heart of all Navarre when it comes to the *Fiestas de San Fermín*, a time when the whole of the region turns its eyes towards the city.

It could be said that the year ends, or starts, in Pamplona on the seventh day of the seventh month, a magical, ritual date which is announced by the optimistic song: "uno de enero, dos de febrero, tres de marzo, cuatro de abril…" (1st of January, 2nd of February, 3rd March, 4th April …) until the festivities literally explode on the day before July 7th. That is how Earnest Hemingway described it in his novel 'Fiesta (The Sun Also Rises)', where he described the atmosphere of the *Sanfermines*: "At noon of Sunday, 6th of July, the fiesta exploded. There is no other way to describe it."

It is true. Explosion… Rupture… The Baroque front of the City Hall is like an altar-piece which serves as a background. A rocket streaks through the air over a cloud of red neckerchiefs, the champagne flows, music sounds and this serious, hard-working and slightly austere city changes colour and mood. People forget about the rules of daily life, leave their watches at home, dress up in red and white clothes and let their hair down for eight days, during which time the only things that matter are the people themselves and having a good time. Anyone can enjoy themselves and there are a lot of programmed events, although it is really a case of everyone 'doing their own thing', if possible in a *peña* (a kind of social club). Everyone should join in, but there are many things to enjoy just by watching and listening. Since their origin the *Sanfermines* has been both a religious holiday and a market fair in honour of a Bishop Saint, one whose historical existence has not been proven but who has given rise to a long tradition of worship dating back to the Middle Ages. San Fermín is a dark-skinned saint who turns the red pluvial of his martyrdom into a bullfighter's cape every morning of the fiesta 'to be ready' and protect those who run in front of the bulls.

A San Fermín pedimos,
por ser nuestro patrón,
nos guíe en el encierro
dándonos su bendición.

[We ask San Fermín, as he is our Patron Saint, to guide us in the *Encierro* (the Bull Run) and give us his blessing].

The runners sing this verse three times when there are just a few minutes to go before eight o'clock in the morning, which is six o'clock solar time. A brief, intense spectacle is about to begin, one which does not usually last more than three minutes. People are on edge, with cold eyes but a lump in the throat. A rocket shoots skywards and the gate to the corral is opened. When all the bulls are out another rocket goes off and the entire city holds its breath in respectful silence. The six fighting bulls and the six *mansos* (castrated bulls) instinctively run together, but runners fall over and the animals inevitably end up thrusting their horns at the 'moving targets' in front of them. The runs are fraught with danger when one bull goes too far ahead or gets left behind, and extremely dangerous if a bull turns round and runs against the flow. It's a question of knowing how to run, just a short stretch and then get out of the way. The Run is 825 metres long and has slopes, corners,

wider stretches and also bottle-necks. It finishes with the spectacular sight of the runners fanning out into the bullring after entering the tunnel at the entrance. The third rocket is fired when all the bulls have reached the corral. In the bullring the 'dobladores' save lives, guiding the bulls into the corral by dragging their capes along the ground. The fourth rocket is heard. The bulls are safely in.

The Running of the Bulls is a ritual, a trial of courage and excess. It is an ancient custom which has been lost in other cities, but Pamplona has special permission to maintain it through Article 46 of the Bullfighting Rules and Regulations. Many people have wondered why others run in front of the bulls. "At the heart of it, it's a gratuitous game," is the opinion of the writer Miguel Sánchez-Ostiz. "The Running of the Bulls is the most faithful reflection of the uselessness of the fiesta. You run for the pure sake of it, to see how far you can go, to feel fear at close quarters, to play puss-in-the-corner with death," wrote the journalist José Antonio Iturri. The ethnographer Julio Caro Baroja highlights the attraction in getting away from the monotony of daily life and remarks that "Hemingway was a skilful messenger of a tendency to look for something in life that society has forbidden in many respects. The violent festivities of the ancient societies are rediscovered in this way."

There is some risk in the Running of the Bulls, but it is a relative one. It lies more in the narrow streets crowded with runners than the danger posed by the bulls themselves. Since the 1930s no more than two hundred runners have been gored, and over the last century thirteen people have died in the Running of the Bulls in Pamplona.

In the eight bullfights of the 'Feria del Toro' the *trapío* (power) and corpulence of the bulls are virtues which are jealously preserved. The bullfighters are contracted depending on how well they perform in Seville (April) and Madrid (May). City councillors in top hats and tails (or special evening dress for the ladies) preside the spectacle, which is preceded by a horseback procession of *caballeros en plaza* (riders) dressed in the style of the Mediaeval burghers, with the jingling of bells on adorned *mulillas* (small mules) and the sound of the 'Pamplonesa' (the Municipal Band of the city) which draws and drags the crowd along to the rhythm of its lively *pasodobles*. The

The peñas (social clubs) with their deafening percussion and metal instrument bands. Good humour and fun are guaranteed.

peñas then raise the roof with their noisy percussion and brass bands. Whether the bullfight is up to standard or not, a good time is to be had by all.

The mornings belong to the children, and indeed to anyone young at heart. The *gigantes* (giants), *cabezudos*, *kilikis* and *zaldikos* (different types of processional dwarves) are full of Baroque elegance and fantasy; they dance and play through the streets accompanied by *gaiteros* (pipers), *txistularis* (Basque flute players), folk dancers and a masquerade.

The Fiesta mostly takes place outdoors and runs non-stop for 200 hours from the *chupinazo* (inaugural rocket) at 12 noon on July 6th until the *Pobre de mí* (literally, 'Poor me', a lament to end the fiesta) at midnight on the 14th. The bands are out on the streets from early morning and there are night-time firework displays. It is an exquisite ritual and a very anarchistic way of enjoying oneself. There are concerts by the most popular artists together with noisy drum-banging sessions (the *Estruendo*). Top-class acts and popular sports take place simultaneously. Alcohol is consumed in enormous quantities and its effects are basically neutralised by dancing and jumping around the place. People get together for street lunches and then sleep off their effects in the parks. Age is no obstacle to enjoyment, there really is something for everyone. As the writer Patxi Larrainzar put it, "This is the people's party, and the people are in charge."

The four routes that lead to Santiago de Compostela converge in Puente la Reina, leaving it as a single path", wrote the pilgrim Aymeric Picaud in the mid-XIIth century. The most beautiful Romanesque bridge along the whole route to Santiago de Compostela gave its name to a town built "in a good, spacious place." The Franks designed the layout of the town, which has been admirably preserved. The whole of the main street is a continuous monument.

PUENTE LA REINA

Crossroads on the Pilgrim's Way to Santiago

The swallows sang
To the banks of the Arga
And their trills repeated:
What a beautiful land
Is my Navarra!

Halfway along its course, and after having made its way through a narrow pass where holm oaks grow, and cut out its meanders between the loam and sandstone, the Arga reaches the plain. A torrential course called the Robo joins it from Valdizarbe on the left bringing angry waters and fertile mud with it. They converge, and the first stretch of land irrigated by the river is formed on the Campollano terrace which yields generous crops of peppers and is renowned for its fine beans.

The light and the atmosphere are Mediterranean. There are black poplars, narrow-leafed ash trees, white willows and a few elms along the banks of the river. Poplar groves have been replanted among a tangle of bushes and brambles. Coots and mallards find refuge in the rushes, bulrushes and reeds. Storks fly overhead, their nests close by in the towers of an abandoned factory chimney and a co-operative granary. There are vines, clusters of almond trees and evergreen olive trees on the distant slopes.

Towards the end of the Middle Ages, Carlos III de Evreux, a monarch with exquisite taste, noticed the beauty and grace of this spot situated in the centre of his kingdom. He gave it, complete with all its revenues, to Doña Leonor ('his beloved companion') as a gift. He made improvements to the palace near the river, which his father frequented during the grape harvest, and also to the beautiful gardens of *La Grana* where he could hear the water flow and see the squirrels jump among the almond trees. He ordered a boat to be built in which he went fishing for eels and barbels. He also took great care to establish olive plantations in order that they would grow into 'trees', forbidding any livestock to enter the parts of the estate where he had planted olive stock, as well as anyone to "pick, cut or touch the branches for Palm Sunday or at any other time."

Although the vineyards have been renewed, cereals now dominate the land used for dry farming and irrigated farming, together with the market gardens, and they now only occupy a tenth of the farmland. The river is now much cleaner due to the fact that the industrialised Pamplona area now treats its waste, but at low water the river is still too warm, slow-moving and contains an excess of organic matter.

It is here that the Arga embarks on its lower stretch and widens out. It is no coincidence that a fine, solid, emblematic bridge was built on this plain and crossroads on the Pilgrim's route — 'la linda puente' (pretty bridge) referred to by Calixtine's Code.

[PREVIOUS PAGE] *The pilgrimage routes that cross the Pyrenees at Somport and Roncesvalles come together near Puente la Reina. The town takes its name from the bridge over the river.*

In the XIth century when King Sancho el Mayor repaired the roads in the south and made them safe, the pilgrims preferred them to the old route along the Roman Road through Arakil and Alava. The two great Pilgrim's Routes to Santiago that cross the Pyrenees through Roncesvalles and Somport converge next to Puente la Reina, the town that gets its name from the bridge that crosses the river.

The oldest mention of *Ponte Arga* dates back to the year 1085 and by 1090 both the bridge and the town were connected with a 'Regina'. In the XVIIth century, the official chronicler of Navarre, José de Moret, recorded a conjecture in his annals with no documentary foundation to back it up stating that it was the Queen and wife of Sancho el Mayor or his daughter-in-law Estefanía who had ordered the bridge to be built. Moret's opinion has since been repeated as if it were fact. In 1993, having studied the historical names of the Arga, the historian Jimeno Jurío suggested that the toponym 'Puente la Reina' was not derived from *Regina*, but from *Runa*, which is the old name for the river that also flows through Pamplona. In his opinion, the intervention of a Queen in the construction of the bridge is merely a legend.

For Santiago Sainz de los Terreros, who has catalogued the more than 500 bridges in Navarre from all eras, this Romanesque construction, built with square-cut stones and ashlar, in the mid-XIth century, is "the finest example of the mediæval bridges." Aesthetically, the magnificence of its arches opposes its size. It is 110 metres long and 4 metres wide. It rises in the middle and slopes down steeply to each side. It is made up of six arches of varying size, the largest measuring 20 metres and the smallest only 6 metres. Smaller arches open out on top of the piers, lightening the aspect of the structure and allowing the river to flow freely when the water rises. The current, broken by a cutwater both upstream and downstream, rounds off, duplicates and reflects the profile of the monument like a mirror.

The abutments of the bridge were once defended by fortified towers, and in the centre there was a small turret that housed the stone figure of the Virgin, *La Virgen del Puy*. There is an XIXth century legend associated with this statue involving a rare bird, the *txori*, which appeared from time to time and displayed its devotion to the Virgin Mary by collecting water in its beak with which to wash her face, and by flapping its wings to remove all the dust and cobwebs. The *Virgen del Txori* may still be visited today in the neighbouring church of San Pedro.

The historians Martín Duque and Goñi Gaztambide state that in the year 1049 a town existed on the plain on the left bank of the river Arga. The town, situated at a safe distance from the catchment area of any flooding, was called *Murugarren* and was inhabited by the indigenous people of the area.

The Franks, who arrived at the end of the XIth century, repeated the practice they had used in other areas. They settled alongside the Pilgrim's Way near the original population centre but at a short

distance away, as if to point out other, more deep-seated divisions: language, lifestyle, economy and organisational systems. By the year 1085, the *Villa Nova* (new town) inhabited by Frankish people had grown up between the *Villa Vieja* (old town) of *Murugarren* and the river.

It was King Alfonso el Batallador who put the place on the map in 1122 with his letter of donation granting it the *Fuero de Estella* charter: "Through the desire I have that all the peoples come to settle there and that it becomes a large and spacious town, I give and concede to you a good, extensive and spacious place, that is, from that bridge already named to the meadow of Obanos that is above *Murugarren*, in order that you may build your houses the best you can. And more, I grant to you the land so that you may work it where best you can and in all directions as far as it is possible to journey there and back in one day. In the same way I grant that you may graze your livestock and cut wood."

The town was divided into five neighbourhoods and there was also a Jewish quarter, the layout of which still exists today. The Navarrese people of *Murugarren* took a long time to move into the area of San Pedro in the new area of the town.

A well-defined town plan with a regular layout similar to that of a small fort was designed. It can still be seen with astonishing clarity in modern aerial photographs.

It forms a rectangle measuring 453 metres by 182 metres enclosed by a fortified wall with towers along it, many of which

The most beautiful mediaeval bridge in Navarre has six semicircular arches with an elevated roadway in the centre.

are still standing, and with four gates. The main street, which forms part of the Pilgrim's Way to Santiago, leads to the bridge and there are two smaller streets running parallel to it as well as several crossing it.

The church of Santiago is situated in the centre, and what is now the atrium was the site of a small daily market in mediaeval times. The large square, which was also designed for bull fights, was opened in the XVIIth century, and one hundred years later la *Casa de los Cubiertos* was built to house the town hall and the market in its gallery. At the end of the XVIIIth century, sanitary conditions were improved: the paving was renewed, and sewers and rainwater drains were put in. At the beginning of the XIXth century, the *Paseo de los Fueros* with its gardens and copse was constructed to the south, running parallel with the main road.

The mediæval houses were terraced, built from stone, with only one storey. From the XVIIth century on, one or two more floors were added in brick. They had narrow façades and stretched back a long way with enough room for a kitchen garden or a corral inside. Sometimes, adjoining houses were demolished and a new one built on two gothic plots, but without changing the mediæval layout. From the XIVth to the XVIIIth century, the population of

Moorish masons worked on the façade of the church of Santiago.

Puente la Reina multiplied by five without spilling beyond the surrounding walls. Outside the wall lay a suburb, around the church of *El Crucifijo*.

The people of Puente la Reina have maintained the institution of the *hauzolan,* or communal work, for works of public interest. In recent years, collective effort has permitted resurfacing work in the square, *La Plaza de Mena,* and the construction of the Municipal Sports Centre. The *puentesinos (*the people of Puente la Reina) are very proud of the work carried out and see it as their own.

The journey of a pilgrim

After the two main routes that lead from the Pyrenees have converged into one, the pilgrim enters Puente la Reina and sees that the road passes under a cross vault that forms a common portico between two buildings. Both buildings bring the Knights Templars to mind. The one on the left is a convent with a severe façade built at the end of the XVIIIth century on the same site as a famous XIIth-century hospital. On the right there is a church with two naves, one Romanesque that was the old church dedicated to *Santa María de las Huertas,* and the other is Gothic, built to house the large crucifix of pathetic beauty with its tortured body hanging from the wooden cross to form a 'Y'.

The walled area of the city is reached along *Calle del Crucifijo.* Two large fortified towers mark the entrance to the *Calle Mayor,* the '*Rua de los rumeus'*, which is Puente la Reina's main marvel. It attests the wisdom of those who planned it and has built up a lasting yet ever-changing cultural inheritance over the centuries. In winter it is sheltered and in the summer it is cool. The passer-by can admire the architecture, the superb palaces, cobbled vestibules, craft shops, solid carpentry, railings and ironwork. It all blends well together, and eyes that are accustomed to observing are turned time after time,

fascinated by the sheer scale of the sights and the meticulous detail. There is no hurry. The inhabitants don't know what a rush is. The setting invites prolonged conversation during the break from work in the bars, *tabernas* (taverns) and *bodegas* (wine cellars). During the town's annual festival in July, the street is the scene of processions, choirs singing the *Aurora* (at dawn), noisy street dances and the running of the bulls to the bull-ring where there is also a ritual salute with flags and the traditional Basque dancers, the *dantzaris.* During the annual fair, which transformed Puente la Reina into a tax-free market once a year from 1498 on, races on *layas,* (a long-forgotten farm implement) are held, and *pochas* (local white beans) and *gorrín* (suckling pig) are consumed with great enthusiasm.

The quality and yellow tone of the church of Santiago's solid Renaissance square-cut stones makes them stand out against the original church's damaged grey Romanesque features that still remain, above all the monumental facade. The first archivolt forms an 'engrailed' foiled arch like those in two other churches along the Pilgrim's Route, San Román in Cirauqui and San Pedro in Estella, where Moorish stonemasons worked. In the second half of the XVIIIth century, during the period of transition from late Baroque style to Neo-classicism, Santos Ochandátegui took on the task of realising two beautiful designs by the great architect, Ventura Rodríguez,: the atrium, with its fine railings, and the octagonal lantern bell tower.

The spacious parish church contains a Baroque altarpiece and two extraordinary Gothic sculptures of St. Bartholomew and Saint James (*Santiago*) facing each other on opposite walls. They are called *beltza* because of their brown colour. The Dominican order introduced the Virgin Mary of the Snows, *La Virgen de las Nieves* ('*la Soterraña')* relatively late. This Virgin is capable of bringing snow in August or of storing hailstones, and the peasant population sought her protection and placed the wine harvest in her custody:

> Rare miracle and feat!
> Flashes of lightning and thunder
> Leave us later serene
> Uttering the name of La Soterraña.

Almost opposite the parish church is the Baroque façade of *Los Trinitarios (*home of the Trinitarian religious order), which was a hospital and convent in the XIIIth century. At the western end of the city walls, the late-Medieval church of San Pedro preserves a restored organ which is not used but is a jewel among Navarre's Baroque instruments.

The Pilgrim bids farewell to the town in the neighbourhood of *Zubiurrutia* which, as its Basque name suggests, is situated away from the centre of the town and beyond the bridge. Zubiurrutia grew up relatively early, immediately after the bridge had been built, and there are records of it dating back to 1089. Until it was incorporated into the town in 1416 when it was left with no population, it had its own church, council and district, and did not belong to the *Merindad de las Montañas* (Navarre was divided into areas called Merindades, similar to counties) as did Puente la Reina, but to Estella. So close yet so far away, a community of hospitaller nuns of the order of the *Sancti Spiritus* continue to lead their secluded life in Zubiurrutia.

The buildings represent a fine example of Baroque conventual style and contain five Rococo altarpieces.

All the streets in Puente la Reina are both monument and thoroughfare, in the town that Basque speakers call *Gares*, with the accent on the second syllable. Since when? It is not easy to say because the common people of the town, untutored and illiterate, left no written records of the language they spoke. It is splendid however, for a town along the Pilgrim's Way, that a road in the district of Pamplona, *Gares bidea*, mentioned in a notarial record of 1596, should be the key to knowing that this name is not a recent invention. *Gares* belongs to the surrounding area of Valdizarbe, which formed the linguistic frontier at the beginning of the XIXth century. A century and a half earlier in Uterga, another village in the valley, the Abbot Juan de Beriain wrote a treatise and a catechism in Basque "because there has never been a nation in the whole world that does not feel proud of its mother tongue and of teaching it to be written and read in the schools. So, this is the reason we hold our Basque language in esteem."

The composer from Puente La Reina Luis Morondo, who was the first director of the chamber music choir *'Agrupación Coral de Cámara de Pamplona'*, signed his compositions *Garestar Koldo*. He also composed the musical score for the theatrical work 'Misterio de Obanos' set at the crossroads of the routes to Santiago. Morondo spread a cultural message throughout Europe and America with his choir of proverbial perfection for more than thirty years, daring to perform the avant-garde numbers of the time. A century later, when "all the musicians in Madrid were Navarrese", as stated by Pérez Galdós, another son of Puente la Reina called Emilio Arrieta triumphed. He was a teacher and prolific composer of *zarzuelas* (Spanish operettas with a spoken dialogue and usually a comic theme). One of these works became the opera 'Marina', which immortalising him. To mark the centenary of Arrieta's death in 1994, a choir from Valdizarbe revived the *seguidillas* (the music to a Spanish dance in triple time) and the 'Brindis de 'Marina' (toast to Marina) in the square next to the house where he was born in 1823.

Another son of Puente la Reina was Friar José de Baquedano, whom the musicologist López Calo referred to as "the best epresentative of Spanish Baroque music." He composed a 'Sonata a tres',

The ring of arches around the church at Eunate. A covered cloister used to be supported on these arches, now uncovered.

which is the only known example of its type from the XVIIth century. As in instrumental music, Baquedano was a forerunner of *bel canto* in his religious vocal pieces.

EUNATE AND ITS ENIGMAS

"One must arrive in Eunate at either dawn or dusk when the air and the light are at their most subtle. And alone if possible, because Santa María de Eunate is also alone, isolated in the atmosphere of the clear sharp valley, only just hearing the faint sound of the river Robo. She is protected by the solid transparency of her open cloister. Like a clinging veil of stone and light, it both adorns and defends her." We owe this piece of advice and twilight observation to Juan Ramón Corpas, an expert on stones, esotericism and the traditions of the Pilgrim's Route to Santiago.

Four kilometres from Puente la Reina, in the very centre of Navarre, this octagonal Romanesque church was built at the end of

the XIIth century by noblemen from Valdizarbe who had made the pilgrimage to Jerusalem and wanted to construct a unique building. The church has been object of many unfounded interpretations repeated by both dilettantes and strong meticulous treatise writers alike. The historians Lacarra and Jimeno Jurío and the architect-restorer Yárnoz Larrosa have freed this building, which is both beautiful and impressive on its own merits, from its cloak of false suppositions.

The geographer Julio Aldadill put forward the theory of breaking down the name to Eun-ate, translating it as "a hundred doors." Although there are only 33 counted, this could represent a fine literary image. However, Eunate is a modern euphonic word that does not date back any earlier than the XIXth century. The original name, *Onat*, has nothing at all to do with any number, but it would appear that it does have something to do with 'door'. It would be 'the pass that is underfoot', the gateway to a path that leads up to Las Nequeas. The arches, which nowadays are open, once formed part of and supported a covered cloister that ran parallel to the wall.

Prestigious art historians have repeated that this was a church of the Knights Templars. It was also a funerary building used as a tomb for pilgrims. In place of the bell gable there was a lantern bell tower where a fire was lit as if it were a lighthouse, signalling to distant pilgrims.

Nothing has ever been found in any records to relate Eunate with the Order of the Knights Templar, nor were any remains of the lantern tower found during the restoration work.

However, there are graves among the columns of the cloister. There is also a single tomb at the entrance containing the remains of one person, perhaps the founder, together with a Pilgrim's shell.

Eunate has always been more of a meeting place for the living than a resting place for the dead. The representatives from the six *cendeas* of Valdizarbe (in Navarre a *cendea* is a group of several village councils that make up a district council) as well as clergy from all the town councils, always including Puente la Reina, held occasional meetings here. There is a popular pilgrimage to Eunate to ask for prosperity, sufficient rain and the end of crop diseases.

La Cofradía de Nobles de Santa María (a brotherhood), to which only the most distinguished people of the area belonged, owns the building. Here the brothers found a place for their meetings and for their tombs.

Eunate is a place of Christian worship, a centre of devotion, a very popular church for weddings, and a place of silent contemplation for art lovers.

Oriented or perhaps confused by certain biased guides, some who seek esotericism come to get telluric (earthy) energy under the vault of stars, and even to carry out complex rituals in extravagent dress.

In the equinoctial late afternoon and with autumn yellowing the poplar leaves, the pilgrim can make out the unmistakable silhouette of Eunate, Navarre's emblem of the Pilgrimage to Santiago de Compostela, at the height of its beauty.

The singular, octagonal-shaped church of Eunate, at the geographical centre of Navarre.

E stella, la bella" (Estella the beautiful), says a XVth-century adage, a reflection of the picturesque setting and abundance of monuments in the town. It marks the end of a stage of the Pilgrim's Way to Compostela, which made a slight diversion to include it as it was a 'healthy place', strategic from the point of view of defence and its market, and a pleasant and hospitable city where the mediaeval pilgrim found "good bread, excellent wine and plentiful meat and fish." Prior to the foundation of Estella a Frankish borough and Jewish quarter known as *Lizarra* stood on this spot. It was a hamlet populated by Navarrese that became a neighbourhood of the town council. Head of a *Merindad* (similar to a county), State and Court of Carlist Pretenders, a statutory reference for political autonomy, a treasure trove of traditional music and dance, an active marketplace for industry and services, Estella is hardly large enough to hold all it contains.

ESTELLA
Monument and Market

All beautiful cities have their medieval *laudes*, and those of Estella were written in the XIIth century by a Chaplain from Poitou and an Abbot from Cluny. In them they praise the food, the river, the castle, the setting, the fertility of the land and the dense population, in that order. "It is not in vain that it is called Estella", concludes Pedro el Venerable in his elegy. He refers to a *Stella* (star), a crossroads that will embellish heraldry and legends.

The glittering city illuminates its literary fire which is transformed into the 'Sonata de Invierno' (a winter sonnet) by Valle Inclán, and which an *Estellés* by adoption, Angel de Miguel, invents as a fantasy of carbuncles and unicorns and the origin of the ash tree when the first couple, created from this wood by the god Odín, discovered the Tree of the World on the left bank of an unknown river, "and the people who at that time had begun to colonise the hillside sometimes called it *Fraxinus*, and, with obstinate insistence when they used the coarse language of the mountains from whence they came, *Lizarra*."

Lizarrara or *Lizarra*, the home of Basque-speaking *navarros*, was a small settlement which already existed in Roman times, situated in the neighbourhood that preserves its name. In the Middle Ages, a *castro* (Ibero-Roman fortified settlement) was built there which remained in use in the middle of the XIIth century. It was as strategic in the fight against Islam as the Deio castle that was situated opposite on the conical peak of Monjardín, and which gave its name to the whole area, *Deierri*, the centre of which is known as 'Tierra Estella', the land of Estella.

As early as 1174 there is mention of the church of Santa María del Puy: 'Above Lizarra'. The devotees of the Virgin Mary, people of Auvergne from the *Puy-en-Velay* region of the Upper Loire Valley must have established it here. They brought with them their tanning trade and a plant rich in tannin called 'zumaque' *(Rhus coriaria L.),* which characterises the landscape of the area around Estella.

The Franks, free men who had mainly come from Auvergne, Limousin and the Midi during the latter quarter of the XIth century, created the Borough of San Martín under the crag of Peña de los Castillos on the right bank of the river Ega. King Sancho Ramírez granted it *Fueros* (code of laws, or charter) in 1090 and decided to make a diversion and go there following the course of the river and the Jacobean Route (Pilgrims Way to Compostela), which at that time crossed the river further downstream to the south-east beside the Benedictine Monastery of Zarapuz. The name 'Estella' was given to this Frankish borough founded on the territory of *Lizarra*. The linguist González Ollé believes that the Occitan-speaking immigrants who did not know Basque soon changed the pronunciation of the toponym, and the 'ash tree' that gave it its name became *L'izarra* with an article, a 'star' written *Estela* in Occitan

[PREVIOUS PAGE] *The Church of San Pedro de la Rúa. The demolition of the Castle at Estella in 1572 ruined two spaces in its beautiful cloister.*
[OPPOSITE] *The Romanesque portico of the Church of San Miguel has a great richness of icons, carved by three different people.*

The new districts that grew up on both sides of the Borough were not sufficient. The city expanded during the second half of the XIIth century onto the other side of the San Martín bridge. In 1164 the market was moved and the neighbourhood of San Miguel developed. In 1187, on the decision of Sancho 'el Sabio' (the Wise), the new nucleus of San Juan was born on the land at El Parral and it became the home of both Franks and Navarrese.

The city was completed with the 'El Arenal' neighbourhood to the east of San Miguel, and the Jewish quarter, Elgacena, which had its first synagogue on the land which is now the site of the Romanesque church of Santa María Jus del Castillo. Elgacena, which was established around 1081, was the earliest re-population of Jews in Navarre, and ranked third in terms of inhabitants. When it was at its most prosperous it accounted for more than ten per cent of the population of Estella. The flourishing community of powerful merchants and moneylenders provided a source of suspicion and distrust that was stirred up by the extremist Franciscan, Pedro de Ollogoyen. The houses were sacked and burned down on the night of 5th March 1328 and several Jews died. The revolt was soon quelled, but not with equal justice. Juan Carrasco tells that "the assailants were ordered to return what they had stolen and pay numerous fines, whilst the murderers and those who had induced them were sheltered by a conspiracy of silence." The Jew, Menahem ben Zerach, the famed commentator of the Talmud, managed to escape the massacre.

TIMES OF WAR: CASTLES AND CITY WALLS

There is a detailed reconstruction of the complex fortification of medieval Estella on display in the Municipal Tourist Office. Some stretches of the XIIth and XIIIth-century city walls still remain, as does the Portal de Castilla with its ancient representation of the city's shield on its pediment, the eight-pointed star. The three principal neighbourhoods were separated by ditches and each one was surrounded by its own wall, which stretched from the highest point right down to the river bank.

The solid defence system of castles is impressive. The largest castle was reinforced by three separate bastions, Zalatambor, La Atalaya y Belmecher, which were built in the XIIIth century to protect the different flanks separately. In 1512, the year of the conquest of Navarre, the Agramonteses (a political faction) held out in the fortress until the last day of October, three months after Pamplona had surrendered. The castle lost its strategic value and King Felipe II ordered it to be demolished in 1572. The demolition also damaged the roof of the Parish Church of San Pedro de la Rúa and destroyed two sides of the beautiful Romanesque cloister. The low tower of this church and the corridors that are visible over the naves in the church of San Miguel are evidence of how these religious buildings also contributed to Estella's defence.

The city, which had seen out the end of the Middle Ages with the tortuous memory of civil war and local factious confrontations, was to live through more prosperous times during the Renaissance and Baroque eras. The economy of the nearby valleys was not as strong as that of others in the north of Navarre, but the

The façade of the Holy Sepulchre is the best example of Gothic architecture in Estella, and marks a milestone in the evolution of this style in Navarre.

traces of these centuries are considerable. The city remained within its old walls, but its squares were extended and replanned. Its two main streets, Calle de la Rúa and Calle Mayor are lined with palaces and numerous large XVIIIth-century houses. To the south, outside the city walls, lies 'Los Llanos', a pleasant walk through fields on the banks of the river Ega, where in the XVIth century there were workers who took care of the planting and maintenance of the poplars, walnut trees, elms and willows. When the old regime fell the wool industry went into decline, but 82 master *pelaires* (people who prepared the wool for the looms) still survived with fifty mills producing cloth in the city. At the end of the XVIIIth century, Estella had less than five thousand inhabitants, but the ecclesiastical population remained high: six parishes with forty secular clergymen, four monasteries with forty-eight friars, and three convents for nuns. Half a century later the city became a Carlist bastion.

THE COURT AND THE CARLIST PHASE

The motto of Carlism, the movement that defended the old regime, was 'Dios, Patria, Rey y Fueros', (God, Homeland, King and Historical Rights) was made up of 'Integristas' who were the advocates of the preservation of national traditions, and 'Ultramontanes', who were in favour of supreme Papal authority, within a socialist, federal and almost anarchist tendency. Karl Marx himself was interested in this movement and said: "Carlist traditionalism was based on the authentically social and national foundations of the peasants, lesser noblemen and clergy in so far as the fact that liberalism was embodied in militarism, capitalism, the landed gentry and secular interests."

Estella and nearby Montejurra were both the tragic and privileged scenes of the two bloody nineteenth-century wars between Carlists and Liberals. Tomás de Zumalacárregui was promoted to supreme commander in the Plaza de San Francisco. The sanctuary of El Puy guards the memory of the execution of four Carlist generals, at the back of the church and without trial, who opposed Rafael Maroto's plans. The two Pretenders to the Spanish throne, Carlos María Isidro and Carlos María de los Dolores, the fifth and seventh of the dynasty according to the calculations of their supporters, took their religious and ceremonial Courts to Estella. Carlos VII made Estella the capital of a Carlist State complete with ministers and law courts, a penal code, a postal and telegraph service, a Royal Mint, a Police Force and Customs Officers.

As well as the interest they hold from a historical point of view, the Carlist wars and their setting in Estella have been the source of inspiration for some fine literature.

"For me, Carlism holds the same solemn attraction as the great cathedrals, and even in times of war I would have been content if it had been declared a national monument", wrote Ramón del Valle Inclán in his 'Sonata de Invierno' where he speaks of the Pretender: "He was a king of ancient times. Carlos de Borbón y Este was the only Prince and Sovereign who could don the ermine robe and ascend the golden throne with dignity, and carry the jewel-encrusted crown with which the Kings of the old codices are pictured."

In 1897, in his first novel 'Paz en la guerra' (Peace in War), Miguel de Unamuno calls up memories of his childhood. The intense story closes in liberal Bilbao amid the booming of the Carlist canons. The action in the centre pages takes place in Estella ('the Holy City of Carlism'), "in the thick mane of sombre Montejurra", and in the deserted village of Urbiola, where "oaths, cries of pain and pleas are to be heard" as the King's cavalry stabs the enemy wounded and those left behind in the bloody streets, whilst on the road, the inhabitants with their carts consider hunting down the liberal soldiers who run like rabbits looking for their burrows as they are chased by dogs.

The Navarrese writer, Pablo Antoñana, a Faulknerian observer of the history of his people, has written masterful stories relating the Carlist wars to the tragedy of war in general and the intolerance of our time.

A capital in the Romanesque palace. Roland defeats the giant Ferragut by wounding him in his only weak point: his navel.

is a large semi-circular splayed arch with five archivolts converging towards the tympanum where the Saviour appears surrounded by an inscription refuting the heresy of the Albigenses. Large, high-quality sculptures in relief flank the door. One represents Saint Michael spearing the infernal dragon. The archangel carries a shield bearing the coat of arms of the Kingdom of Navarre. Are they precious stones called carbuncles? Are they simply rivets? In all events, the representation is pre-1212, the date of the battle of Las Navas de Tolosa from where Sancho VII el Fuerte is said to have brought the chains that figure on the shield of Navarre.

The most outstanding monument in Estella is the Palace of the Kings of Navarre, which dates back to the last third of the XIIth century, and is a unique example of Romanesque civic architecture. The main façade has four large arches over the vestibule with four large arched windows above. Two of the capitals are remarkable for their subject matter and beauty: one represents the legendary fight between Roland and the giant Ferragut, and the other depicts a horse playing a harp.

This Romanesque palace has been converted into the 'Gustavo de Maeztu' Museum. Maeztu, who died in Estella in 1947, bequeathed a major art collection, which had been stored in his workshop, to the city that had become his home in the last years of his life. The work comprises paintings in "wild colours transformed into brilliance, into a glow that is intended to reinforce the quality of the matter." There are also lithographs and "powerful, vigorous, unbounded" drawings. Gustavo de Maeztu was also an uncommon, spontaneous, absurd and melodramatic writer of novels, essays, plays and fantasies which he illustrated himself. He was a regenerationist author, "a spiritual gypsy", as his brother Ramiro called him.

One of the façades of the Palacio de los Reyes (Palace of Kings) leads onto the Plaza de San Martín, the heart of the medieval borough. The water that falls into a pool in four jets from the Fuente de la Mona, a rare Renaissance example, sings in the centre of this beautiful urban space which is shaded by plane trees. The square opens out towards a bridge, the Puente Azucarero, a footbridge over the river which is an integral part of the city, and towards the long flight of steps that shows, under the rock, the tower and façade of the church of San Pedro. A group of XVIIth-century brick houses closes the angle of this public area. On the site once occupied by the Casa de los Francos (House of the Franks) and the Chapel of San Martín there are two buildings with ashlar façades; one has a monumental door and lancet windows, the other is a monumental Baroque construction that was once the

CITY OF MONUMENTS

Estella, a stopping point along the 'French route' to Compostela, is above all a Romanesque city with a host of monuments inspired by the Benedictine models of Cluny, but carrying the stamp of the local masons.

The construction of the church of San Pedro de la Rúa began at the end of the XIIth century with the triple apse of its sanctuary. The main façade with its foiled arch, and the cloister containing a wealth of sculpture date back to the same period. These late Romanesque examples coexist alongside Protogothic forms of Cistercian influence. The height of the tower is impressive; it is prismatic and warlike, topped with a raised brick belfry. The church contains a collection of valuable Romanesque, Gothic and Baroque carvings. The patron saint of the city, San Andrés, is buried in the chapel.

In the church of San Miguel, with its late Romanesque sanctuary and surrounding walls, the north façade stands out, rich in iconography and the work of three different pairs of hands. There

Town Hall and is now home to the local Law Court.

To the right of this square, in the Calle de la Rúa, there is a large Plateresque building that has been converted into a cultural centre: La Casa de Cultura. It is the Palacio de San Cristóbal, which once belonged to the family of the Franciscan ascetic and mystical writer Friar Diego de Estella, a friend of St. Theresa of Jesus, and the author of works written in both Spanish and Latin and translated into Arabic and all the European languages. Examples of his work include: *Enarrationes* on the Gospel According to St. Luke which was seized by the Inquisition, the *Libro de la Vanidad del Mundo* ('Book of the Vanities of the World') and *Meditaciones devotísimas del amor de Dios* ('Very Devout Meditations on the Love of God'). These works were marked by flashes of Franciscan affection and tenderness. Friar Diego, in the wake of Erasmus, sharply reprimanded any type of abuse and reminded the Church about poverty: "God is the father of the poverty-stricken, not of the rich and those who have plenty." Printing and the Golden Age go hand in hand, and the industry was established quite early on in Estella. Miguel de Eguía, born in Estella, and also an Erasmian, worked with his father-in-law, Guillén de Brocar, on the 'Biblia Políglota Complutense' (Bible written in Hebrew, Chaldean, Greek and Latin, published in Alcalá de Henares), and with the help of Adrian of Antwerp he printed up to thirty-two books in his home city in the middle of the XVIth century. Graphic arts, which reappeared in the XIXth century in several family printshops, have undergone significant industrial development in Estella.

There are two important Gothic monuments that are located very close together. The impressive Santo Domingo convent was an important study centre from its foundation in the year 1258. The Holy Sepulchre façade is the most excellent example of Gothic sculpture in Estella and is a landmark in the evolution of this style in the whole of Navarre. A dozen splayed ogives frame a beautiful tympanum portraying the Paschal mysteries, and two rows of niches harbour an eloquent Apostolate in stony silence.

There has been a sanctuary for the Virgin on the hill overlooking Estella ('el Puy') since the XIIth century. It is embellished with

Start of the festivities in Estella, in August. Following the inaugurating rocket, pipers accompany the ancient jota of the Baile de la Era.

wonderful legends in which it rains stars, bells toll on their own, and greedy thieves go round and round the mountain at night believing that they are getting further away until they are surprised and captured by dawn. The present basilica replaces a Baroque one that was destroyed, designed by Víctor Eusa in 1949. Despite the fact that it is unfinished, it is a work of great interest, with the nobility of concrete on the outside, while inside it forms a luminous, star-shaped glass box where brick, wood and metal have been meticulously finished by the great architect. All this surrounds an image of an oval-faced smiling Virgin showing her Child to the people. The Virgen del Puy is a Gothic figure dating back to the first half of the XIVth century. The church is entered through a Baroque courtyard which is closed in by splendid XVIIIth century railings.

A MARKETPLACE

The whole length of the Calle de la Rúa has always been a commercial centre. The Pilgrims' Way to Compostela accounts for much of the economic development of Estella, where during the early Middle Ages the level of commerce "could be compared to that of the Cities of Burgos and Bruges", as the official chronicler of Navarre, José de Moret, tells us.

If Estella has always been a market town, this is due to its location between the livestock and forestry area of northern Navarre and the agricultural *Ribera* of the south. Farmers from both areas came to exchange their products in a marketplace that offered products made by craftsmen as well as providing administrative, financial, educational and health services.

Estella soon established taxes to protect the limited production of its wine-growing neighbours, charging the vendors who arrived at its gates the early tax of 'la palmada' (the handful) which was levied by a civil servant who put his open hand into each sack of cereal and took out the grain that filled it. Fair and market days were tax-free. Fairs were held from the XIIIth century onwards, and the weekly market, which dates back to the XIIth century, first in the borough of San Martín and later in the old marketplace next to San Juan, has been held in the Plaza de San Juan every Thursday from 1467 onwards.

Although commerce spills over into the neighbouring Plaza de Santiago, the real heart of the city is still the Plaza de los Fueros. The Romanesque church of San Juan faces the square with its neo-classical facade and large altarpiece alongside some excellent Renaissance and Romanesque sculptures.

In 1993, the architect from Estella Francisco Mangado conceived a project to recover the central square and turn it into a pedestrian precinct. A continuous pavement of granite underlines its spatial unity and creates an area for civic, economic and festive functions. On one side the trees, buildings and bandstand link, define and incorporate an area situated to the side of the church that used to be on the margin and was used as a car park. The design of the bandstand also provides light for the underground rooms, which are used as an exhibition hall and for other purposes.

Estella is a 'city with a river'. The Ega embraces the town at Los Llanos and then narrows in the mediaeval part between bridges.

adapted to the musical demands of new times. Its social circle was restricted to accompanying processional giants in festivities and some traditional dances. When it was going through a difficult moment with the critics, three families from Estella, Elízaga, Montero and Pérez de Lazarraga, strove to conserve this marvellous instrument, whose sound came to be associated with the city, Today, thanks to the work carried out by a new generation of pipers (*gaiteros*), the Lacunza and Fraile brothers and their students, the instrument is now taught with new methods and there are bands in all the *Merindades* (counties), including Ultrapuertos, the area of the ancient kingdom of Navarre to the north of the Pyreness, now French territory. Its production has been perfected, the volume has been adapted to the different intensity required either for the street or the stage, and the instrument converses with all types of musical groups, from symphony and chamber orchestras to electric and jazz bands.

It is no longer possible to enjoy the modernist view that the 'Andén' (footpath) of the Paseo de la Inmaculada offered from its terraces and series of small railed gardens from where Estella, once the city walls had been demolished, opened up to the modernity of a development towards the Bus Station and the abandoned railway. Town planning standards and the restoration of the historical part of the city arrived too late to avoid dense and disorganised building work. In recent years democratic consensus has managed to preserve and improve the riverside park of Los Llanos. Next to this there is a Municipal Sports Centre which was awarded a prize by the Basque-Navarre College of Architects, which praised the work of its creators Alonso Alvarez, González Presencio and Otxotorena Elizegi.

The Navarrese *gaita* is not at all like the Celtic or Galician bagpipes ('cornamusas'). The Navarrese version is a double reed wind instrument and is the result of the evolution of the primitive oboe which is attractive for its wealth of harmonies. In other areas, it is called 'dulzaina' but here there is no doubt: it is called 'gaita', and 'gaitero' is the name given to its player.

Estella is still the city of the *gaita* due to the high level of skill attained by its players and because the rocket that announces the opening of the festival at midday on the Friday before the first Sunday in August gathers together the best players in a challenge of virtuosity. However, the primary reason for its continued popularity is that in Estella the *gaita* accompanies the most beautiful and elegant *suite* of dances which are very much alive in Navarrese folklore, the 'Baile de la Era' (literally, 'dance of the flat field').

The 'gaita' and the 'baile de la era'

In the mid-twentieth century, Estella was the last redoubt of the 'gaita', a Navarrese type of flute. This is a popular instrument that has remained in the city for diverse reasons, above all perhaps because a native *estellés* of great musical talent, Julián Romano, made considerable technical developments during the last century and made it popular by including the music that was fashionable at that time in its repertory and by composing scores that permitted the instrument to be played solo or together with a woodwind band.

The *gaita* had been played by performers throughout Mid-Navarre, but its sound quality had not been improved nor had it been

Couples of all ages join hands with kerchiefs to demonstrate their affection and happiness and their identification as *Estelleses* on feast days such as May 25, the Feast of the Apparition of the Virgen del Puy. The choreography at the beginning of the dance is the same as that of an *ingurutxo*, a social dance that is common almost all over Navarre. Later on, local tunes such as the *jota* are played, and then newcomers like the waltz, the fandango and boleros. It was Julián Romano who, at the end of the XIXth century, gave the definitive musical form to this collection of dances. In 1929, Padre Hilario of Estella made a successful piano version of the 'Baile de la Era', which has also been adapted for orchestra.

The history of the monasteries of Navarre, like that of any human adventure, includes a series of contrasts: health and depravation, observance and relaxation, poverty and accumulation of wealth, wisdom and ignorance, technical progress and resistance to change, internal democracy and despotic control over servants and serfs. Nowadays, the considerable artistic and cultural heritage and the restored monastic life of the monasteries bear witness to their major contribution to history. They were an integrating factor in the newly-formed kingdom of Navarre, a focus for cultural communication, a place of hospitality and welcome, and a centre of religious contemplation.

MEDIEVAL
MONASTERIES

Monastic life in Navarre

Bernardus valles, Benedictus colles amabat. The beauty of monastery sites always draws one's attention. Their founders clearly sought quiet places, with the possibility of farming the land and providing beautiful surroundings for monks who, as a result of their vows, had to stay in their chosen monastery for the rest of their lives. A common thread is seen in Navarre: the early Benedictine monasteries of Leire, Irache and Iranzu chose locations near the mountains, whereas the *Bernardos* (La Oliva, Fitero or Tulebras) are in valleys. There were good reasons for situating the former against the Arabs from Cordoba, and for welcoming pilgrims. The Cistercians also founded their monasteries on frontiers, but given the dignifying nature of manual labour they chose locations near

[PREVIOUS PAGE] *It is the hour of Vespers. The hymn sings of the evening light. The light projects an image of the Virgin Mary onto the front part of the church at the Monastery of Leire.*
[ABOVE] *Irache stands at the foot of Montejurra. A large dome stands on top of the transept. The tower is also of great beauty.*

fast-flowing rivers to drive their mill wheels and machines. At Fitero and La Oliva the remains of original canals and irrigation ditches are still clearly visible.

Monasticism reached Navarre from Carolingian France, and seems to have begun to implant itself in the early Middle Ages through solitary anchorites who lived in caves and sheltered places at the western end of the Pyrenees until the grouping of monasteries took place under an Abbot. There was a rule which, according to San Benito, did not just conceive a monastery as a simple "school of Divine service" but rather as a community in which mutual love between brothers was the order of the day. At one time there were over three hundred monasteries or small country churches, and in the IXth century the monasteries at Igal, Urdaspal (near Burgui), and above all Leire, flourished. King Sancho el Mayor later called Leire the "first, most ancient and heart of my kingdom."

The martyr from Cordoba, Eulogio, visited Leire in 848, and interesting information is gleaned from a letter he wrote three years later to the Bishop of Pamplona, Williesindo, among other documents. Leire, already located on its present site, had a large community of "men well trained in the fear of God", a thriving centre of study and a well-stocked library. The worship of Saints Nunilo

and Alodia began around the same time (mid-IXth century). Many major donations were made when their remains were brought from Huesca. After the raids and devastation caused by the Muslims in the Xth century, the monastery's heritage reached its high point in the following century, when seventy-two small monasteries, thirty-eight villages and many churches came under the control of the Monastery of San Salvador de Leire. Sancho el Mayor increased the power of Leire by combining the posts of Bishop of Pamplona and Abbot of the monastery. The XIth century marked the dominance of Leire and the start of the admirable Romanesque building work at the monastery, which had almost a hundred monks at the time.

The historian José Goñi Gaztambide tells us that the monasteries were the most important centres of ecclesiastic life in Navarre at the time. The large abbeys and rural monasteries were populated by monks. They all came under the Bishop and lived in a rather backward and isolated manner until Sancho el Mayor freed the small monasteries from the rule of the laity and reaffirmed the Benedictine Order of Cluny.

The rule of San Benito inculcated wisdom, a way of life based on realism and moderation, although with concern for the weak and the sick, the sharing of work and daily tasks, and the laying of more emphasis on contemplation than asceticism.

The hospitality of monks is proverbial. The Abbott of Montecassino once wrote: "Any guest arriving here will be welcomed as if he were Christ. Give a specially warm welcome to the poor and pilgrims." In 1045 the pilgrims' hospital at the Monastery of Irache was completed. It was the first on the Pilgrim's Way to Compostela, almost one hundred years before the great hospice at Roncesvalles (Roncesvaux) was founded.

In the XIIth century the Cistercian reform aimed at returning the monks to a state of original purity. As José Jiménez Lozano describes it, "the Cistercian order is a rigorous process of dispossession and removal of worldly trappings in the search for the basic essential: the least possible power within the organisation and minimum adornment in buildings and books. In their quest, the Cistercians invented parliamentary democracy, as their international *Parliamentum* met as early as 1115. Individual and collective conscientious objection was allowed, and the entire system of monastic rule until the end of the XVth century was based on democratic principles: universal suffrage, majority government, participation in the running of affairs through discussion and voting, the delegation of power and the possibility of reducing the period of an elected mandate by half if the way of managing things was not considered to be correct. The Chapterhouse was the scene of the first attempts at political liberty in the West."

Bernardo de Claraval, a highly cultured conservative mystic who, according to Chelini, "blocked the development of religious structures and ideas for a time", fought against heresy, predicted the Crusades and did not feel at ease among such monastic wealth, as he made clear in his writings: "The Church shines brightly within its walls but is needed by its poor. It dresses its stones in gold and leaves its children naked. People come to marvel at the sight, but the poor do not come to be fed."

The descendants of San Bernardo (St. Bernard) arrived

The Puerta Speciosa at Leire.

times accompanied by local uprisings and the use of the sword. José María Jimeno Jurío has described the deterioration in the customs of the monks at Fitero and the iron-fisted secular dictatorship exercised by the Abbots over neighbouring villages. "The monks led a dissolute life, feeling secure in their privileged situation. In the first half of the XVIth century most of them lived openly with single and married women, some of them even having up to three mistresses. Their licentiousness did not stop there, as many of them were keen hunters and gamblers. When they walked the streets at night they carried weapons under their habits. Brawls, challenges, stabbings and general violence were quite common, and some monks even died in street fights." The constant struggles between the monks

in Navarre from the abbey of *Scala Dei* in Bigorre (France) and from 1140 onwards settled in Navarre under the guiding hand of King García Ramírez. In 1151 San Raimundo, a scourge of the Infidel, started construction of the monastery at Fitero to house a community which had lived in the area for several years, one which must be the most ancient of the Order in Spain and Portugal. Another group of monks arrived at an already existing mediaeval hamlet, Oliva, in the autumn of 1149. A Benedictine monastery dedicated to Saint Adrian had existed since the start of the XIth century in the solitude of Iranzu, at the end of the Aspidea gorge (near Estella). Its community languished until it almost disappeared and was later taken over by another Bernardian order from *Aula Dei* (a monastery near Orléans), whose first Abbott was Nicolás de Artajona, from Navarre. The convent at Tulebras was the first of the Order in Spain and later gave rise to many others, among them that of Las Huelgas (province of Burgos).

Hermenegildo María Marín tells us of monks who "lived in the early days of the Cistercians in high fervour and observance. Worship was the main activity, manual work enjoyed a good reputation in the Order, silence was rigorously observed, the food was very frugal, and generous help was given to the poor."

The level of accumulated wealth, the desire for power and temporal rule, the low level of intellectual development, and the gradual abandonment of the monastic spirit led to dark times for the monasteries. In the XIIIth century there was a prevailing atmosphere of uncertainty which continued at Leire for seventy years. During that period the monastery changed hands on several occasions, alternating between the white-clad Cistercian monks and the black cowl wearers of the Order of Cluny. The raids were violent, some-

and their vassals, who defended their freedom tenaciously, lasted until the *Desamortización* (confiscation of church property) which took place in the XIXth century.

The XVIIth and XVIIIth centuries saw the great cultural development of the monasteries, which had well-stocked libraries and published highly scientific works on their printing presses. From the XIVth century onwards Irache stood out academically thanks to its College of Theology and Arts, which acquired the status of university in 1569 and granted degrees in Medicine until 1753. Irache also fulfilled a humanitarian role in the final Carlist War, as a Blood Hospital capable of accommodating over five hundred war casualties.

The far-reaching confiscation of church property was accompanied by the ruination and sacking of the monasteries. Even the buildings were auctioned off to anyone who wised to use their stones as building material. In an atmosphere of Romanticism, two famous writers described the abandonment and death of monastic life through legends which have an identical basis: Gustavo Adolfo Bécquer set his "El Miserere" on the Mountain in Fitero, sung between the ruins in the dark of night by ghostly spectres of penitent monks, and in 'El Organista Loco de Iranzu' (The Mad Organist of Iranzu) Juan Iturralde y Suit composed a deep *De profundis* against the background of a fierce storm on All Souls' Day. Distinguished figures such as Hermenegildo Oyaga (in the case of Leire), Onofre Larumbe (La Oliva), or Manuel García (Irache), were able to act in time to save and revitalise the monasteries. The Monuments Commission of Navarre and the 'Institución Príncipe de Viana' (the Cultural Heritage department of the Government of Navarre) have supervised their restoration.

Monks and nuns from Benedictine and Cistercian monasteries have continued the work of Benito de Nursia and Bernardo de Claraval. Each monastery is a silent place of prayer, work, and hospitality. The American Trappist Thomas Merton, one of the most widely read contemporary experts on spirituality, says that: "… we should understand monastic life, above all, as a life of prayer. Meditation is not based on anything if it is not firmly rooted in life. You change through prayer. It does not blind you to what is happening in the world, it rather transforms your vision of it, in the light of God. There are times when activity should take over from contemplation, because Man is asked to love God and his neighbour. Within the fast pace of modern life interior silence is necessary to maintain our human and Christian identity, and our freedom."

HISTORICAL MONUMENTS:
LEIRE,
THE BIRTHPLACE OF
ROMANESQUE
ARCHITECTURE

Interior of the abbatial church at La Oliva. The Cistercian order always seeks bare, non-ornate lines, also seen in their art.

The word 'Leire' comes from the Latin *legionarius*, attributed to someone as a surname. Although some people have thought that the Basque name of the mountain range behind the monastery is *Errando*, it appears that this name only corresponds to one particular place on the range. In the Basque dialect of the Salazar valley, however, Leire was certainly called *Lexuri*. At the foot of the range, crowned by a high limestone ridge, is the *legerense* monastery, as it was called in the oldest known document in which its name appears.

To reach the abbey, hidden in the folds of the mountain side, you go up a picturesque road which blends into an old sheep transhumance track (the *Cañada Real de los Roncaleses*) in certain places. The monastery is set back and offers a magnificent view of the surrounding countryside, made even more beautiful by the bluish-green water of the Yesa reservoir below. It is easy to understand the strategic importance of this site in history, as a fortress and refuge for the Church and the young Monarchy of Pamplona (forerunner of the Kingdom of Navarre), which has its mausoleum here.

The rocky outcrops are covered with different types of oak trees, and near the monastery is the legendary 'Fountain of San Virila'.

Virila was an Abbot of Leire whose existence is proved by a document dated 928 and who has been worshipped since at least the XIth century. A delightful legend is attributed to him, one which spread across Europe and which probably had its origin in this monastery, where it is represented in a bas-relief from the end of the XIIth century. An XVIIIth century chronicler describes it as follows: "A holy monk called Virila lived in the Monastery of Leire. Having heard that mysterious verse of the Psalm in Matins, which says: "A thousand years in your glory, Lord, are like the day which passed yesterday", he was left thinking, meditating on the words. A small bird came near him and sang so sweetly that he followed it until it disappeared inside an impenetrable wood, where the saintly monk went into a trance which, thanks to God's grace, lasted for three hundred years. He then returned to his monastery thinking he had only set out that morning, and found almost all the monks dumb with awe."

Leire is one of the most attractive monuments in Navarre. Different epochs and architectural styles succeed each other harmoniously. The foundations of the Pre-Romanesque church, set on fire by Almanzor in the Xth century, are hidden under the floor of the Gothic nave.

The greatest interest lies in the Sanctuary of the church, with its naves and apses, and the crypt, built to support it and overcome the problem of different ground levels. This early XIth century work is the first example of Romanesque architecture in Navarre and was the prototype for the great constructions of Spanish Romanesque. It is earlier than the cathedrals at Jaca, San Isidoro de León, San Martín de Frómista and Santiago. It was completed in 1057, the year when the church was first consecrated. Luis María de Lojendio assures us that "the same stones we see in the crypt today were cut and carved in the reign of King Sancho el Mayor."

A rough Romanesque façade provides access to the crypt, which has an archaic feel to it. It is an unsophisticated, austere construction but is also wise and balanced. It has four barrel vaults, and the extensive space is almost stifled by the presence of a large number of robust pillars with unusually large capitals, decorated with roughly-hewn scrolls. It is a vigorous structure designed to support the enormous weight on top of it.

The church was built in different stages and its Sanctuary is particularly striking: "… a marvellous monument, with spectacular contrasts and singular scenography", in the words of the monk and historian Ramón Molina. The three naves, of unequal width and covered by barrel vaults, end up in semicircular apses. The large ashlars were exquisitely carved by stonemasons. The Sanctuary was a complete early church which was then extended in the Romanesque period, leading to a second consecration of the whole building in 1098. In the XIVth century the Cistercians had the good idea of leaving the Romanesque sanctuary as part of the Gothic nave. Quite a bold technical solution was adopted, the roof being supported on the walls without columns.

The outside of the Abbey is equally beautiful. The rays of the rising sun bathe the stone drum walls of the triple apse, the tower with triple bores on all four sides, and the austere belfry. At Vespers the setting sun lights up the 'Puerta Speciosa', which has excellent examples of the most common themes in Romanesque sculpture. "From sunrise to sunset" is a Gregorian chant the Benedictines sing in praise of the Lord.

Interior of the abbatial church at Fitero. Its is Latin Cross shaped and the main chapel is surrounded by an apse with smaller side chapels.

LA OLIVA, BEAUTIFUL ART FOR THOSE WHO WITHDREW FROM THE WORLD

Legend says that a King of Navarre was wounded in an ambush fighting against the Arabs and died at the foot of a wild olive tree. He was buried nearby, and the village and monastery of La Oliva was located on that spot.

"For Christ, we have renounced the beauty of the world", St. Bernard used to say. It was, however, in the lack of adornment and dispossession that he found the pure essence of beauty.

In his book 'Diversion to Santiago', the Dutch writer Cees Nootebom thought he had seen the birth of Gothic architecture in the façade of the monastic church of La Oliva. There are three arches on the front: "The secret is in the arches. There is a faint sway in the full Romanesque arch at its highest point. This is almost accidental, a rising movement petrified in its pristine flight. However small it might be, at the same time it breaks with anything before it. After that the arched line cannot be complete, it can only escape, fly higher and higher until it becomes the Gothic arch of Amiens or Chartres."

The façade is usually dated at the end of the XIIIth century. On both sides there are Romanesque rose windows which throw light onto the lateral naves of the church. On top of the archivolts there are eaves with symbolic sculptures, among them a curious Wheel of Fortune and a Renaissance tower crowning the façade where storks nest.

Through the wrought iron gate there is a platform eight steps higher than the floor which highlights the size of an imposing church, seventy-four metres long with five sections of cross-ribbed roof. The style is Spanish-Languedoc and its construction began in 1164. There is an atmosphere of peace, simplicity and harmony in the pointed arch naves. The apse of the presbytery is an exact copy of the Chapel of Jesus Christ, the first oratory used by the monks, and which is still preserved to this day. An elegant octagonal dome serves as the bell tower. Every evening after Compline before the monks retire to bed, the bell rings and the church is left in darkness with only the image of the Virgin Mary lit up. The monks praise her by singing the moving *Salve Regina*.

The Mediaeval section of the monastery is located on the north side of the church, around the cloister (XIVth and XVth centuries). The Proto-Gothic Chapterhouse has a beautiful entrance.

The Monastery of Azuelo held more relics than Leire at one time. Converted into a parish church, it still holds the head of the saint to which it is dedicated, Saint George.

THE OTHER MONASTERIES

At the foot of Mount Montejurra, Irache, which already existed in the Xth century, bears witness to the memory of its Saint, Abbot Veremund, He was so generous to the poor that, when he took his ration of bread to them under his habit and the other monks criticised him for this, he opened his clothes to reveal roses and chips of wood he took to keep the frozen beggars warm. The monastery has a Romanesque church with three naves and a large dome in the centre, a tower and a Renaissance cloister. Irache has sufficient material to be a great ethnographic museum. In the nearby village of Dicastillo an image of Santa María la Real de Irache has been kept since the *exclaustración* (confiscation of Church property). It is the oldest statue of the Virgin preserved in Navarre and is dated around 1145. The statute is clothed in a highly representative sample of the garments worn during the Romanesque era.

Iranzu is a jewel hidden in a dark, solitary valley. A Renaissance stone cross welcomes the visitor, a stream flows down the hillside and a three-hundred-year-old walnut tree provides shade over the entrance. Access to the site is through the Gothic cloister, where a number of large windows reflect a period of construction over many years. In the space over a hexagonal shrine is a washbasin, just opposite the refectory. Next to it, there is a large stone chimney in excellent condition, and the stove opens out in the form of four pointed arches. The church, covered in cross ribs, is rectangular in shape and has a flat façade. It is based on the Cistercian models of

Burgundy, and surprises the visitor with its light concentrated in the presbytery, and the clever layout of spaces, which give the building a feeling of luminosity.

The Abbey church of Fitero is also inspired by the Burgundy style. It has a Romanesque facade, the layout is in Latin cruciform and the main chapel is surrounded by an apse with smaller chapels in it. Christian and Muslim masons carved the capitals very carefully. The ancient cloister was replaced by the present one (XVIth century) and has rooms over it which were completed in 1613. The image of the Virgin Mary ('la Virgen de la Barda') is kept in a Baroque chapel — 'Barda' means 'brambles' in the dialect of the area. Legend has it that a bramble grew and entered the chapel to the Virgin Mary through a window. There is a large collection of small Arab chests, Mediaeval coffers, and a beautiful Gothic reliquary made of Limousin enamel.

The monastery of Santa María de la Caridad at Tulebras was restored a few years ago by the nuns who lived there. Worthy of note is the convent museum, located next to the XIIIth century single-nave Cistercian church. In addition to the gold and silver work and a curious painting of the Holy Trinity, it is home to the 'Virgen de la Cama', an original and striking way of representing the Ascent to Heaven of the Virgin Mary. The figure is dressed in embroidered silk, and lies on pillows in a kind of urn-bed of bright colours in the Rococo style. At one time the rather picturesque nuns of Tulebras had many servants and dressed in silks and curls. However, a chronicle from 1686 describes the "Mirror of the saintly and royal Monastery of Tulebras, in which all the writings and memorable things since its foundation", clearly stating that it was a place in which eminent examples of austerity and virtue were to be found.

There were over a hundred castles in Navarre at the beginning of the XIIIth century when, according to Altadill, *Sancho el Fuerte* (Sancho the Strong) saw the need to 'turn this land into a dense forest of fortresses, a rocky jungle of castles, the perpetual keepers of calm and order throughout the kingdom'. This imposing heritage fell into decay as the years went by, thanks to the constant wars and the three campaigns conducted by the Castilian conquerors to demolish them, and also as a result of the negligence and plundering of the local inhabitants themselves. The buildings still standing are scarce and precious. Unlike other European regions, today we know more about the castles in Navarre by consulting the abundant documentation to be found in the archives than by carrying out systematic archaeological work.

CASTLES
OF THE KINGDOM

The Castles and mediaeval walled towns of Navarre are often used as settings for films, *son et lumière* shows, and for contemporary art festivals.

However, two thirds of the towers and fortifications are located in rural areas or isolated spots. There are few things as pleasing to the eye as contemplating a castle built on a rocky crag, like the *Peña* castle. First from a distance, on the escarpment, and then close-up in order to view its solid stone blocks. If the outing is made in the company of children, climbing walls, crossing bridges, hiding in look-out posts, throwing money in wells, making echoes and waving from the towers become part of an exciting adventure.

The governor of the castle is almost sure to appear. You just have to knock three times on the door and then shout:

–'Is anybody there? Who's the keeper of this castle?'

And, once silence reigns, we will receive an answer:

–'I, Sancho Pérez de Agorreta, am the keeper. Do you have the royal command? Well then, come inside and have a look'.

Then he informs us that he was born here in this kingdom and is obliged to continuously live with his family here in the fortress as he has solemnly vowed to defend it until death or until seriously wounded.

After that, he informs us of the occupational hazards and comments that he feels he is well paid, because this is a border castle and his job is very dangerous. Although he has to wait for months to receive his wages, until Candelmas in February and the mid-August Virgin, he does not complain since he always gets paid in the end.

He is glad that it is peacetime because, when the Great Companies of mercenaries passed by, they sent him forty lancers and crossbowmen from the neighbouring town of Sangüesa to help with the defence. At that time, it was necessary to operate the winch located in the Great Tower to bring up supplies of bread, wine, bacon, salted fish and mutton. Now he is not too worried about arms, he is more concerned with fighting off leaks, checking for cracks and maintaining the tower, which was almost destroyed by lightning.

Once we are in his confidence, he shows us the outbuildings: the courtyard with its well, the church, the stables, the kitchen with

A German traveller who visited the castle at Olite around 1442 wrote: "I am sure that no king has a more beautiful palace or castle, with so many gilded rooms."

its oven and storage rooms. Everything is very sober: in the chapel there is a lead chalice, a large register and vestments for mass. In the rooms there are several beds, an old chest with no lid, three shields and four crossbows. In the kitchen, with the table and stools, a grinder, a table for making bread and a bucket for getting water. He has his doubts, because of the children, but finally he also shows us the prison. It is a dark and sad dungeon with mantraps and shackles in the corners.

'And now you must forgive me but I have sentry duty and must stand guard'.

A castle, no matter however much in ruins, always exudes a certain atmosphere and arouses one's fantasy.

Colonel Villalba (the mentor and physical executor of the political order to demolish castles and walled enclosures in 1516) had a very different idea of fantasy, a word he considered equal to pride or rebelliousness. As he wrote to Cardinal Cisneros: 'Navarre has so little fantasy left after your Lordship ordered the walls to be demolished that no man can hold his head up high'. However, these words were written at a time when developments in artillery were making castles obsolete as a defence system. Those fortresses fulfilled many military and civilian functions during mediaeval times. The towers, a permanent observation point, were also real communication posts which could send or receive visual smoke and fire signals or sound messages using cymbals or horns, day or night. Castles presided over districts, defined borders and safeguarded the territory, whilst defending both people and property. They acted as prisons for captured enemy soldiers, political detainees or delinquents and as a place for executing prisoners who were either hanged or thrown from a great height. It was also a place for negotiations and agreements, a mint for coining money, a guarantee for loans, an archive, a place for storing taxes, an office for the clerks, an arena for tournaments and the occasional or permanent residence of the monarchs.

[PREVIOUS PAGE] *The Castle of Javier is one of the oldest in Navarre. It was originally an isolated watchtower in the IXth century. On 7th April 1506 Francisco de Jaso y Azpilicueta was born, later to become the most universal figure and patron saint of Navarre, Catholic missions and sport: San Francisco Javier.*

FROM THE UNYIELDING ROCK TO THE CASTLES

More than twenty Navarrese writers and historians from this century have studied both the castles and the complete defence system of the kingdom. One should not forget the well classified monuments nor the legacy of wonderful traditions and legends, of which Fernando Videgáin has collected at least fifty. Juan José Martinena Ruiz has made decisive contributions with his direct handling of valuable documentation on the late mediaeval public accounts, the 'comptos' or treasury, and modern cartography.

Since ancient times Nature has offered refuge and defence to those men who have known how to take advantage of and fortify a few high and rough positions, locations almost inaccessible to possible attackers.

Place names still reveal numerous signs of ancient hill-forts or fortifications. The syllable *car*, of Celtic origin, has left its mark on important settlements in Navarre, such as Cárcar, Carcastillo or Santacara. There are abundant '*Castellones*' and '*castellares*' which coincide with archaeological sites. The generic name of the 'Peña' castle comes from the Latin *pinna* since, as Corominas explains, 'the rocks which stand up on the crest of a rocky mountain are compared to the battlements of a fortress'. In the Basque language, many mountains were given the name *Gaztelu* (castle) as is the case

There was already a defensive tower at Ujué in the Early Middle Ages. A pre-Romanesque church also stood in the shadow of the castle.

with one which can be clearly seen from Pamplona and on whose summit the cylindrical bases of a mediaeval defence tower are still preserved. Maybe this tower, or perhaps the neighbouring Garaño, corresponded to that favourite fortress of the Pamplona monarchs which was destroyed in 924 by Ab al Rhaman III, and which the Arab chronicles called *Sajrat Qais*.

During the Reconquest against Islam it was necessary to protect access routes and consolidate borders and this gave rise to the construction of several castles. In the face of the Cordovans, who came as a punitive expedition, the strategy of the defenders was elemental: to attack with a surprise skirmish and then to quickly withdraw to the mountains. The Monjardín castle, which is Arab in origin, must have been very important by the IXth Century. Its old name is *Deio* and this extended to cover a great area, *Deierri*, which is the present Land of Estella. The Castles of that time, or those which still have something left of them, must have been those of Falces, work of the Moslems, Leguín and Garaño, near Pamplona, and those of Ujué, Aibar, Peña and Javier.

Those castles were more like watch-towers than fortresses. They were either cylindrical or prismatic with a square base. They were free-standing towers with just one door, situated quite high up and not at ground level in order to prevent a surprise attack. A hanging wooden bridge led to the first floor where there was a small room for occasional use. In Arellano there is a tower still standing of this 'dungeon' type. The structure of the castles gradually became more complex until, in the XIIIth century, stretches of wall with towers in the corners appeared and which formed a fortified enclosure with

different outbuildings opening out onto the parade ground.

The Moors were gradually pushed back from the middle area of Navarre towards the Ebro plain. In the IXth century, the Moslems had outposts at Falces, Caparroso and Valtierra covering the important fortified town of Tudela, which remained under their control until 1119. Of all the present day sites in Navarre, the only one to preserve an unmistakably Arab name is Azagra, which comes from *Al Sajra* ('the crag'). Great towers were built on the highest points of these Moorish towns and villages and, in the crags directly below the towers, they excavated caves to store food and take refuge in difficult situations. Miranda and Milagro, two small towns conserve the memory of a border marked with watchtowers, which continue to be, as their names indicate, real balconies and observatories.

Feudalism as such never existed in Navarre. If anything, just a late neo-feudalism was present from the XIVth century onwards when, unfortunately for the kingdom, the kings of the Evreux dynasty wanted the territory divided up amongst the noblemen. This led to factional fighting which put an end to independence and exclusive monarchs. As Yanguas y Miranda wrote, 'each of these men became so powerful that he alone was sufficient to endanger the monarchy, with the help of his relatives, friends and vassals'.

The majority of the castles belonged to the crown, whilst very few were owned by the church or nobility. Until well into the XIIIth century, they were included in a regime of 'tenancies' which were military and administrative districts at the same time. The seat of the tenancy was a fortified castle or town, from which a specific *comarca* (territorial area or basin) was defended and ruled. The king granted his barons this 'honour', which was understood to be the government of the tenancy, but this was always for a limited period of time. By means of this mobility of tenancies, the king prevented the post from becoming hereditary and the nobility from accumulating patrimony. The system of tenancies evolved under the kings from the Champagne dynasty who imported French models and developed a more modern administrative system, based on *merindades* (similar to counties) which were larger, better defined territories.

Once the Reconquest was over, the borders of Navarre were defined in relation to the neighbouring kingdoms of Aragón and Castile. They were consolidated during the reign of Sancho VII *el Fuerte* towards the end of the Middle Ages, at the beginning of the XIIIth century. The king had border towers built in La Bardena,

strengthened the fortress of Sonsierra in Alava and created a defence system along the Ebro river, where the new town of Viana played a key role. During his reign the number of free-standing castles came to total one hundred. During his final years, Sancho VII was called '*el Encerrado*' (a person who shuts himself off) since he spent his time in solitary confinement inside the walls of the Castle of Tudela, one of the most important if not the most important castles in the kingdom.

Scarcely any new castles were built during the final three centuries of the Middle Ages. Instead, a great effort was made to improve and repair some of the existing ones. During the Champagne dynasty, the castles of Tiebas and Castillonuevo were constructed, and the complex defence structure of Estella was completed with the Belmerchet castle. During the first decade of the XIVth century, under Luis Hutín, King of France and Navarre, the first castle at Pamplona was built. This was located between the present streets of Chapitela and Estafeta. Under the kings of the house of Evreux, a great deal was spent on repairs, and they improved the residential conditions of some castles, such as those at Tudela and Monreal, and the two distinguished Gothic castles of Tafalla and Olite were built.

After the wars with Castile and the civil war between the *Agramonteses* and the *Beaumonteses* many castles were left in ruins. An extreme example was the Rada castle, which was attacked so violently by the *Agramontés* Martín de Peralta that none of the inhabitants were left alive 'and the blood of its defenders stained the waters of the Aragón river red'. The Crown was obliged to curtail expenses, and considerably reduced the number of fortresses considered useful for defence. Artillery, used for the first time in Navarre in 1378, marked the decline of the castles. At the same time, there was a general process in the villages of fortifying the towers and bell towers of the churches, taking advantage of their solid walls. Some castles were still built in the time of Juan II, in the middle of the XVth century, namely those of Lumbier, Eslava and Miravalles, although they had a very short life.

[PREVIOUS TWO PAGES] *The Walls of Artajona were finished in 1109. It is the most important and complete example of mediaeval fortification in Navarre.*

There are few aesthetic sensations comparable to seeing a castle on a rock like La Peña. In the background, an escarpment. In the foreground, the castle's ashlars.

After the conquest of the kingdom by the Duque de Alba, the king Fernando *el Católico* was told that there were some twenty five key fortresses in Navarre, although only seven of them were in a fit state to face artillery attacks. There then followed three campaigns to demolish them.

In 1512, in order to remove the castles which could be detrimental to his control of the conquered territory, Fernando ordered the demolition of the castles of Arguedas, Aguilar, Belmerchet, Cábrega, Cáseda, Castillonuevo, Eslava, Javier, Legúin, Mélida, Murillo, Oro, Ozcorroz, Peña, Petilla, San Martín, Sancho Abarca, Santacara and Ujué. At the same time, the King of Aragon concentrated his defence strategy on the new castle of Pamplona which was located on the plot now occupied by the *Palacio de la Diputación* (seat of the Government of Navarre). In 1516 Cardinal Cisneros began further action to remove the fortresses in Navarre. His objective, rather than the castles themselves, was the demolition of the walled enclosures which defended the towns and cities. In 1521, further to the unsuccessful attempt made by General Asparrot to recover the kingdom, the castles of Monreal, Tafalla and Tudela were demolished by order of the Emperor Carlos V. The last bastion of the *Agramonteses*, the fortress of Amaiur, was razed to the ground after heroic defence in June 1522.

The second castle of Pamplona, where Iñigo de Loyola, founder of the *Compañía de Jesús* (Jesuits), fell wounded as he defended it at the side of the Castilians, was soon declared a 'ruin' by the Italian engineers advising the House of Austria. The construction of the *Ciudadela* (citadel), which began on 11th July 1571, converted Pamplona into a fortified town close to the Pyrenees. Its five bastions were used to control both the citizens as well as possible external enemies, which did not manage to set foot inside the walls until the XIXth century. In 1877 work began on the construction of the fort of San Cristobál on the high hill north of Pamplona for the purpose of defending the city from a distance.

Thanks to its restoration, the Royal Palace of Olite is the most attractive and best preserved castle in Navarre. It began life as a military building in the XIIIth century. All that remains of this period are the towers of San Jorge and 'La Prisión' which housed the arms room and the chapel. In the XIVth and XVth centuries the nucleus of this primitive fortress, which has now been converted into a *Parador de Turismo* (state-owned hotel), was extended to house the Court premises. These included beautiful landscaped galleries and a large number of rooms which still preserve the delicate work of masons and plaster workers. The exterior brings to mind the Papal Palace at Avignon and presents a beautiful ensemble of up to twenty two towers and turrets. This impressive Gothic monument is dealt with in greater detail in the chapter on the town of Olite.

The castle of Tiebas is nowadays just a venerable ruin, although its cellar is well preserved. It was built in the middle of the XIIIth century at a strategic location on the royal route from Pamplona to Zaragoza. It was used as a preventive prison and an archive. It was set on fire in 1378 by troops from Castile and this caused the writer Iturralde y Suit to write a legendary account in which a valiant defender was to die, accompanied by his faithful dog. The reality, however, was rather different. The defence of the castle by the Navarrese soldiers was halted due to the negligence of the governor, who was accused of being a coward. A well preserved early XIXth century drawing has enabled the image of the Castle of Tiebas to be reconstructed. The watchtowers of the castle at Olite were restored on the basis of the lookout posts and pointed lead spires of the old castle at Tiebas.

The stately castle of Marcilla managed to avoid demolition by order of Cisneros because, as the legend goes, a brave woman, Doña Ana de Velasco, boldly faced up to the people who were going to carry out the order. This stately castle, constructed at the beginning of the XVth century, was built of brick on stone slopes.

The walled town of Artajona is the most important and complete example of popular mediaeval fortifications. Other places which had enclosures, such as Aibar, Larraga, Monreal or Mendirgorría, have all lost them. The one at Artajona is characteristic of military architecture of the XIth and XIIth centuries. It was completed in 1109. The enclosure stretches out and tries to adapt itself to the shape of the hill. The prismatic flat-walled towers were linked by lengths of wall with a castellated sentry walk. The Gothic Church of San Saturnino was used as a bastion and completed the defence system of the town.

Scattered around Navarre are towers pertaining to the nobility and fortified palaces which were built during the decline of the Middle Ages. The noble tower of Zabaleta at Lesaka, Ayanz at Lónguida and Jaureguía at Donamaría, which still preserves its primitive wooden scaffolding, are of particular beauty and interest. Amongst the stately fortified palaces, the ones at Arazuri and at Artieda, with a square shaped ground plan and a parade ground and towers at the corners, are worthy of note.

The Castle of Javier

After Pamplona, no other historic corner of Navarre (not even Roncesvalles, or its French name, 'Roncesvaux') receives as many visitors as Javier which is, above all, a sanctuary and missionary centre. The greatest concentrations of pilgrims occur during the '*Javieradas*' (popular pilgrimages to Javier) during the month of March, when thousands of people gather together, many of whom have walked a great distance to get there.

On 7th April 1506, Francisco de Jaso y Azpilcueta was born at the Castle. His own family was affected by the disasters of war during his infancy and, perhaps because of this, his mother guided him towards books and away from arms. He attended the University of Paris where he obtained the qualification of *Maestro en Artes* (Master of Arts). He then refused a canonry in Pamplona cathedral in order to follow Iñigo de Loyola in the first days of the Jesuits. He was ordained as a priest and named Papal Nuncio, and was sent by the King of Portugal to the West Indies. From 1541 until his death due to pneumonia, on the island of Sancián at the gates of China on 3rd December 1552, he converted many people in Asia to Christianity. He created a school in Goa for training native priests, he wrote a catechism in the Tamil language and founded the first Christian communities in Japan. He was cheerful, fervent and always humble, but energetic when it came to taking decisions. His aim was to lay the basis for long-lasting missionary action and, according to the scholar, Dominguez Ortiz, 'the tactic of this apostle of the fishermen and the poor was to establish close relations with the people and preach a religion which honoured poverty and humility'. San Francisco Javier is the patron saint of Navarre, which celebrates the Day of the Community on 3rd December, the Feast day of the Saint.

The Castle of Javier is one of the oldest in Navarre. It was originally built at the beginning of the XI century as an isolated tower for signalling and defence. The base of the keep is Romanesque, and the castle was always important as a result of its position on the border with Aragon. In the XIIIth and XIVth centuries, the nobles built around the high tower dedicated to San Miguel. They erected some residential buildings at the front and another building at the back with a wall around them and a sentry walk, where the cellars and stores which opened out onto the parade ground were situated. In the XVth century the polygon-shaped tower, named Undués, was added with a projecting gallery with holes in the base. In 1516 the walls were razed to the ground by order of Cardinal Cisneros, the towers were cut off, the moats were filled in and the defences were made useless.

A restoration initiated in 1892 and completed from 1952 onwards with the excavation of the moat and the base of the exterior wall, has enabled the castle to recover its mediaeval appearance. The building has an interesting art gallery, a letter signed by San Francisco Javier and, in a small chapel located in the *Torre del Cristo* (Christ's Tower), frescos of a 'death dance' and a large, late Gothic, walnut-wood sculpture of a smiling Crucifix are to be found. This Christ was already considered miraculous even before Francisco de Jaso was born but, each Friday during the final year of the Saint's life and on his deathbed, drops of blood appeared on it and 'very important and righteous people were witness to this', according to the kingdom's chronicler, Padre José de Moret in 1686.

The unexpected dieresis on the Romance form of the name of this town is already a reminder that, even in linguistic terms, Sangüesa is on a border, a strategic situation both for peacetime and during the wars which affected the town just as much as the river Aragon, which was responsible for its wealth and occasional ruin. Sangüesa is the most important town in the area and the main source of income nowadays comes from industry and services, as well as agriculture. The town continues its market activity and the pedagogic tradition of the Grammar School, and it was here that the future saint, Francis of Javier, like many other local people, received his education. For the thousands of pilgrims who visit the nearby castle where the saint was born, and for those following the Pilgrim's Way to Santiago de Compostela, this town is a hospitable crossroads, with a monument in every street.

SANGÜESA

Frontier Town on the Way to Santiago

Standing among the foothills of the surrounding ring of mountains, Sangüesa reflects a mixture of features from the mountain region to the north and the flatter area to the south known as the *Ribera*. The geographer Alfredo Floristán comments that "this land has always been generous in cereals and wine, but most ungenerous in oil; in short, sub-Mediterranean." The Aragon and Irati rivers, which come together at Entrambasaguas (literally, 'between two waters'), the Onsella and several ravines have shaped great hills, covered with vegetation reminiscent of the Pyrenees, in the chalk and clay, and levelled fertile terraces. One such irrigated area is Pastoriza, where the farmers have cultivated the exquisite beans known as *pochas* a speciality of Sangüesa. The warm, dry climate contributes to the quality of the crops grown in the area. In winter, fog usually hangs over the town, covering it in a sea of white. The north wind also plays a part —in the words of Tomás Moral "it brings the countryside to life and sets it moving to the point of making it dance, when it doesn't make it howl."

The name of Sangüesa, which has greatly interested linguists, tells us much about its past. The meaning of the name is not clear, but it would seem to be related to *Sanga*, a woman's name. The earliest form of the name would have been *Sancosa*, from which the present name is derived. The Basque name for the town in all the surrounding area was undoubtedly *Zangoza*. Spanish has long been spoken in the region, but place names show a strong Basque influence, especially on the left bank of the river Aragon.

The area has many traces of human settlements dating back to the Bronze Age. The customs and knowledge of these people, who predominantly lived off animals rather than crops and whose culture was Basque in origin, mingled with the more advanced techniques brought across the Pyrenees by peaceful Celts in the Iron Age. There followed a period of intense Roman settlement.

Julio Caro Baroja emphasises that the mountains were never a real barrier: "The people from Jaca passing through this area brought the eastern part of Navarre into close contact with Aquitaine. This situation continued in the Middle Ages. The route from Jaca to Pamplona via Sangüesa was of exceptional importance. Historically the Basques in the east had close contact with the people of Aquitaine. There is little doubt that their languages were originally the same or very similar. We should also mention the Celtic and Romano-Gallic penetration of Aquitaine, and there are reasons for believing that this extended to the Basque area, as the place names suggest. This process was later significantly affected by increasing Romance influence, and this may have been an important factor in the increasingly clear distinction of Aragon as a separate territory."

THE TWO MEDIAEVAL SANGÜESAS

A few kilometres from the city, close to the paper factory, stands the town of Rocaforte, situated on a rocky outcrop. The name dates from the middle of the XVth century and mediaeval documents refer to it as "Old Sangüesa." Since the IXth century there had been a fortified watchtower and stronghold on this peak which played

an important role in the wars between the fledging Pamplona monarchy and the Moslems. Two Roman roads, later to become part of the route to Santiago, crossed at the foot of Rocaforte. At the end of the XIth and beginning of the XIIth centuries there was a determined effort on the part of the monarchy to stop people fleeing from the area and to increase the population of Sangüesa with an influx of Franks. As a result three different parts of the town grew up, known (depending on their position on the ridge) as upper, middle and lower. However, in the years that followed the number of inhabitants diminished and those who remained effectively became servants of the king. The town was really one large fortress and the remains of the walls and the castle on the top (demolished in 1516) were still visible at the end of the XVIIIth cetury.

In the XIth century the dangers to travellers through raids by bandits had gone and Europeans were making pilgrimages to Compostela. Two monarchs, who were simultaneously kings of Navarre and of Aragon, Sancho Ramírez and his son Alfonso el Batallador, initiated the re-population of the town. In the words of the historian Jimeno Jurío: "Sancho Ramírez had carried out an extraordinary experiment at the beginning of his reign in Aragon. Attracted by the special privileges granted to the settlers in Jaca, a large number of foreigners came to settle in the city, thus renewing the institutions, customs and language of the Frank inhabitants. When he became king of Navarre in 1070 he wanted to try the same thing there. The road through Somport, Jaca, Yesa and Monreal was busy with pilgrims journeying to Santiago. The villages and hamlets of Navarre were inhabited by farmers and herdsmen whose language and traditions meant they were unreceptive to the outside world. There were no hospitals and very little means of guaranteeing the safety of the pilgrims. Sancho Ramírez and his successors started what can only be termed a social revolution by organising the re-population or development of important towns along the road to Santiago. For the first time in our history, strange customs and unfamiliar professions, such as craftsmen and merchants, made their appearance. The monied classes of Sangüesa, the borough of San Cernin in Pamplona, Estella or Puente la Reina also brought their Provençal speech, which was to be maintained for several centuries, in isolated pockets surrounded by Basque speakers.

The need to open up a route that would link Aragon and Navarre was clear: the population had to be settled, the cultivation of fertile meadows had to be improved, and it was important to renew the economy and provide hospitality.

At the end of his reign, between 1089 and 1093, Sancho Ramirez started the building of a bridge across the river Aragon. Next to it (on the left bank) he built the royal palace, with a church dedicated to Our Lady. Beside it was a small village. Alfonso el Batallador continued his father's work and in 1122, under the

[PREVIOUS PAGE] *"My admiration for Romanesque art did not fall from Heaven. I have been enchanted by Vézelay and Conques, Maastricht and Sangüesa" (the great Dutch writer Cees Nooteboom).*

[OPPOSITE] *The portico covers the entire façade of the church of Santa María with high-quality sculptures. It has two parts as the final result of two fronts built by different stonemasons.*

jurisdiction of Jaca, he founded the town which came to be called "New Sangüesa".

The direction taken by the bridge and the road towards the village of Ull meant that the Rúa Mayor was the street which became the backbone of the town's development. For Juan Cruz Labeaga, Sangüesa is a good example of mediaeval town planning. All the streets are organised around this main thoroughfare, which gives the town its marked character as a stopping place along the road. A plan of the town shows it to be a grid system, almost square in shape, with one main street and others parallel and at right-angles to it. The houses form deep, narrow, rectangular blocks."

What had grown up as a city around a bridge became a city defending a border when the people of Pamplona chose García Ramírez as their king, and the destinies of Navarre and Aragon were once more separated. Frequent discord between the neighbouring kingdoms led to the building of defensive walls around the city.

The city then spread on the other side of the bridge. *Ultra pontem*, near the Romanesque church of San Nicolás, the quarter with the parish of San Andrés del Arenal, continued to grow and in 1171, by order of Sancho el Sabio a third town appeared on the high ground of Arangoiz, where a monument to the Sacred Heart of Jesus now stands. This town, known as El Castellón, had its own fortress and parish church.

The XIIIth century was a period of peace and saw the arrival of four mendicant orders. The Descalzos appeared in 1210 and fifteen years later built their Carmelite monastery outside the city walls to the right of the river, next to the chapel of Santa María de la Nora. The Virgin, who took her name from the Spanish word (*noria*) for the waterwheel situated nearby, was a Carmelite virgin, protector of shipwrecked sailors and the men who travelled downriver to the sea accompanying their cargo of floating timber (expeditions known as *almadías*). The Lesser Friars settled in a chapel in Rocaforte, which was still standing and the subject of many legends. Almost all the Franciscan chroniclers insisted on the belief that it had been founded by St Francis of Assisi himself, and that he conferred miraculous powers on the wood of a mulberry bush which cured the fainthearted and on the water of a fountain which worked wonders with women in labour. In the interests of safety the Carmelites and Franciscans soon moved their monasteries to the new Sangüesa, in which the Dominicans and Mercedarios had also founded theirs.

The four monasteries became part of a new quarter, known as La Población, which had extended beyond the limits of the city walls in the second half of the XIIIth century to almost double the size of the original town. The church of San Salvador was built for its inhabitants. In the battles which resulted from the worsening relations with Aragón Sangüesa gained the motto "The city which never failed" on its coat of arms, and the situation made it necessary to build a second line of defensive walls in the XIVth century and fortify the towers of Santiago and Santa María. The Renaissance building which housed the Grammar School, still stands in a street in the quarter of La Población; this educational establishment, already famous throughout the kingdom in the mid-XIVth century, had a monopoly of education in the whole area until new laws were introduced in the XIXth century.

The hermitage of San Zoilo stands in the village of Cáseda. It was built in the first half of the XIVth century.

The end of the Middle Ages and the period up to the French Revolution brought with them a great surge of private building. The numerous noble houses bear witness to the high standards achieved by local craftsmen.

In the XVth century Carlos III 'el Noble' gave orders for changes to be made to the Royal Palace. Sessions of the legislative assembly were held here and the last Navarrese monarchs in their own right, Juan de Albret and Catalina de Foix, frequently stayed here. Their son, Enrique, the last Prince of Viana, was born and baptised here. The town remained loyal to the rightful kings and took part in the uprisings against the invaders from Castille. The walls around the city were pulled down on the orders of Cardinal Cisneros, but the castle was left intact to house the garrison and the walls facing the river were preserved as a defence against flooding. The council of Sangüesa acquired the castle/palace and decided (in 1569) to knock down the south wing, which faced onto the Rúa Mayor, in order to build a new town hall on the site. "Las Arcadas" (the arcade) offer access to what was previously the inner courtyard of the palace and which now serves a multitude of purposes. A detailed reproduction of this town hall, one of the oldest in Navarre, has stood since 1929 at the entrance to the "Pueblo Español" in Barcelona, a collection of the best typical architecture of Spain.

CHAPELS AND HOSPITALS

Vicente Villabriga listed as many as thirty-one chapels in Rocaforte and Sangüesa, and Jimeno Jurío, who is extremely knowledgeable about the religious institutions in Sangüesa, added still more to the list, with information about their history, who they belonged to and the traditions surrounding them. Some of them were the parish churches of villages which have since disappeared. Most fell into disrepair, though efforts at restoration have kept a large number of these chapels in use. In Las Navas, facing towards Aragon, a rustic-looking building contains the Gothic statue of the Virgin of Succour who, tradition has it, appeared above an olive tree to encourage the Christians in their fight against the Saracens. On the road to Sos stands the little Romanesque church of San Adrián de Vadoluengo, previously a Benedictine monastery. San Babil, built under royal protection in 1503, is a basilica to which the seriously ill, some of them bedridden and some even at death's door, came to be anointed with the miraculous oil from the votive lamp. It was a hospital for cholera patients during the epidemic of 1885, during which sixty people from the area died here. Local retired people have taken on the renovation and upkeep of the chapel, one which holds memories for them of an unforgettable date in the calendar of local festivals. The Saint's day (24th of January) was a day of carnival masks, a day for buying fruit trees in the market and for young couples whose parents had promised them in marriage to go and see each other.

The town which grew up on the road to Santiago is today, as it was then, a place which welcomes pilgrims and travellers. No other town in Navarre has so many centres offering assistance to people passing through and there is documentary evidence of more than a dozen different types of hospitals.

A TROUBLED YET HAPPY HISTORY

Sangüesa, though the administrative centre for the surrounding area from the middle of the XIIIth century and a town with a seat in the Parliament of Navarre, did not receive the title of city until 1665, and it only achieved this by arguing the merits of its historical past and paying 6,500 silver ducats.

The people of Sangüesa shed their blood in more recent wars, and the armies, with their demands for food supplies, ruined the borough and looted its artistic heritage. The livestock of a farming village could be requisitioned on the spot.

However the greatest nightmare for the people of Sangüesa, until the building of the Yesa reservoir in 1959 controlled the waters of the river Aragon, was flash flooding. There are accounts of various such events in the Middle Ages, shocking reports of others in more recent times and photographs of the floods which have occurred in this century. None, however, was as catastrophic as the flood of 25th September 1787, described in several apocalyptic accounts which have survived to this day: "Some made holes in the dividing walls in order to get into other houses which they thought might be safer, while others climbed through windows or over roofs. It rained and there were continuous thunderclaps. Many had the great misfortune to be buried in the ruins of houses to which they had run for shelter and which collapsed." 665 people died, the crops were washed away and 2,000 people were left destitute. Out of a total of 485 houses, only 39 were left standing.

The river, then, brought both prosperity and ruin. The mountain of Arangoiz was also a mixed blessing, because as well as overlooking the city and thus contributing to its defence, it also channelled the raging waters towards the houses. There was a plan to move the city to the El Real plain, a much safer place, but money

The artist Leodegario left his mark in Latin on the lower part of the façade of Santa María, on a book held by the Virgin Mary: Leodegarius me fecit

was not available and the plan was never carried out. The people did what they could: they built defences and in 1892 they knocked down the three central arches of the stone bridge and replaced them with a metal bridge spanning sixty metres.

September brings with it the lively festivities which have always helped the people of Sangüesa to forget the problems of the rest of the year. Music plays an important part. Groups of singers and musicians spring up and there is a long line of local composers, of whom the most famous is Juan Francés de Iribarren, the Baroque composer of thousands of religious "Cantadas" which can be heard in the best concert halls in Europe and America.

Christmas is increasingly a focus for consumerism and little else, but it is still possible to find the traditional flavour of the season in Sangüesa. There is Franciscan simplicity and popular feeling in the "Three Kings Mystery Play", a religious verse play written in 1900 by the capuchin, José de Legarda. On the 6th January every year the dawn chorus greets the arrival of the Three Wise Men who arrive on horseback from the East, voice their anger at Herod, and join with the shepherds in worshipping the Christ Child.

Details from the façade of Santa María. The gaunt figures at the top represent a sculpted bestiary and occupations and legends from Nordic tradition.

A CITY OF MONUMENTS

Some travellers will never forget the impression produced by a thoughtful examination of the great gate of Santa María and this makes them want to return to admire it again. For example Cees Nooteboom, the great Dutch writer, in his "Detour to Santiago":

"My admiration for Romanesque art didn't happen just like that. My interest was captured by Vézelay and Conques, by Maastricht and Sangüesa. This is the first great European art since the classical period, radiating its own character and cosmic vision, and so totally linked to what people thought and believed that you could say that here it has become a stone image of the world itself.

Once, perhaps twenty years ago, I was in Sangüesa. I even wrote an article which I now cannot find. Memory has reduced this town to the only thing I know Y wish to go back and see: a Romanesque portico in the church of Santa María la Real. You have to stand in the middle of the street to get a good view of the tympanum, but I experienced again the same feeling of ecstasy.

Whether I believe or not is of no importance: to the man who chiselled this dead stone into living, flowing, moving, lines it was as obvious what it represented as wars, illness and change are obvious to me today. My understanding means that this is a world to which I still belong."

Santa María was built in several stages. The XIIth century apses and the portico, built at the beginning of the XIIIth, are in the Romanesque style. Well into the XIIIth century the naves were covered with Gothic cross ribs and a slender lantern. The XIVth century saw the erection of the last section of its crenelated tower with its pyramid shaped steeple.

The portico occupies the whole facade with sculptures of great quality. It is in two sections as a result of there being originally two different doorways designed by two different people. The upper part is the work of San Juan de la Peña, while, in the lower section, the artist Leodegario left his signature in a book held by the Virgin: *Leodegarius me fecit*. In the upper frieze the Majesty of the Lord, surrounded by the symbols of the four evangelists, stands over a double arch which shelters the apostles. The entrance is flanked by three pairs of finely worked sculptures, has a scene from the Last Judgement in the tympanum while the upper right shows an episode from a Norse legend, which also appears in churches in Norway: Regin, the blacksmith forges the sword with which Sirgud will kill the dragon Fafner.

Inside, the main silver-plated altarpiece with its Gothic image of Santa María de Rocamador, dating from the end of the XIIIth century, is remarkable for its colour and size. The church also has a processional monstrance from the XIVth century, a masterpiece from the workshops of local silversmiths, designed as a model of a Gothic building.

In a town on the Pilgrims Way the church of Santiago (St. James) is of great importance. The influence of the Pilgrims Way on the church is apparent, both in the oldest Romanesque features which link it with the cathedral in Jaca and the development of the building itself, which marks the first hesitant steps towards the Gothic style. Two stone images show the saint as a pilgrim: one Gothic monument is inside the church while the other, polychrome, presides over the tympanum in the entrance. There are two beautiful altarpieces linked with well established guilds: that of San Eloy,

patron saint of silversmiths, holds paintings from the XVIth century, and from his Baroque chapel, San Román still blesses the albeit dwindling number of market gardeners.

The entrance to the gothic church of San Salvador, dating from the end of the XIIth century, shows clear signs of the modifications carried out at the beginning of the XVIth. At that time the irregular portico with its high vault was built to protect the facade. The tympanum of the doorway shows Christ in his majesty, with the wounds of His Passion. He stands in judgement over all of humanity, depicted on the lintel awaiting their sentence. On the left, the dead arise from their graves, and on the right demons throw the condemned into the furnace and jaws of the infernal dragon. Inside the church is the chapel of San Sebastián, patron saint of the city, a Gothic stone side chapel, a Romance altarpiece with first-class carvings, another with Gothic Hispano-Flemish paintings and an organ box from the XVIth century, the oldest still existing in Navarre.

Of the four mediaeval convents, only two have survived. Their churches, with a single nave, and their twin Gothic cloisters with pointed, trilobite arches follow the conventional model established in the XIIIth century by the mendicant orders. The Franciscan cloister contains a collection of disc-shaped gravestones. The Carmen convent has now become the Music School. The cloister is a wonderful museum where the machinery from old clock towers is carefully preserved, and in summer it is also the setting for mediaeval banquets which provide the opportunity to taste the gastronomic delights recovered, *cum mica salis,* from old menus by chefs and pastry cooks from Sangüesa.

The list of palaces and noble houses dating from the XVth to the XVIIth centuries is extensive and includes Gothic, Renaissance and Baroque styles. The building style consists of stone masonry on the ground floor and clad brickwork upstairs, a coat of arms on the front of the main floor and the arches which decorate the windows of granaries at the top. The Palace of Vallesantoro, now the Casa de Cultura, has features of Colonial American art added to its original Baroque style. The façade with its Solomonic columns and a spectacular wooden eave with thirteen protruding corbels carved with human heads, fantastic animals, Indians, grotesque figures and exotic flowers. The three floors of the building are arranged around an interior staircase with a beautiful balustrade.

The *Valle de Orba* (Valley of Orba), remote and sparsely populated, is an old and noble valley, as witnessed by the hundreds of coats of arms engraved on its palaces and stone houses. It contains superb examples of Romanesque art, has many villages with Basque names, and has seen its harsh surroundings returned to their natural state as a result of the exodus from the countryside. There are two Natural Reserves in the Valdorba, an area which becomes a botanical garden every Spring in a blaze of orchids and honeysuckle.

VALDORBA

Rural Romanesque in Mediterranean woodland

The Valdorba is the southernmost valley in Navarre, and we can distinguish two main parts. To the west, the flat Valdorba where roads between Pamplona and the south run, an area which was defended from castles and strategic sites and witnessed many battles and ambushes. Then there is the hilly Valdorba, a extensive and remote area which silently hides a rich historical heritage among its hillsides: over twenty forgotten hamlets along the modest river Cidacos. Its Romanesque churches, houses with coats of arms, Gothic palaces and Mediaeval bridges have seen the emigration of a large majority of the population, people who only return to what are now their second residences at the weekends and on holidays. In just 15 years, from 1960 to 1975, the village of Leoz lost 73 per cent of its population. As the poet Angel Urrutia wrote: "Valdorba ... a plain and hills… an age of silent stones grows there."

The exodus from the countryside has occurred not only in recent times. In the Middle Ages there was constant emigration southwards by the dispossessed people of the valley. A stable population was only achieved towards the end of the XVIIIth century, because agricultural poverty was offset by a relatively large variety of resources: livestock, forestry and firewood, and because the relative isolation of the area kept its people free from major epidemics.

The Valdorba had been populated since prehistoric times, as many remains show. A Roman road crossed the central area of Navarre at the southern end of the valley and there were many Roman farms and settlements. The hamlets of the area are very ancient, dating back to the Early Middle Ages. In the IXth century fortresses were built against the Muslim invasion, the first being the stronghold on top of the hill at Pueyo. Near Unzué stood the castle of Guerga, from where the whole valley was governed in the early Middle Ages. During the Civil War which split Navarre in two in the XVth century, all the villages of the valley were on the side of the Agramonts. People became poorer and the situation worsened, sixty four families and five villages disappearing in the process. In the XIXth century the Valdorba was the scene of four wars. The people rose up against the French and young men joined the guerrilla groups of Javier Mina and his uncle Francisco Espoz y Mina, taking part in several ambushes at the pass of El Carrascal. On 4th October 1822 the Royal *Junta* watched the victory of their troops over the Liberals in the decisive battle of Barasoain from the heights of San Pelayo. Of the two Carlist Wars, the second was the most devastating for the valley because the military commanders were particularly vicious against the civil population. Cruchaga says that "although the wounds have healed over one hundred years, bits of shrapnel can still be seen on the *Peña* (rock outcrop) of Unzué."

History has been hard on the Valdorba. In this hidden land certain social and cultural systems emerged which are now only studied by ethnographers. José de Cruchaga y Purroy wrote of what has disappeared for ever in his interesting book *La vida en el Valle de Orba* ('Life in the Valdorba'). He points out that the valley suf-

fered another painful mutilation a hundred years before the exodus: the loss of the Basque language, which was maintained for centuries in the northern part of the area. Prince Louis Bonaparte, who passed through the Valdorba, published a map of the Basque language in the area in 1863, with only a minority of people in nine hamlets still speaking the language. "These people —wrote Cruchaga en 1977— changed their language a hundred years ago. With the disappearance of Basque a whole series of legends and traditions were also lost ... the translation of Basque into a Romance language is very difficult, especially when dealing with spiritual concepts, indeed it is often impossible."

The historical and geographical area of the Valdorba has never been an administrative entity. Its 209 square kilometres were divided into seven municipalities in the middle of the XIXth century. Nevertheless, since the XIVth century, when King Carlos II created the *Merindad* (county) of Olite, three separate entities were distinguishable: The Valle de Orba, Leozarana and Pueyo. Administratively, the Valdorba has also been divided into four *cendeas* (administrative grouping of villages): Basondoa (or Barendoa), Marquesado, Leozarana and Barasoain. The Sanctuary of Catalain was a secular meeting place between the governors and the clergy of the Archbishopric. Nowadays, during the *romería* (popular pilgrimage) in September, it is used to celebrate the 'Day of the Valley' and revive the traditional bar-throwing games of the adults, 'la calba' and 'la barra'.

Caro Baroja writes that "the Valdorba is a land steeped in nobility", the seat of important families. There are about a dozen Late Gothic (early XVIth century) buildings in a similar number of villages, the so-called 'palacios de cabo de armería'. In a compilation of noble properties published at the beginning of the XVIIIth century there are drawings of over one hundred coats of arms. Society was not equal: the palace owners had special seats in the churches and at official ceremonies and they did not have to pay dues, which were passed on to the peasants. The people of the Valdorba, however, while accepting their unequal situation, did not tolerate excessive abuse. They would appeal and stand up for their rights when required.

The Renaissance palace which was the home of the most famous *valdorbés*, Martín de Azpilicueta ('the Doctor of Navarre') still stands in the village of Barasoain. He was a canonist and Professor at Salamanca and Coimbra, and was also the uncle of San Francisco Javier. He lived during a difficult era, that of the conquest of Navarre by Castile which meant the loss of Navarre's independence and its integration into Spain. A jurist of international renown, he avoided the subject of the legitimacy of the manner in which the Spanish monarchs had obtained Navarre. A descendant of the Agramont family which had suffered in exile, his writings and work attempted to help in calming things down and mentally preparing people for the fact that the Kingdom of Navarre would not be returned. Other notable people from the Valdorba were Martín de Ursúa y Arizmendi, an officer in the armies of Felipe III and Felipe IV who became Governor of Yucatán (Mexico) and freed the area from piracy, and José Julián de Aranguren, of Barasoain, Archbishop of Manila in the XIXth century. The popular musician Manuel Turrillas was also born in Barasoain. He is the author of most of the

[PREVIOUS PAGE] *In Catalain the first striking thing is the facade: the belfry on top, divided into three round spans, and the front in a projection of the wall.*

songs and dances that liven up the streets of Pamplona in the festivities of San Fermín.

THE LANDSCAPE

To the north, the mountain ranges of Alaiz and Izco act as a climatic barrier, holding back the rain clouds from the Atlantic. All the Valdorba, except for the sources of its streams, has a Mediterranean climate with cereal fields, some vineyards, and olive groves. Demographic pressure led to over-ploughing of the land. The countryside of the hills of the Valdorba is very similar to the *bocage* of the Mediterranean: small areas of cropland surrounded by copses or (as they are called here) *cerradas*, tiny terraced hillside plots surrounded by stone walls. What was initially a means of survival eventually brought serious problems. Rainwater washed away the earth on the steeper slopes and with it the few fertilisers available, the abandoned fields now being called *llecos* or *faitíos*. The soil is highly eroded and evolves towards natural pasture which becomes increasingly poor, because sheep only like eating some the plant species. These then disappear and others emerge in their place. Lavender, thyme and gorse grow in these pasturelands, and orchids are abundant in the Spring.

Animal husbandry was the complement to a mixed economy. Even today there are *facerías* (pastures) which are common land, where sheep, goats and cattle graze. The Garinoain ram was always

The Romanesque art of the Valdorba is not a catalogue of simple popular art, but a body of fine sculptures and masterpieces.

well-known for its delicate taste. The ilex and oak woods led to much pig rearing activity. In his book *Historia Valdorbesa* Francisco de Olcoz y Ojer refers to an agreement reached in 1643 whereby the village of Olleta rented hill pastures for an unlimited number of pigs until the day of the 'Circumcision of the Lord' to a person from Ibarrola, in Lower Navarre (the area to the north of the Pyrenees which is now French territory). The transhumance of pigs across the Pyrenees is thus documented in Navarre. One activity which has increased rather than decreased since the days of exodus from the land is the practice of bee-keeping.

The Valdorba is a paradise for botanists and ornithologists. There are some areas which have a special natural value: the sources and banks of the rivers, the holm oak grove of El Carrascal and the two Natural Reserves of Monte de Olleta and Monte del Conde.

The headwaters of the Arlusia stream at Unzué are situated in a beautiful beech wood. A dam has been built across the river Mairaga to provide water to thirteen villages. Plantations of Monterrey pine (*pinus insignus*) dotted with gall oak cover the nearby slopes and the wire fencing has become the backdrop for a 'carpet' of brambles, clematises and wild roses. The upper reaches of the river Leoz are located among beech and oak groves, an area which has always been used for hunting. Nowadays only boar are hunted, although wolves, deer and roebucks were fair game until well into the XIXth century. The Fountain of the *Tercianas* springs forth in the same wood, and legend has it that it cures fevers. It is not the only medicinal fountain in the Valdorba. The Fountain of Yesal in Solchaga was usually visited on the day of San Juan (Midsummer Night) at dawn, because the water was not only good for the kidneys and stomachs of horses, but also excellent for cooking chick-peas and beans. Finally, the legend says that anyone who drank the water and washed their face in it would not feel sleepy for a whole year.

The El Carrascal pass (at the north-west end of the Valdorba) is the gap between the Perdón and Alaiz mountain ranges where the road to Pamplona runs through. It is called 'carrascal' because it has always been covered by a dense wood of ilex (kermes oak). The area was devastated during the last Carlist War, and what can be seen today is no more than a remnant of the woodland which once covered the whole of central Navarre. It has a rich undergrowth of box trees, juniper and kermes oak, even thicker since the traditional activities of acorns for livestock, firewood, charcoal and tannin (from bark) were abandoned. In geological terms El Carrascal is a glacis, i.e. a gently inclined plain. The Arlusia and Mairaga rivers have left a deposit of red earth and stones of unequal size and shape. These short, torrential streams did not have enough course, strength or flow to round off sharp stones through erosion. The materials deposited reach a depth of up to seven thousand metres.

There is a small crypt at Orisoain. Access to the church is through a simple but beautiful Romanesque entrance.

The river Cidacos runs north-south through a landscape of Mediterranean crops. It runs low in summer, but livens up in the winter and overflows its banks about ten times a year. To the east, it collects water from streams and gullies running down from the hills. There is a small gully called Linares, which evokes textile crops: flax grows spontaneously along its banks, and also black poplars and willows. On the earthy banks of the gully the striking bee-eaters make their nests. It does not run dry in a normal summer, but holds freshwater fish and is visited by green frogs and water snakes.

The Natural Reserve of Monte Olleta is located below the Linares gully. On its south-east slope and river bed it covers 28 hectares, mainly consisting of conglomerates and sandstone. It is a well-preserved gall oak wood which also contains stripped oak, maple, service trees, privet and kermes oak among the rocky ledges, and scrubland of gorse, thyme and different types of honeysuckle. The population of birds of prey is high: Egyptian vulture, eagle owl, kestrel, goshawk, sparrow hawk, black and red kite, booted eagle and buzzard. Among the mammals found here are genet, marten, wild cat and boar.

The Natural Reserve of Monte del Conde, located in a shady spot at Sansoain to the south of the farmhouse of Musquiliberri, has the symbolic value of being the first Nature Reserve in Navarre (in 1971) through the initiative of its owner, the Marqués de la Real Defensa. One of the best-preserved Mediterranean woods in our Community, it covers 130 hectares with well-structured masses of kermes and gall oak groves in the deeper, fresher soils of the lower areas. There are also maple trees, and (among the bushes) white beam, kermes oak, juniper, savin, box and honeysuckle. Beautiful primroses, daffodils, orchids and irises flower here. The owner's decision not to cut down vegetation has saved this natural remnant, whose firewood was always much sought-after. Ilex is suitable for burning, and particularly good for charcoal. The remains of up to twenty charcoal 'mines' can be seen around the Reserve. The paths there were traced by shepherds, woodcutters and charcoal burners. Charcoal burning as such ended in the last century, although not the *leñateros*, who exploited scrubland such as kermes oak until 1955. Animal life is very much present in Monte del Conde. From the road you can hear birds singing and watch the struggles and flights of the warlike birds of prey. When evening falls, the two-toned call of the owl can also be heard. Among the birds of prey in the Reserve are short-toed eagle, booted eagle, kite and hobby hawk. Reptiles include snakes and lizards, and other mammals such as genet, marten, dormouse, fox and boar are also present in abundance.

Next to the Reserve of Monte del Conde is the *Coto de Caza* (Hunting Reserve) of the Valdorba, established in 1986 and visited by hunters from all over Spain almost all year round. They are attracted by the game released every week which is easy to hunt. For example, over 20,000 pheasants are released every year. This has led to four times the previous number of foxes in the area and has stimulated the appetite of the birds of prey there, many of which have been shot down by rather ignorant hunters.

FIVE JEWELS OF RURAL ROMANESQUE ART

Of the twenty-four Parish Churches in the Valdorba, all are of Mediaeval except that of Echagüe (XVIIth century). Five are Romanesque, two Late Romanesque, seven Proto-Gothic, five Gothic and one Gothic-Renaissance. Many have been considerably modified over the centuries, although without destroying their original identity. Around 1200, during the prosperous times of the reign of King Sancho VII ('el Fuerte'), work was started on nine parish churches. Mediaeval religious architecture, however, also covers buildings which were always hermitages or parish

Near Olóriz. All the Valdorba, except the heads of its streams, has a Mediterranean climate and landscape. Stretches of shrubs can be found among ploughed fields.

churches of villages which have since disappeared and remain as a testimonial presence in isolated places.

The densest concentration of Romanesque architecture in Navarre is found in the Valdorba. Surprisingly, however, it is not just a case of simple popular art, but of true masterpieces. The teams that worked on the construction of large monuments also left their mark in small villages. The sculptor from the village of Echano surely had the Cathedral at Jaca in mind, or perhaps the beautiful façade of Uncastillo also evoked its forms but interpreted them in a more personal way.

The oldest building of the whole group was the large *caserío* (farmhouse) of Eristain (the people of the Valdorba now call it 'Tristain'), the heir of a Roman villa. It is a small church dedicated to St. John the Baptist. According to Clara Fernández-Ladreda, "the rectangular nave may correspond to a Pre-Romanesque structure from the Xth century. This hypothesis is backed up by a Roman funeral inscription in the foundations, the bond of relatively large ashlars (keystones) joined together and, above all, the door (now hidden from sight) of the western front, which used to be a horseshoe arch, although the stones were scraped to form a semicircular arch." The bond of the apse is different, small ashlar joined by lime mortar. This is surely a case of a later date. The circular shape of the both the exterior and the interior suggests Romanesque, but the total lack of sculpture makes early Romanesque more likely. Strangely, the lintel of the window of the apse is a reused mill wheel. Towards the end of the XIIth century there was a reform which converted the triumphal arch into a pointed one, also incorporating two columns crowned by sculpted capitals. The previous roof of the nave was made of wood, although only a short section has been preserved. The rest of the roof is now of pointed barrel type.

In the restoration, which was finished in 1994, partly lost Gothic murals were discovered with their colours changed. In the vault of the apse there is a Pantocrator with the Tetramorphous accompanied by a cortège of angels. The twelve Apostles are on the walls under arcades which represent Celestial Jerusalem, plus drapes with a two-headed eagle. On the wall over the triumphal arch there is a Crucifixion, a Resurrection, and representations of Heaven and Hell, angels and devils. It is possible that these paintings are contemporary to those of Olleta, dated between 1340 and 1360. Several tombs have been located in the earth, probably of the people who lived in the palace of Eristain. In the church there is a Romanist carving of St. John the Baptist (c. 1600), and a copy of a Romanesque Virgin Mary represented as *Seeds Serpentine*. The original can be seen in the Diocesan Museum of Pamplona. Opposite the church is the Palacio de Cabo de Armería de Eristain, from the XVIth century.

In the municipality of Garinoain the hermitage of the Holy Christ of Catalain is located next to a very old large farmhouse with some Roman remains. It is a simple, splendidly beautiful building from the middle of the XIIth century. It was a *clavería* (treasury) under the collegiate church of Roncesvalles from the start of the XIIIth century to the *Desamortización* of the XIXth century, a place of governors of the valley and the clergy of the Archiprestry, a hospital for pilgrims travelling to Compostela, and the destination of local and major pilgrimages. From a stylistic point of view Catalain belongs to the peak of the Romanesque period and to a very extensive type in Navarre, with a single nave and semicircular apse. The first thing that draws one's attention is the façade: above is the belfry with three round openings, below three small grated windows with their projections, and the façade in a ledge of the wall protected by a slate roof. The door (domed rounded arch) consists of three archivolts with two pairs of columns and capitals representing three lions, three seated persons, three standing figures with birds on either side, and two knights fighting each other. The tympanum is decorated with the three letters of Christ. Only in the apse, with its oven-shaped vault, has the original covering of the building been preserved. In the restoration carried out in 1979 care was therefore taken to build everything new in brick and wood: the cover of the roof and the dome on pendentives, hypothetically imitating what was there before. On the exterior of the apse and the brackets and the cornice which runs round the perimeter of the building there are also interesting sculptures: birds, monstrous figures, whole-bodied animals, heads, embracing couples, musicians, and plant and chess motifs.

The carving of the Christ of Catalain is a crucifix from the first half of the XIVth century. It is completely Gothic, with an expression of pain close to anatomic naturalism, a style which appeared much later. The Romanesque virgin of Catalain is in the Diocesan Museum of Pamplona. The Gothic baptismal font (c. 1300) is appealing, the cylinder-shaped shaft and cup being

The hórreo (granary store) at Iracheta has been carefully restored. According to Uranga and Iñiguez it was built in the IXth century, or the Xth at the latest.

decorated with rich symbols: a star with eight points which dissipates the mists of darkness, interpreted as sin; an eight-spoke wheel, the symbol of regeneration through baptismal waters; a six-petal flower, a figure of Paradise; a fleur de lys, symbol of purity; and between two coats of arms, those of the Houses of Champagne and Roncesvalles.

A few miles further along the road to Catalain you come to the village of Orisoain. Above the village is the church of San Martín, built in the second half of the XIIth century. Its originality lies in the small crypt, located under the presbytery to correct the slope of the land. The vault is supported by thick ribs on short columns with capitals decorated with plants, birds, snakes and angels' heads. The entrance to the church is through a simple and beautiful Romanesque door. Inside, the nave has three arches supported on six large capitals (similar to those in Jaca) with plant scenes and others with fighting animals and Sagittarian Centaurs.

On arriving at Olleta you have the impression of being in an oasis. The parish church of the Assumption is cleverly located between two streams with abundant vegetation and impressive willow trees. You reach it by crossing a delightful Mediaeval bridge. The church (second half of the XIIth century) seems to be based on Catalain, although its square tower is different. The entrance is through a door with a rounded arch with tympanum and the three letters of Christ. Inside there is a single nave, a semicircular nave, and the structure of a dome on pendentives with a hexagonal base which is gradually rounded until it ends in a small lantern added during a reformation in the XVIIth century. There are eight large capitals, some of them with plant themes and others representing men prepared for war. The figures in the angles carry bags around their necks, which is how misers are characterised in Romanesque art. The church at Olleta was completely decorated with Gothic *al fresco* murals which are now in the Museum of Navarre. They are two superimposed cycles, the oldest corresponding to the middle of the XIVth century and related to the cycle of Maestro Roque de Artajona. The second cycle (end of the XVth century) belongs to a highly popular Spanish-Flemish style. The church contains a Gothic image of the Virgin Mary from the XIIIth century. In the village there is another place of interest to visit: on the track leading to the *Fuente del Caño* (Fountain of the Spout) there is a monolithic Cross-Calvary with sculpted details of the Passion of Christ and an apocalyptic skeleton with the tibia and perone crossed. It is the work of a popular mason of the end of the XIXth century.

In the village of Oloriz, between kermes and other oaks on the banks of the Mairaga stream, there is an unsurpassable example of simple beauty and harmony, the hermitage of San Pedro ad Vincula (the church was initially dedicated to Santa María) at Echano, a village which has since disappeared. It was built towards the end of the XIIth century. When observed from a distance, the belfry is a graceful spire pointing skywards. The decoration sculpted on the north-facing portico is the most interesting part of the hermitage. It is the work of an anonymous craftsman who worked with Maestro San Martín de Artaiz, the archetype of all rural Romanesque architects in Navarre, and with the creator of the portico of Santa María de Uncastillo. The domed door has seven archivolts. In the centre, twenty-six carved figures attend a Mediaeval charitable get-together. Some of them play flute and tuba. They are all seated with their hands on armchairs or the tablecloth, and below their legs (seen under the table) it is clear that two are crippled because they have wooden prostheses. Julio Caro Baroja tells us that "musicians and minstrels livened up celebrations in the distant past. Sometime they were crippled, people on the payroll who could not do other work. The 'lame' musicians shown in the hermitage at Echano illustrate many Mediaeval texts very well." Agustín Gómez Gómez has studied the iconography of this façade in depth. Regarding the musicians with their left leg amputated and the right on a wooden leg, he states that this type of prosthesis does not appear in other images in Spain, although it is found to the north of the Pyrenees. He points out that most of the diners have long, loose hair and unkempt beards, and concludes that they "are characters which were identified in the Middle Ages with poor, miserable, excluded people... the façade shows a groups of poor people with no other narrative reference but themselves. The poor become a subject in their own right." These figures evoke the parable of the discourteous guests from the Gospel.

This Asturian-influenced *hórreo* (granary) is a singular work of art in the Valle de Orba.

Uranga and Iñiguez say that it "survived through luck, its good construction, and its exceptional interest, based on the fact that both here and in other areas where *hórreos* have been preserved (Asturias, Galicia, Navarre Oriental, Aragón or Ribagorza) there is no other dating so far back, around the IXth century or the Xth at the latest. This date is based on the arrangement of irregular but well-carved stones, similar to those found in Asturias. The influence of Asturias was felt in the art of the time as a result of the arrival in Navarre of people loyal to the Asturian kings Alfonso III and Ordoño II, both of them married to princesses from Navarre. If this theory is to be accepted we are talking about a Pre-Romanesque monument. Other art historians say that it was built in the Romanesque period (end of the XIth century or the start of the XIIth). It is difficult to establish a date, however, because its utilitarian nature means that it does not have decorative elements. From documents, we know that the granary first belonged to the Monastery of Irache, then to the Crown until 1187, when it came under the Order of St. John of Jerusalem, where it remained for the whole of the XIIIth century. Its use as a parish granary is also documented, covering the period from the XVIIth century until our era.

The building has been carefully restored. It is rectangular in shape and has a gable roof made from slabs. The only things that were changed are the eaves and the door, both made larger at an uncertain date although quite late, perhaps in the XVIth century. The stone is well carved, with strong corners. The ground floor is bright: it opens out through three rounded arches on the longer sides and two arches on the shorter sides, on pillars. The upper and ground floors are supported on these pillars, and only have three grated windows for illumination and ventilation. The top floor is reached via a stone staircase separated from the main part of the building in order to stop rodents entering. Access from the top floor to the interior is via a door with a rounded arch.

At the gateway to a range of hills, situated on a platform that opens out onto the plain, Olite etches its Gothic profile of elegant, high palatial towers and an even higher and daring arrow of stone. Roman and mediaeval walls squeeze together to form a double boundary that surrounds a well-planned layout of streets and squares together with fine, carefully finished monuments. Outside the city walls, the long-established vineyards have inspired a flourishing co-operative movement as well as up-to-date grape-growing, wine-making and ageing techniques. This historic town, the ancient seat of the Court of the Kingdom and the Head of a *Merindad* (an ancient administrative division of Navarre), Olite is also the wine capital of the region. The distinguished writer Arturo Campión assures us that "not to know Olite is not to know Navarre."

OLITE
Gothic splendour

The musician from Olite, Jesús García Leoz, composer of the soundtracks of more than eighty films including 'Bienvenido Mister Marshall', one of the best Spanish films ever, carried out his work during the mid-XXth century. At the same time, the architect José Yárnoz was directing the restoration work on the Royal Palace based on historically accurate criteria, making it a fabulous stage for reliving and filming mediaeval sequences.

The castle, completely burnt down and demolished during the wars against the French, was regarded by romantics as a glorious ruin. In 1866, Gustavo Adolfo Bécquer wrote in his Traveller's Notes: "Today it is difficult to make out the precise design of this construction. Only isolated walls covered in moss and ivy remain, together with the odd tower and some foundations in ruins." The famous poet from Seville penned a reconstruction of the ruined walls and imagined them thus: "the drawbridge creaks, the battlements are crowned with crossbowmen, in the silent courtyards one can once again hear the cheerful racket of the licentious pages, the coarse men-at-arms and the plebeians of the castle as they train the goshawks to fly, leash their dogs or draw their horses to a halt."

In 1870, Juan Iturralde y Suit criticised the negligent state of the ruins and chided the people: "The splendid abode of Carlos el Noble is in ruins. Venerable ruins! You have never been a threat to the people, just their aegis. You do not symbolise oppression and tyranny, just the greatness of the Navarrese people who have known how to maintain their independence throughout the centuries. People who regard the monuments of their past glories with indifference are not worthy of occupying a place in history."

This XVIIIth century fervour had documented foundations and tradition. Mention was made of an old castle at Olite in the XIIth century. At that time it only occupied the area that is today the site of the *Parador*, and was called the Palace of the King of Navarre. It was the grandiose construction work carried out during the first third of the XVth century that inspired an anonymous German traveller who visited it around 1442 to write: "I am sure that there is no other King who has a more beautiful palace or castle, with so many gilded rooms. I saw it very well. One cannot express or even imagine how magnificent and lavish it is."

The monarchs chose an ideal site for their Court: in the centre of the Kingdom with good communications, fertile land, a medium-sized population, a sunny climate and a plentiful supply of game in the surrounding area. The ambitious project, put forward by Queen Leonor, was carried out on a lofty scale by King Carlos III. Both King and Queen were directly involved in the construction work. They gathered a great deal of information on contemporary developments in France and Castile and produced sketches. They personally drew up the programme and selected the most highly-qualified artists and craftsmen to carry out the work.

The work was carried out non-stop and did not even pause on Sunday, because among the tradesmen there were Christians, Jews and Moslems alike, all of whom took their day of rest on a different day of the week. The first work on the so-called 'Queen's Palace' with its delicate Gallery and the *Jardín de los Toronjales* (orange tree garden), was followed by the construction of a central prismatic body, where the *Gran Torre* (Great Tower) and the *Galería Dorada* (Gilded Gallery) were located, together with a south wing including a large fortified lookout tower open to the four winds, and another tower, the *Torre de la Atalaya*. Carlos III himself christened this last tower 'Joyosa Garda' ('Bright Guardhouse'). In fact, all the elevations of the building have their own names, such as *Torre de las Cigüeñas* (Stork's Tower), *Torre de la Prisión* (Prison Tower), *de Ochavada* (Octagonal) or *de las Tres Coronas* (Three Crowns), *de la Vit* (Vine), *del Aljibe* (Dungeon), *del Retrait* (Retreat) or *de las Tres grandes finestras* (three large windows). The watchtowers that give out onto the square have been restored with conical roofs based on old plans of the castle at Tiebas. Some of the castle walls, which now have battlements, were covered arcades.

More than a mediaeval fortress, the building was a Gothic palace bathed in light that filtered through its large openworked windows. It was finished in brick, decorated with fine tiles and set with plaster, had panelled roofing, was painted in gold and silver and was paved with cold tiles that were covered with rush mats in the winter. In the courtyards and even in the *Torre de la Fuente* (Fountain Tower), there were orange trees and hanging gardens. In one courtyard, to which it gives its name, the stump of a five-hundred-year-old white mulberry tree still remains. It is listed, and the object of very special care; it still blooms and gives fruit every year. There was also once a large aviary and a small zoo with exotic creatures such as swans, ostriches, lions and camels. Greyhounds were kept for hunting and goshawks and falcons were trained for Carlos III's favourite sport, falconry. Delicate fruit for the royal table was harvested in the nearby gardens and kitchen gardens: lemons, oranges, strawberries and early morello cherries. The King took great care of his wine cellar, which is still well preserved today, where rosé wines, spirits and also *verjus* (a wine made from sour grapes used for cooking) were made.

At Olite, annual festivals, family events, visits or the reunion of the Court, or *Estamentos* (the estates into which the Court was divided), were celebrations with great pomp and circumstance. Carlos III had a choir with portable organs and dozen precentors, mainly laymen. Tournaments and bullfights were also staged in the square. The King liked to make gestures to the people: he would lay his hands on the sick, who trusted his curative powers as he had been anointed with consecrated oil. On Maundy Thursday he would wash their feet and give alms to thirteen poor folk. His kindest act, however, occurred every 6th January at Epiphany, with the feast of 'Rey de la faba' at which a child chosen from among the humble families became 'King for a Day'. The spirit of that Yuletide festival has been revived on a travelling basis thanks to the interest shown by the *Muthiko Alaiak* Society of Pamplona.

A TOUR OF THE MONUMENTS OF OLITE

In 1932, José María Iribarren drew a literary picture of the city in the autumn light: "Olite is a city of stone, of regal stone. The stone of the big rambling ancestral homes, of the marvellous coats of arms,

[PREVIOUS PAGE] *A stone Apostolate on the façade of Santa María de Olite.*

The church of San Pedro has a paired-column cloister on its north side.

the city walls and the porches of the square. But in Olite, the heart of Navarre and the transition point from the mountainous north to the *Ribera*, houses built from brown Aragonese brick with arched verandas under panelled eaves stand alongside stone houses with monumental doors and wide voussoirs. How enchanting are these long streets with a Gothic arch at the end! Looking out from the balustrade of the church of San Pedro, a beautiful tower pierces the sky with its French octagonal stone spire, and Olite is a patchwork of roofs. How small the square looks from this Olympian height! Around this isolated sunny square and the Castle, the history of Navarre unfolds in the blue of deep waters, of luminous pleats."

The agricultural village was transformed by gradual repopulation and the concession of the *Fuero de Estella* in 1147. Work on the church of San Pedro was initiated on the site of the old parish church at the end of the XIIth century. The church has long since lost its original front, but it has retained its elegant, sober Romanesque façade portraying scenes of the life of St. Peter. There is an adjoining cloister with pairs of columns on the northern side of the church. A Gothic tower forms the platform to support the 21-metre XIVth-century octagonal spire. Inside, there is a magnificent Gothic figure of St. James, and in the sepulchre, also Gothic, there is a polychrome alabaster relief representing the Holy Trinity. In Pamplona the Museum of Navarre houses a collection of XIIIth-century Gothic mural paintings from the belfry of the church.

In spite of the fact that it is next to the Palace, the Gothic church of Santa María was not the Royal Chapel, although it was used for certain occasions such as that of the marriage of the Prince of Viana to Inés of Cleves. The construction work, which started in the XIIIth century, was not completed until the late XIVth century when the façade was finished. It is formed by a large window, a frieze of arches each housing a stone Apostle, and a door decorated with plant motifs designed to draw the eye towards a tympanum holding the Virgin Mary seated under a canopy. In front of the façade there is a three-sided open cloister. The building contains a Renaissance altarpiece by the Aragonese painter Pedro de Aponte, with panels dating from around the year 1515. The XIVth-century figure of the Virgin Mary presides over the church and is a contemporary of the dramatic *Cristo de la Buena Muerte*, to whom the city dedicates its local festival in September.

Olite began its expansion on a large scale from the XIIIth century onwards, when neighbourhoods grew up outside the city walls. They join together on both sides of the Rúa Mayor from the Capital Tower, and are surrounded by the new outer city wall. The XVIIIth-century convent churches of San Francisco and Santa Clara are worth visiting for the sculptures housed within. The XXth century has also given Olite some interesting architectural

The castle at Olite has a Gothic profile of elegant palatial towers.

works. The City Hall, inaugurated in 1950, was designed by Victor Eusa and reproduces the style of other noble houses of the city. It combines stone on the two first storeys with brick on the third floor and for the small arches of the top floor. A classic pediment supports a clock over the projecting eaves. The Health Centre is the work of Fernando Tabuenca and Ignacio San Juan. It has two floors, each used for a very different purpose, and with its cornice it equals the height of the rest of the buildings in the block. The high vestibule with its zenith lighting separates its functions, and the waiting areas open out onto a courtyard with gardens. On the lower floor, the use of brick highlights the horizontal forms which compete with the vertical carpentry of the upper floor.

The award-winning architect Francisco Mangado has designed three different types of building work in Olite. They combine a reflection on space and form with an austere, purist style of design. His work in the main square, the *Plaza de Carlos III*, is remarkable. The challenge was to organise and provide an irregular space, give distinction to the castle and provide access to the underground mediaeval galleries that had been recently discovered. As Luis Fernández Galiano says: "In this dialogue with history, Mangado lays a carpet of stone on which he positions an urban still life of objects that have been found. There is 'land art' at both ends of an avenue flanked by minimalist benches and lamps. A pyramid and a circle made of iron provide a geometrical railed access to the Gothic dungeons, paving spills over into steps like a surreal mass of ordered lava and a conical fountain evokes the sharp-pointed towers of the magic castle in pop-art style." Using the historical brick façade of the *Casa de los Leones*, built in the second half of the XVIIth century, Mangado and his colleague Alfonso Alzugaray created a new building inside it, destined to be the Cultural Centre of Olite. The staircase, with its zenith lighting both relates and separates the old and new constructions. The third design, a wine cellar in the middle of the plain of vineyards, rises to the challenge of the landscape with a sober box of stone, and the cellar where the wine rests is buried under a great mass of concrete.

THE WINE OF NAVARRE

Vineyards require constant, careful attention, but they reward and remunerate the wine producer who, caught up in a system of agriculture that is becoming more and more competitive and technical, contemplates the whole process and the fruit of his work. There are few happier occasions than the wine harvest, when the grapes reach their exact degree of ripeness.

Navarre has undergone a major process of modernisation of wine production thanks to a combination of factors: the proven quality of its vines, diversity of grape varieties, mechanised harvesting methods, careful wine-making processes, the use of new technologies such as temperature-controlled fermentation, and the opening up of a market that both appreciates and demands quality.

In Navarre the wines are covered by two Regional Denominations: *Rioja* and *Navarra*. The Rioja Designation (DOCa) covers

1,639 wine producers in 8 areas of Navarre, with a total of 4,749 hectares of vines. In 1996 the harvest totalled 30 million kilos of grapes, which were converted into 9 million litres of wine. Almost half of this was labelled and directly marketed by several of the 18 *bodegas* (wineries) that produce the wine.

The Navarra Designation of Origin covers 6,700 wine producers from 103 administrative districts with a total of 12,675 hectares of vines. Red grape varieties dominate: *Garnacha* represents 46% of the total, *Tempranillo* 26%, *Cabernet Sauvignon* 9%, plus a small proportion of *Merlot*, *Mazuelo* and *Graciano*. *Viura* is the most important among the white varieties (8%). There are also smaller plantations of *Chardonnay*, *Moscatel* and *Malvasía*. Ninety-four million kilos of grapes were harvested in 1996, to produce 68

The ancient castle at Olite, referred to in the XIIIth century as "the palace of the King of Navarre", is now a Parador.

million litres of wine: 40 million red, 23 million rosé and 5 million white. The wine was made in 35 co-operative *bodegas*, accounting for more than 75% of total production, and in 29 private *bodegas*. The sale of bottled wine has almost doubled over the last decade and now exceeds 31 million litres, of which two thirds are consumed by the domestic market and the rest is exported, mainly to EU countries. The main markets are UK, Holland, Sweden, Germany and Denmark (in that order). Wine from Navarre has reasserted its tradition of full-bodied reds with a characteristic bouquet and taste.

EVENA, the Viticultural and Œnological Centre of Navarre, is based in Olite. It experiments with different vine-growing and winemaking techniques, and circulates its findings to winemakers. The Centre also advises the Regulatory Boards of the Rioja and Navarra Designations of Origin, carries out analyses and tests, assesses batches of wine sent for quality control, carries out and evaluates programmes, proposes sales norms, keeps the vineyard register up-to-date and supervises methods of transport.

AGRICULTURAL CO-OPERATIVES

Olite is an inevitable reference point in the agricultural history of the region. The growth of the population and the wars in the XIXth century gave rise to the conflict of the *corralizas* (large communal areas of grazing land with corrals). In 1865 the *corraliceros* (owners of the *corralizas* that had once belonged to an administrative district) confronted the *comuneros* (those who believed that the *corralizas* should be communal and owned by the districts). The socialist ideal of free

ploughing of communal land was opposed by the legal offensive of the powerful *corraliceros*. The controversy, which came to a head in 1884 and was rekindled in 1914, caused the loss of several lives. During the years of the Second Republic, the *Unión General de Trabajadores* (UGT) was still demanding the expropriation of 1,524 hectares of land in order to parcel it out.

Olite was also the birthplace of the rural co-operative movement. In 1896, phylloxera was declared in Navarre. This parasitic insect of American origin destroyed all the vineyards, which at that time occupied 42,300 hectares and provided two million *jornales* (working man-days) each year. The moneylenders lent money for replanting and supplies at exorbitant rates of interest. To confront them, the agricultural movement appeared, which was inspired by Catholic Social Doctrine and was backed by the clergy. This movement was doctrinal, politically conservative but advanced, and encouraged co-responsibility regarding social matters, as is expressed by the motto written on the façade of the Olite Co-operative Bodega: *'Unos por otros, Dios por todos'* (One for Others, God for All).

The leaders of that initiative were Antonino Yoldi, a lecturer in Sociology at the Seminary in Pamplona, and Victoriano Flamarique, the Parish Priest of Santa María in Olite, who from 1907 managed to convert the city into a redoubt of co-operative economy with wineries, a flour mill, an electricity production and supply station, a loan bank, and centralised purchasing, marketing and machinery facilities. Yoldi set up a printshop, and when he put forward the idea of a co-operative factory for chemical fertilisers he received strong opposition from private capitalists. This egalitarian spirit was gradually lost as the presence of the landowners in the co-operatives increased, and that of the *jornaleros* (day labourers) decreased. In 1935, the Navarrese Catholic Social Federation grouped together a total of 106 Rural Co-operative Banks. Only the dairy and wine sectors remained strong in the following years.

As the historians Emilio Majuelo and Angel Pascual point out: "(…) a modern style of co-operatives orientated towards business development, representing the strongest organised force in the agricultural sector has stemmed from that agricultural Catholicism that is so deep-rooted in Navarre." In 1995-96, the movement covered 144 co-operatives with 22,923 members and a total turnover of 54.9 billion pesetas. Some co-operatives have various sections. There are 41 registered wine co-operatives, 67 dedicated to herbaceous

crops, 7 to oil production, 38 to horticulture/fruit growing, 2 to dairy production, 3 to livestock and poultry, 3 to animal feed production and 22 to machinery co-operatives.

The Plaza de Navarra, in Tafalla. It covers the area previously occupied by the Royal palace, which was demolished in the mid-XIXth century.

OLITE AND TAFALLA, THE FLOWER OF NAVARRE

This popular saying from the XVIth century reflects the desire of the two towns to be good neighbours despite being rivals throughout history. Tafalla, an industrial and services centre, was favoured by King Carlos III, who had a lavish summer palace there with gardens and fountains. In 1418, he granted it the privilege of celebrating a fair in February, always very busy and still held today.

An ambitious architectural project in the time of Queen Isabel II was carried out on the site of the Royal Palace, which was demolished in the middle of the XIXth century. This was a period of population explosion and new ideas on urbanisation. In 1856, Tafalla City Council commissioned the architect Martín de Saracíbar to design a municipal building, a grain store, butcheries, fishmongers and a marketplace. The artist designed a symmetrical rectangular square, with the City Hall situated in the centre of one of the sides, a design based on the main square of Vitoria. The fountain forms part of the project for the water system drawn up in 1844 by José de Nagusía, the architect and Director of Roads and Water Systems of the Kingdom of Navarre. An obelisk marks the spot and there is a jet in the form of a barrel, a metaphor representing the agricultural wealth of a town that produces quality wines.

The great sculptural treasure of Tafalla is to be found in the church of Santa María. The main Romanesque altarpiece is considered to be the masterpiece of Juan de Anchieta, a sculptor from Guipúzcoa who studied in Italy and came into contact with the finest religious image makers from Valladolid. Anchieta, who donated his work *Santo Cristo del Miserere* to this church, also left important pieces to the Cathedrals of Burgos and Pamplona as well as to the parish churches of Cáseda and Aoiz.

Tafalla is a musical city. The beautiful Baroque organ in the church of Santa María, which had a choir, was used by the great composer of religious music, Felipe Gorriti, between 1858 and 1867. The *Banda de Música*, which celebrated the centenary of its foundation in 1985, dates back to the fourth decade of the XIXth century. This love of music is translated in the form of choral expression and the popularity of the *jota* (traditional Navarrese dance and song). Tafalla has its own school and style of singing *jotas*. Among the records made by *joteros* from Tafalla, those by the quintet 'Los Pajes' and the voices of Juan Navarro and the Flamarique sisters stand out. The most celebrated of all the Navarrese *joteros*, Raimundo Lanas, often alluded to the town and paid compliments to its women in his songs:

> By the way she walks
> and the light in her face
> by the way she loves
> it is obvious that she is from Tafalla.

Pilgrims make their way to the church of Santa María in prayer and song amidst Easter hallelujahs and crosses of penance adorned with poppies and ears of corn. They wear tunics and sometimes walk barefoot or drag chains along. They have continued this ancestral pilgrimage since at least the XIVth century. The Kings of the House of Evreux also went there on foot from their Palace in Olite. The Lagoon at Pitillas is a noisy, lively wetland and is a strategic resting-place for migrating birds.

PILGRIMS TO UJUÉ

It can be seen from a great distance, up there on high. The silhouette of the Sanctuary-Fortress breaks the long straight profile of the mountain plateau like a crest. Whoever contemplates the sight will understand that Ujué did not arise in a convenient spot or a pleasant valley next to an abundant source of water, like so many other villages. On the contrary, it is a vantage point for observation and protection.

"Ujué, lost in solitude, without rivers to refresh it, without trees to shade it... on an immense pedestal of rock, is impregnated with the poetry of memory." This is Juan Iturralde y Suit's romantic vision that cannot ignore the starkness and aridity of the landscape.

The most intensive deforestation took place during the XIXth century, although there are records showing that charcoal and juniper oil were produced and that large quantities of firewood, pine

and oak were taken from the mountainsides during the XVIIIth century. Going up to Ujué along a winding road, the woodland of holm and gall oaks is soon left behind. The slope is a staircase of narrow terraces that were cultivated, even though in some cases it seems hardly possible. These terraces were called *aborrales*, the term given to the land on which livestock was allowed to graze temporarily after harvesting. Modern agricultural machinery does not fit in these tiny inaccessible fields, but there are still some olive trees and vines there as well as a few almond plantations.

Man moulds the landscape and vice versa. For the historian Jimeno Jurío, Ujué, which "still keeps watch from the knoll of its dehydrated, wrinkled skin", has the same austerity as its people, subjected to a life of suffering and deprivation. They were farmers of poor soils, accustomed to strong winds and affected by frequent rockfalls that destroyed the crops, in addition to the epidemics that decimated the population. Time after time they begged their landlords for a reduction in taxes, and this was finally granted. The philosophy of the Kings was to maintain a stable population, the guarantee of strategic defence. But what serves for war and military control is not necessarily the most appropriate as far as civil life is concerned. Ujué, which at the end of the Middle Ages was on the verge of total depopulation, is one of the villages that has lost the greatest number of residents in Navarre over the last century.

[PREVIOUS PAGE] *This shot clearly shows the apses of the church. All art historians relate this church to the front part of the Monastery of Leire, the most outstanding example of early Romanesque in Navarre.*

[ABOVE] *Ujué did not arise on an easy site, but one chosen as an ideal lookout and protection point.*

In addition to having rough uneven land, the municipal district is extensive. It covers 112 square kilometres and descends from the top of the hill range right down to the banks of the river Aragón. The town, situated at a height of 840 metres above sea level, appears as the combination of a multitude of small hamlets, some of which existed in Roman times. A document from the year 1530 sets out the names of 23 deserted places under Ujué's jurisdiction. The hermitage of Santa María la Blanca still stands in one of them, eight kilometres south of the village. Roman votive altar stones have been found there, one of which was dedicated to Jupiter and another to the local god *Lacubegi*. The attractive strength of a large defence tower, which was already in existence in the late Middle Ages, was the reason for such a concentration of population. However, many *Ujuetarras* (the people of Ujué) were accustomed to living in their corrals, dispersed in isolated spots, for a large part of the year.

Ujué is a national monument. The centre still preserves the mediaeval atmosphere and layout with a tortuous map of streets adapted to the slope. The narrow descending streets are crossed by others that form transversal rings. On the corners, which are never uniform, there are narrow and wide places that create surprising perspectives. The tightly packed old houses with their ashlars and the coats of arms that ennoble many facades can be best appreciated from the church on top of the hill.

THE SANCTUARY OF SANTA MARIA

There was once a small pre-Romanesque church that was protected by the castle. According to the IXth-century Islamic chronicle of Al-Himyari, the fortress, the church and the village were placed under the patronage of the Virgin Mary.

Sancho Ramírez, King of Aragon and Navarre, who gave Ujué its *Fueros* (code of laws and privileges) in 1076, proclaimed in 1089: "With full liberty and spontaneity we build the Church of the Mother of God, Santa María de Ujué." This document refers to a Romanesque building with three naves that was demolished in the XIVth century. The sanctuary still remains, together with its semicircular apses. The first body had lateral barrel vaults and a central pointed vault. Art historians compare it to the sanctuary at the monastery of Leire, the pinnacle of early Romanesque style in Navarre. They point out, however, that the fact that it was started 32 years after the monastery was first consecrated resulted in the inclusion of later influences that came from the Pilgrims Way to Santiago de Compostela, from León and Jaca, particularly with reference to the sculpture of the capitals which is schematic but attractive: there are crosses, small roses, racemes, vine leaves and human figures. The Benedictine monk, Luis María de Lojendio, underlines the fact that "the most important feature of Ujué's Romanesque art is without doubt the sculpture. This is not due to the objective value of the coarse primitive decoration of some of the capitals, but the relative value it holds with regard to the evolution of Navarrese art during the second half of the XIth century."

It was in the second half of the XIVth century that Ujué's church acquired its splendid Gothic solemnity, the fruit of an ambitious project of King Carlos II, who visualised a large basilica, a royal residence, a university and a hospital for the poor and pilgrims. The great Gothic nave ended up being positioned slightly to the northeast in relation to the central point of the old church. The construction, inspired by contemporary buildings in the south of France, aimed to achieve a single large space. The three main bodies, built with balanced proportions, reduce the appearance of the enormous 15 metre span, the widest Gothic nave in Navarre. The high vault rests on a fine series of arches supported by columns that are embedded in the walls. The shield of the House of Evreux figures on the keystones of the arches which still bear their original rich colours. The shield portrays a seated Christ giving his blessing, and a relief of the Virgin Mary. The capitals are decorated with plant motifs, hunting scenes, wild animals, fantastic animals and a scene from the Bible: Delilah cutting Samson's hair. The nave also includes an elevated Gothic chancel complete with its Rococo choir stalls and Gothic mural paintings behind the organ.

The main south-facing façade has ten splayed pointed archivolts and a rich range of sculpture. The consoles show warriors fighting lions and dragons symbolising the struggle between vice and virtue, as well as episodes from the life of the Virgin Mary and the childhood of Jesus. The tympanum has two scenes: the lower one portraying the Last Supper complete with cockerel; and the upper one is of the Epiphany with a star overhead and a fourth person dressed in priest's clothing, rendered in a naturalistic style. The figure is kneeling next to the three smiling Kings and some consider him to be King Carlos II, the patron of the work.

The north façade is plainer and has only five archivolts with a labarum instead of a tympanum. The sculpture shows winemaking scenes, some rather indecent nudes and a rudimentary visualisation of the punishment of the Damned: the devils are conveying the souls of the Condemned and the infernal dragon is devouring them.

Santa María de Ujué. Serene and beautiful, sober and inscrutable. An outstanding Romanesque image,

The church was finished around 1376 and resembles a fortress more than a sanctuary, with its crenellated towers, covered passages, buttresses, lookouts and solid square-cut stone construction. The highest tower, which is joined to the sanctuary, is a robust late-Romanesque construction. The other tower is Gothic and has a large elegant window that gives a courtly air to the place. A rampart runs round the whole of the church and on the western side there is a gallery-lookout with a splendid balustrade. The consoles that support the ribs of the vault are sculpted with circus scenes: two men in a hand-to-hand fight, a contortionist and a monkey wearing long robes. The outbuildings of what was once the royal residence built by Carlos II still stand alongside the sanctuary, together with the ruins of a large hall which Carlos II may have intended to be the seat of the projected university. The exterior of the Romanesque apses can be observed in comfort as they are protected by a covered corridor.

Carlos II also built the eastern walls of the hospital that provided shelter for the poor and pilgrims until the mid-XIXth century.

THE LEGEND OF UJUÉ

There is a graphic and phonetic relationship between the place name 'Ujué', or rather its mediaeval forms *Uns, Unse* or *Uxua*, and the Basque word *Uxoa* which means 'dove'. This is the probable link with the legend of the Apparition which, although it is age-old, does not seem to date back any further than the XVIth century. In the middle of the following century, the author of the Annals of the Kingdom of Navarre, José de Moret, recounts it in the following way: "A shepherd was grazing his flock on the stark mountainside. He noticed that a dove repeatedly flew in and out of a hole in a large rock on which the church now stands. He tried to frighten it several times by throwing his crook at it. Impressed by the fearlessness of the bird he decided to explore. He climbed the rock with difficulty and reached the mouth of the cave. On entering he was met with the sight of the Virgin Mary before him, with the bird that had led him there at her feet. Once he had worshipped the image he had discovered, the shepherd ran to the village to give the news to his neighbours. They all went to the mountain and identified the effigy which had apparently been hidden by Christians who had escaped from the Moors. The dove was still at her feet..."

The sanctuary of the church of Ujué is separated from the nave by Gothic railings. The image of Our Lady presides over the church from the main apse. She has been the object of tremendous devotion since 1886, the date which marked the millennium of her apparition, and the patroness of the Ribera region of Navarre (the southern part, along the Ebro river).

The Virgin is a masterpiece of Romanesque religious imagery, carved in alder wood at the end of the XIIth century. Comparable to other images to be found in the eastern Pyrenees, Francisco Iñiguez says that "this is an exceptional statue, sweet and pleasant, without the least trace of dryness or hardness, worthy of praise in a piece that is as schematic in its detail as it is upright in posture." Serene and beautiful, sober and inscrutable, facing forward, sitting on a backless stool, she herself is the very throne of Christ, *Sedes Sapientiae*. He who regards her admires the beauty of her oval face with its arched eyebrows framing the almond eyes and penetrating stare, and the small mouth with its fine lips. The original figure has been greatly transformed. Carlos II ordered her to be plated in silver and added an enamelled shield and medallions in bas-relief. The piece that now forms the back of the stool and the halo and crowns, a copy of those of the Romanesque figure of Christ in Villamayor de Monjardín, are modern.

Carlos II's heart was preserved in a glass container and is to be found in a small niche in the main apse. It is set on a wooden case which was decorated with hearts and the Navarrese coat of arms by the painter Jaymet nineteen years after the monarch's death in 1406. The sovereign's last wish was fulfilled in the following way: his body was embalmed by the Jew, Samuel Trigo, who took out his heart and intestines. His body was buried in the Cathedral in Pamplona, his entrails in Roncesvalles and his heart was taken to Ujué.

PILGRIMAGES IN NAVARRE

Between April and June, when the fields turn green, Navarre embarks on pilgrimages to sanctuaries and hermitages. This could be a pre-Christian custom that sought the fertilising and curative virtues of fountains and wells. These pilgrimages are preceded by the Supplicatory Processions held on Rogation Days during the feast of Saint Mark and three days before Ascension Day, when rain and protection from hailstorms are implored. In the Middle Ages,

People taking part in the popular pilgrimage to Ujué make an early start along the route. The men wear a black tunic down to their feet and carry a wooden cross.

these marches were made to distant places and at least one person from each household was obliged to go. The journey was sometimes so long that it was necessary to spend a night either in the sanctuary or nearby. People of both sexes spending the night together was not considered to be at all appropriate by the ecclesiastic authorities who, through the *Concilio de Trento* (Council of Trento 1545-63), prohibited processions that did not allow a return home in one day. However, the road home was often still very long. The Town Council's custom of offering bread and wine to pilgrims has survived in many Navarrese pilgrimages. The wine was sometimes served in *barquillas* (silver cups), an ideal way of reviving the walkers and giving them strength to make the journey home.

Many of the modern pilgrimages date back to mediaeval times and are those which most clearly preserve the sense of penitence. Others, in particular those held at Pentecost, must be more recent inventions as the atmosphere is more festive: vehicles or trailers are decorated and there is dancing and merry-making.

All the pilgrimages fulfil one new function: to gather all the people of one valley or village together, and they have taken on a new value for those who wish to return to their roots. Many people do not attend the village feasts but they do go on the pilgrimages without fail. There is rivalry between villages in brightening up and reconditioning their hermitages and sanctuaries.

The Navarrese pilgrimages, particularly the penitential ones, are a redoubt of authenticity, favoured by photographers seeking an anthropological theme. LIFE magazine made Cristina García Rodero's photograph taken during the *Trinidad de Lumbier*

The romería (popular pilgrimage) to Ujué is an expression of religious fervour and combines festive and penitential elements.

pilgrimage famous throughout the world. The popular songs and the discovery of variations of quarter tones that are impossible to transcribe on the stave also attract musicians. Folklorists come to study the rites, superstitions and costumes. Gourmets come to sample the delicacies of the seasonal cooking such as *migas de pastor* with *perretxikos* in the mountain areas (a traditional dish eaten by shepherds made from breadcrumbs, fried larding bacon and wild spring mushrooms); and in the Ribera, *empanadas* (savoury pastry turnovers) and *culecas* (sweet bread with a hard-boiled egg cooked inside it).

There are records of the pilgrimage to Ujué from Tafalla and several other towns and villages in the Ribera region that date back to the XIVth century. It is held on the Sunday following 25th April, St. Mark's Day. The pilgrims get up very early to set out on the long journey. The men wear ankle-length black tunics tied with an esparto grass cord around the waist and a pointed hoods on their heads. They carry heavy solid wooden crosses on their backs. The groups of pilgrims who come from the different villages and from different directions converge within sight of the sanctuary at *La Cruz del Saludo*, which has been the junction since the XVIth century. The bells ring. On entering the village, the Priests exchange copes and the Mayors of Ujué and Tafalla exchange rods. On reaching the church, each village hails the Virgin with its own song. After the Mass the groups disperse for lunch, and first thing in the afternoon the farewell is made in the form of a spontaneous acclamation of compliments made to Our Lady of Heaven complete with cheers and shouts of primitive tenderness. The hand of the great XIXth-century composer Felipe Gorriti, who was the organist at Tafalla for many years, is manifest in the music that is played from daybreak until the farewell.

Another imposing pilgrimage is that of *La Hermandad de Esclavos de Nuestra Señora, Apostolado de los Doce* (Slaves of Our Lady, Apostolate of the Twelve) which dates back to 1607. The pilgrims walk through the night praying in silence accompanied by their priest. They wear black tunics, crosses that hangs from a purple cord around their necks, and carry staffs and lanterns.

Ujué's devotional attraction seems to date from the reign of the Navarrese Kings of the House of Evreux, who made pilgrimages from their Palace in Olite from 1364 onwards. Carlos II regularly went to pray for help in triumphing in his complicated political ventures in France. Carlos III, his wife and three daughters made a pilgrimage on foot in 1395 and slept in tents. At the end of the journey they made an offering of a beautiful enamel-gilded silver chalice, now on display in the Museum of Navarre. Princess Blanca, who was then ten years of age, kept up this family custom every year. As she was in a delicate state of health, she was carried to Ujué on a stretcher. Right up until the moment of her burial she was always shrouded in the same rich robes she wore for her coronation, and which she ordered to be used to decorate the church after her death. Prince Carlos frequented the sanctuary to pray for an improvement in his mother's state of health.

The records state that the Prince of Viana never forgot to buy the famous *sanjaimetas*, sweets that were sold in the village. Nowadays the visitor must try the *garapiñada* almonds. The *garapiña* is the equivalent of *praliné* in France, i.e. a coating of caramelised sugar around an almond called *largueta* typical of this area.

The pilgrimage ends with spontaneous flattering comments to the Virgin of Ujué. The custom has been followed since the XIVth century.

The village of Pitillas was already established at the base of the Ujué slopes at the end of the XIth century. It was populated by peasant farmers who worked the land of the plain, which was more fertile and easier to cultivate than the higher land. The people from Pitillas harvested more wheat than the whole of the village of Ujué, on which they were dependent. The village, which did not obtain municipal autonomy until the middle of the XIVth century, was a 'village and tower' and was in dispute with Ujué, situated higher up the mountainside. The *pitillejos* (peasants of Pitillas) refused to work on the maintenance and repair of the hilltop castle, and those from Ujué imprisoned them in order to force their compliance.

Three kilometres from the village, on the border of the district with Santacara, there is a Nature Reserve of significant interest. The Pitillas Lagoon occupies an area of 216 hectares and is no more than two metres deep at any point. It originated as a saltwater lake that covered the whole Ebro valley in the Tertiary Era. It is the most northerly non-mountain lake in the Iberian Peninsula, and one of the areas with the densest bird population. This marshy area provides shelter for around seventy species, which ranks it in second place in Navarre for nesting birds and in first place as a resting place for migratory species.

This lagoon was once royal property and there are records of it dating back to 1348, when a meeting of the council of the village of Pitillas studied the farmers' complaints that were lodged because the guards fined them for "allowing their livestock to drink from the Sabasan pond." An agreement was made and an annual payment of wheat and barley was made to the Crown. In exchange, the residents of the village observed and supervised the hunting of birds and were permitted to take their animals to drink. The lake is supplied with rainwater collected in the ravines that descend from the Ujué Sierra. The present dam is the successor of a mediaeval one, the purpose of which was to increase the capacity of the reservoir in order to use the water to irrigate the surrounding fields. In 1843, the geographer Julio Altadill wrote the following about the area, which is very close to its current appearance: "It is the lagoon, two kilometres to the east of the village, with constant waters that filter through the bed with a periphery of between eleven and twelve kilometres; an irrigation channel leads from its lowest side providing water to an area of farms." In 1971, the lagoon was dried out in order to cultivate the land. The salinity of the soil, together with the protests about the ecological damage caused, dissuaded the promoters from the idea. The Regional Government leased the whole area and established it as a Protected Area in 1976.

La Laguna de Pitillas, situated at the edge of a main road, is a Nature Reserve with easy access. It has good observation points around the dam or on the hill where the San Gregorio hermitage overlooks the whole lake. The lagoon varies in size depending on

the rainfall. It is largely lined with bulrushes and reeds and is fenced off with barbed wire. However, walkers and cyclists may go round it, and if they are discreet and come during the right season at twilight armed with patience and a pair of binoculars, they will see and hear a rewarding spectacle.

With the method and tenacity of all true ornithologists, the photographer Xabi Otero and the journalist Pili Yoldi have given the general public an insight into the secrets of life over the four seasons in this cool spot set in a coarse grassland landscape.

During some winters the lagoon has been known to freeze over. Birds gather in the centre of the ice looking for a crack through which to eat and drink. Even in this hard season they come seeking shelter: the grebes dip their long white necks into the water to fish, the common pochards dive, the shoveler ducks and the garganeys explore the lime trees and the red-crested pochard can also be spotted. The storks arrive around the feast of St. Blas, and February heralds the arrival of the early geese who are always the first visitors as they stop off on their long journey from the Guadalquivir Marshes to the tundra of Lapland. The reed-beds provide a winter home for the marsh harrier, the only bird of prey that nests in Pitillas and of which there are more than a hundred examples.

The green fields of March mark the start of the mating rites and the bird calls. In April, the lagoon is at its most resplendent. Yoldi has closely observed the inhabitants of the reeds and has observed how the birds hide their nests from the predators, snakes and foxes that come in search of eggs: "The variety of constructions prepared by each one of the birds in which to lay their eggs converts the study of the nests into a treatise on architecture." The great reed warbler builds its nest in the centre of the lagoon supported by several stems at a height of one and a half metres above the water. Pairs of bitterns build large platforms of up to one and a half metres in diameter from bulrushes and reeds. The grebe braids plants together so that they float on the surface. In the shallow areas of the lagoon, stilt birds pile up dry grass to make an untidy nest, and on the banks the white wagtails lay their eggs in hollows between the stones without bothering to build a nest. Ducks and garganeys leave the water to nest in the sown fields or thickets. Far from the water, colonies of bee-eaters breed, using their feet to dig tunnels of up to two metres in length in the steep sides of the ravines.

In high summer, life in the lagoon is lazy. At dusk, the 'cheep-cheep' of the cicada dies out to give way to the croaking of frogs and toads. Once night has fallen, the birds come and go from the lagoon in search of food. "It is the time of day when there is most movement, when the heat has died down and the birds are the lords of the air. Some swallows come to drink. The lanner falcon leaves its nest in the nearby pines and comes to hunt insects, swallows and swifts. A solitary stork pecks at some food before leaving to roost. The ringed snakes that have spent the whole day in the sun come to the banks to lie in wait for frogs. The small sulky sparrow owls look on from the telephone posts. The crickets and glow-worms come to help the birds to sleep. Only the whisper of the air among the rushes and the splash of a frog diving into the water can be heard through the silence. Suddenly the calm is broken by the quack of a baby duck frightened by a fox who is still there, taking advantage of the cover of night to have a duck dinner..."

Only the summer storms relieve the excessive heat, and the long summer months exhaust the lagoon. The arrival of Autumn is announced by the departure of some of the birds. When the turtle-doves and the majority of the insect-eating birds have left, the first of the pigeons begin to fly over. In the skies over the yellow and reddish grapevines fly flocks of cranes and the V-formations of geese. The last migrants to fly over are the rooks. Once the grape harvest is over, the starlings, or *tordos* as they are locally known, finish up any forgotten grapes left in the vineyards. Wild boars also come down from the hills at night to wallow in the mud.

[LEFT AND ABOVE] *The lagoon at Pitillas is the northernmost steppe-type lake in the Iberian Peninsula and one of the most important in terms of concentration of birdlife. It provides shelter for about seventy species. It is also the major 'stopover' place in Navarre for migrating birds.*

Tudela was founded by order of Al Hakam, to whom God gave Paradise, and it was established by Amrús. Everyone marvels at the goodness of the district of Tudela. Its bread knows no equal. It has many houses and orchards and good lands. The fruit trees bear such tasty fruit that it is above praise. Its waters flow into the river Ebro. There is a bridge at the entrance to the city with waterwheels under its arches. There is abundant water." This eulogy was written at the beginning of the Xth century by the Islamic chronicler, Ar-Razi, and describes the strategic position that continues to be the great advantage of a rich city and its surroundings, with abundant economic and cultural assets. Throughout history Tudela has been a loyal town, a cultural melting pot, a defender of civil liberties and entrepreneurial in spirit.

TUDELA
AND THE SURROUNDING AREA

A THOUSAND ROUTES THROUGH NAVARRE

The word *'Ribera'* (riviera) comes from the Latin *riparia* and refers to the area along the banks of a river. The word is found in the chronicles of Navarre as far back as 1280, and appears in XIVth-century censuses in reference to the southern *riberas* of the larger rivers, the counterpoint of the northern 'valleys'. There are Riberas of the rivers Ega, Arga and Aragón, the three rivers that "make the Ebro a man." The Ribera of Estella is also referred to, but there is just one main Ribera, one extensive alluvial plain, and that is the Ribera of Tudela, the *Ribera Tudelana*.

The earth of this plain, where rainfall is sparse and irregular, is treeless, abundant in tiling clay, difficult to work, thirsty and parched by the icy north wind and burning summer breezes. Sunshine and aridity abound. Canals and irrigation ditches make use of water from the rivers while thickets and highly fertile market gardens trace small oases between the extensive areas of dry land.

Mediterranean agriculture supplies the classical trilogy described by Greek and Latin writers 2000 years ago: wheat, vines and olive trees, complemented by bread to soak up the aromatic wine and oil. The irrigated lands, which yield a little of almost everything, are a feast to the eye and the nose as well as to the palate.

This is not an area of isolated houses. Urban life predominates. It is an *agora* of bars, streets and squares, where conversation is torrential, loud, clear, direct, sharp, and at times brutal. It is an area of large, defensive villages located close to each other where life seems to go on in slow motion. These are rather ugly, yet rich, towns that have long been established near the river Ebro and its tributaries, the Alhama and the Queiles. Sometimes they are close to the river plains, or at a wise distance on the chalk and sandstone slopes to avoid the fury of the floods or the surprise of the *'aguaduchos'* (flash floods) from the irrigation ditches.

Francisco Escribano, a writer from the area, assures us that "the desert shows its visor over the exuberant river plain", and, dazzled by so much burning sun, he was right when he captured the sensuality of the August night: "What beautiful nights when the sparrow owl sings in a secret olive tree. The frogs croak in the pond and the crickets play the strings of the earth. The poplars sway, rocked by the fresh north wind, rehearsing true-blooded *jotas*. Far off, the timid sound of a small bell can be heard and the lights of the towns shimmer like a ruby necklace. Up above, the Milky Way swathes the Universe in a great spiral. The Pleiades look down on us from their golden height and suddenly a shooting star streaks across the polished sky. What a sky, pierced with clarity! And what smells! The warm breeze carries the fragrance of the slopes with it: thyme, lavender, oregano, fennel, rosemary and gorse. In

[PAGE 193] *The Puerta del Juicio (Door of Judgement) is an imposing sculpted entrance which illustrates (for an illiterate people) the punishment of the reprobates and the triumph of the Blessed. Initially it must have been completely polychrome.*
[PREVIOUS DOUBLE PAGE] *The Ribera holds a large number of wetlands. Some pools and lakes are remains of the immense Tertiary Age lake that flooded the entire Ebro depression. The largest are linked to the history of disappeared mediaeval towns.*

replica, the north wind lifts the bouquet of the mature muscatel grapes or the perfume of the tomato plants from the fertile plain. Both winds cross on the hillsides and pick up the bittersweet smell of stubble where ants gather their harvest for the winter and quails fatten their breasts before returning to Africa."

The thickets are green belts of poplars, ashes, elms, willows, tamarisks, osiers, rushes, bulrushes and reeds. They limit erosion, reduce the effects of floods, provide a welcome resting place and contain a range of ecosystems. The thickets of Murillo de las Limas, Traslapuente, Ramalete, La Remonta, El Quebrado and El Ramillo are close to Tudela and are protected as Nature Reserves or Areas of Interest.

Erosion makes incessant changes to the river and accentuates the curve of its meanders, scratching away at one bank and depositing material on the other. This has brought about technical and legal challenges, most marked in the river Ebro, the historical frontier of kingdoms and which still had customs officers until well into the XIXth century. The mighty river caused problems in Castejón in 1970 during the construction of Navarre's motorway when it invaded the embankment of the bridge that was being built and a new course of more than two kilometres in length had to be planned. The challenge is by no means a new one. In 1420 the people of Tudela were forced to take measures to prevent the Ebro changing its course and leaving the great 17-arch mediaeval bridge at the entrance to the city high and dry. In the XVIth century they worked feverishly to avoid the formation of what would later be the river's most famous irrigated plain, La Mejana. They finally obtained a Declaration of Public Interest for the ambitious channelling work undertaken at the end of the XIXth century.

There is a series of wetlands on the right bank of the great river. Some pools are the remains of an immense Tertiary Age lake that occupied the whole of the Ebro basin, and the largest of these are linked to the history of mediaeval villages that have now ceased to exist. Valpertuna, next to a farm called Bonamaison, must be very salty because there are no fish, just newts and frogs. Purple herons observe the flocks of sheep that go to drink at the Laguna de Lor close to the olive groves and used by the 'Huertas Mayores' Syndicate from Tudela for irrigation. In the Montes del Cierzo, lake Pulguer looks like a sheet of silver, lined with tamarisks where tens of thousands of starlings spend the winter, screaming and darkening the twilight like the violent scenes from Alfred Hitchcock's film 'The Birds'. In Corella, there are the Estanca y Estanquilla lakes, whose volumes are increased for irrigation purposes.

CANALS AND IRRIGATION

Irrigation is made possible by the land, the sun and water. However, the action of the market gardener is more important because there are similar resources available in other parts of the Ebro Valley, but the farmer from the Ribera has always been resolute, advanced and progressive, and this is very helpful if one wishes to be successful in agriculture.

The farmer who irrigates is someone who possesses great experience over the centuries, going back to Roman times. The Arabs later left their mark very clearly. This inheritance from the Mudejar market gardeners (the Mudejars were Moslems who stayed in Castile after the Reconquest) can still be seen in the wise regulations of the farming communities, in the vocabulary that still refers to the person in charge of watering as the '*alhamín*', and the right to take water in turn as '*ador*' or '*almóceda*'. Place names in the area include *Almajares, Almenara* and *Azut*, meaning 'marshy land', 'canal' and 'dam' respectively.

La Mejana is beautiful, whether viewed from the height of the old castle of Tudela or from the middle of one of its fields. '*Mejana*' means 'fluvial island'. It was divided up and shared out and is the symbol of market gardening in the Ribera. It is not the best nor the most extensive farmland, but it is an emblem of agricultural progress.

The bridge over the Ebro, at Tudela, has great symbolic value. It is even on the city's coat of arms. In the distance the towers of the Cathedral and the church of La Magdalena can be seen.

Water has been drawn from the Ebro for irrigation since the early Middle Ages. The region's agriculture benefits from three large, modern canals that also serve the neighbouring regions of Aragon and Rioja. Two of them, the Canal de Tauste and the Canal Imperial, were built in the era of Carlos V. The enlightened spirit of the XVIIIth century modernised these great works and laid the groundwork for a third, the Canal de Lodosa.

The reason for the construction of the Canal Imperial de Aragón, one of the largest and most impressive public works in Spain, was twofold: irrigation and navigation. Two hundred years went by before the canal took on a leading role once more following the construction of the Renaissance dam built from square cut stone; it still exists, complete with its valve house. The Canon and engineer Ramón Pignatelli was able to realise his dream of increasing the area of cultivated land, defending market gardens from floods, promoting livestock farming and industry, developing interior trade and supplying the city of Saragossa with water. The dam called *El Bocal* was completed in 1790 and is the largest in Navarre. 1,500 labourers, 400 convicts and five infantry regiments worked on its construction.

Even when the sun is at its most oppressive breezes blow around the *Bocal*. There is a coolness in its 'jungle' of willows, poplars and ashes. The song of chaffinches, goldfinches, great tits, thrushes and nightingales can be heard. It is a great, austere construction, and the valve house still has its 11 original modules. There is a large house of discreetly severe architecture and some well laid-out, romantic gardens that both relax and shelter the spot as well as protecting it from noise from the nearby roads.

An admirable love of trees is noticeable along the Canal; around 100,000 line its banks. Not far from the *Bocal* is a great 35-metre high oak that is listed among Navarre's monumental trees. Those interested in the Industrial Architecture of the Enlightenment may admire the bridge at Cortes (20 kilometres from the *Bocal*), one of the few that conserves the original design with stone bonds and brick courses.

THE EXQUISITE KITCHEN GARDEN

Large expanses of maize, forage crops and tomatoes can be seen in the fields irrigated by the larger canals. There are also many small patches of intensive farming near Tudela, yielding a great variety of vegetables to make up the delicious *menestra* (minestrone), a dish that is at its best in the middle of spring.

Asparagus, at one time exclusive to the Ebro valley, has extended northwards almost as far as Pamplona. Strong competition from the Andes and Asia has meant that asparagus production has dropped by a third in just 12 years. In 1996 Navarre produced 12 million kilos from 3,300 hectares, half of it on irrigated land. Careful selection of varieties and the promotion of the consumption of fresh asparagus are crucial to the future of the crop.

"The artichoke from Tudela is all heart", remarked the journalist Antonio Díaz Cañabate when he was served a plate of tender *cogotas* (the local name for artichoke head). Eighty per cent of Navarre's production of 'white' artichokes comes from Tudela and

The cortados (crags) of Peñalen rise up near Funes. At their foot, the Arga flows into the Aragón among irrigated fields.

the surrounding area, with a total of 1,200 hectares and an annual production of 17,000 tons. The farmer renews the plant stock each year and reaps two benefits: the fruit and the plant. The season begins at the end of the winter with the sale of the fresh vegetable and closes with production for the canning industry. In July, at the end of the season, the market gardener pulls up the plants and cuts them into four parts. One is kept for his own use and the other three are sold to the market gardens of Valencia and Murcia, in south-eastern Spain.

Small lettuce hearts (*cogollos*), ripe tomatoes, baked broccoli, tender peas, bitter chicory, the humble chard, strong–tasting broad beans, green runner beans and the delicately peeled borage are, lightly seasoned, among the delicious dishes from the area.

The pepper is another culinary treasure, green, red or '*entreverado*' (streaked red and green). It is the companion of the tomato in the '*fritada*' (fried peppers and tomatoes); the smell of autumn roasted on a wood fire, the winter stock drying out in the sun on the balconies. Five towns in the Lodosa area produce the

slightly sweet *pimiento 'del piquillo'*, universally recognised as the best of its kind.

Three specific Navarra Designations of Origin guarantee the quality of the asparagus *'Espárrago de Navarra'*, the artichoke *'Alcachofa de Tudela'* and the red pepper *'Piquillo de Lodosa'*.

CHRISTIANS, JEWS AND MOORS

Minorities left their mark on the area, but did the three cultures cohabit or coexist? Carrasco Pérez, from historical research, and Salinas Quijada, from reading the *Fuero* (specific code of laws and privileges) of Tudela, are of the opinion that tolerance was more of a desire or maybe a fashion.

The three groups were a minority in Tudela because, during the period of Moslem domination, there was already a Jewish quarter and a neighbourhood of Mozarabs (Spanish Christians), the population of which was reduced by the fanaticism of the Almoravides. After the conquest of the city by Alfonso el Batallador, the Moors surrendered and their properties, way of life and religion were safeguarded, although they only occupied a marginal area outside the

city walls, in the Moorish district. The Jews who had fled returned when they were conceded the *'Fuero de Nájera'* (code of privileges and rights). New Christian settlers arrived and joined up with the Mozarabs. The Mudejars and Jews had direct access to the King, but according to the thinking of the time the Christians were superior and 'others' were marginal, although their legal status and governing bodies were respected.

Salinas concludes that "without doubt there was a civilised level of cohabitation between the three cultures. Jewish or Moorish jurisdiction took temporary primacy for civil, and even penal, matters before this was passed on to the Christians. In the *Fuero* there is a certain degree of distrust regarding the honesty of Jews and Moors, and the Christians were definitely privileged with regard to judicial, family and inheritance law. In social matters, certain obligations put the Moor or the Jew on the same level but not the serf, who was often on the verge of slavery or considered as a mere irrational or inanimate object."

When more accurate data began to emerge in the middle of the XIVth century the Moslems accounted for almost 3% of Navarre's population. This figure was highest in the Ribera, where the census put it at 20%. Almost half the Navarrese Moors were concentrated in three Moorish districts in Tudela, Cascante and Corella. There were excellent carpenters, bricklayers and blacksmiths among them, but their strength lay in their farming skills. Christian predominance reduced the land they were allowed to work and many were forced to emigrate to the neighbouring Moncayo area in Aragon. The Arab quarters had their own bylaws and the Islamic group had a political and religious leader appointed by the King (the *alcadí*) whose official residence was in Tudela.

The 35 Navarrese Jewish areas were concentrated into five: Estella, Funes, Pamplona, Tudela and Viana. Communities from the other side of the Pyrenees established themselves in the new settlements along the Pilgrim's Way to Compostela, but in the Ebro corridor other Jewries with Islamic traditions were already in existence. Tudela had the most prestigious and important Jewish neighbourhood in the whole Kingdom. There were some 800 families there before the Black Death of 1348, which reduced the population by half to 27% of the inhabitants. At that time there were around 1,900 Jewish families in Navarre, a minority that represented 8.5% of the total population. The bylaws of the Jewish neighbourhoods of Tudela and Puente la Reina have been conserved and they provide information on their organisation, social systems and even the way in which they celebrated their feasts in their synagogues and homes. The Rabbis, at first purely spiritual leaders, took on political responsibilities comparatively late. The figure of the Chief Rabbi appeared in 1390 in Navarre, later than in other Kingdoms in the Iberian peninsula. The Jews traded in cereals, woollen cloth, skins, jewels and medicines and they were also moneylenders and tax collectors.

Professor Carrasco questions the idyllic image of the ethnic minorities and does not conceal their internal difficulties and tensions. He also underlines their role from an economic and taxation point of view and points out the contribution they made to the structure of the landscape, as a result of the major presence of the Jews in the vineyards and Moslems on the irrigated plains. "These lands of the Ebro valley cannot have lacked variety and colour, due to the colourful clothing of their settlers and the very different ways of life and religions."

At the end of the Middle Ages the Jewish and Moorish minorities were substantially reduced. When the Decree of Expulsion for all who did not convert to Christianity was applied in Navarre in 1498, around 200 Jewish houses were left uninhabited in Tudela. A small minority was baptised but they were considered to be 'new Christians' and did not attain the position of *hidalgo* (gentleman). Years later, the names of the converted would still remain on a large panel displayed in the cathedral.

The Moorish and Jewish quarters of Tudela produced four figures of universal fame, whose biographies partly overlap during the XIIth century.

Al Amá al-Tutilí, a blind man from Tudela, the son of emancipated slaves, jester and beggar, was a great popular poet. 149 of his *'moaxajas'* (poetic compositions in Arabic) have been preserved. They travelled around the world at a time when classical Arabic poetry was on the decline.

Yehuda ha-Leví, doctor and poet, wrote amorous, bacchanal, mystical love poems for Sion in Hebrew with *'jarchas'*(verses forming part of a *moaxaja)* in Arabic and stammering Castilian Romance. Writers from all periods, including the great German poet Heine, praise him and concur that he was the master author of the Hebraic-Spanish Golden Age:

I will climb the palm tree and take its bunches of dates
and for me your bosom is like the bunches of grapes on
the vine.My honeycomb and my honey between your lips,
My nard and my myrrh between your two breasts
What I want are years that add to those of your life,
Although your steal my dream at night on loving you.

Abraham Ibn Ezra, a philosopher and scholar, was another ingenious poet who wrote treatises on Arithmetic, Astronomy and Astrology.

Benjamín de Tudela, Rabbi and polyglot merchant, wrote the 'Itinerary' of the journey which took him within sight of the Himalayas a century before Marco Polo. It has been translated into all the world's major languages. This "errant Jew" who visited his brothers in the world of Jewry offers an enthralling documentary on the cities he visited and their peoples, trades, customs, festivals and economies, with some early references to "an oil called petroleum."

At the end of the XXth century, Tudela has once again opened its doors to a new minority. In 1996 the Social Services recorded the presence of 200 immigrants, mainly from North Africa. Almost all of them were unmarried, bilingual or trilingual and generally well-educated. They emigrated from their countries of origin for political or economic reasons and are looking for work, housing, and social and legal protection. History, with its new challenges, is once again showing that cultural diversity is an asset and an opportunity to make progress in terms of humanity and democracy.

TUDELA'S ARCHITECTURE TELLS ITS HISTORY

Tudela is now Navarre's second largest city, although its population was larger than Pamplona's in the Middle Ages. The name of the city is related to the protecting divinity of the Latin world, *Tutela*. The enclave is both a point of defence and strategic communications. The hill of Santa Barbara, where a castle stood before the arrival of the Arabs, and the bridge over the Ebro (represented on the municipal coat of arms due to its symbolic value) are prominent.

An agricultural and market town, in the Xth century it was also the most important cultural centre north of Al Andalús. Only a few small stone remains have been conserved from its Mosque, the focal point of intellectual dissemination. They are related to the Cordovan style of art: battlements, capitals, modillions and pilasters.

According to the architect Juan Antonio Ridruejo, it is "one of the most important urban examples of Islamic origin in the country, and perhaps in Europe." The old part of the city has an irregular layout with narrow winding streets, sometimes leading to a dead end. Humble houses and great palaces alike benefit from the skilful use of brick.

The Romanesque or Proto-Gothic churches that existed in the city have disappeared. Fortunately the Magdalena church remains, built at the turn of the XIIIth century in the same style as the fine collection of small churches: rectangular in shape, with an elevated barrel vault, pure Romanesque façades and a bell tower. The tympanum of the parish church of San Nicolás still has a Holy Trinity of unique beauty.

The great monument of the city is the church of Santa María, which was converted into a cathedral in 1783 on the occasion of the foundation of the diocese of Tudela. The jurisdiction of the diocese was limited and its autonomous life was short, as it only ever had four bishops in residence.

The cathedral is a large building of calculated proportions, highly influenced by Cistercian art. Building work started during the reign of Sancho el Sabio and continued through the greater part of the XIIIth century after its Consecration in 1188. The façade and cloister are Romanesque and the luminous central nave Gothic. The *Puerta del Juicio* is an imposing sculptural work portraying the punishment of the Condemned and the triumph of the Blessed, for the enlightenment of the illiterate.

The main altarpiece, dating back to 1489, introduced Hispano-Flemish art into Navarre and is the work of Pedro Díaz de Oviedo. It is made up of 17 panels and a large Gothic canopy that crowns

The Chapel of Santa Ana in Tudela Cathedral. It has sumptuous polychrome plasterwork and is covered by a dome that produces theatrical lighting effects, from semi-darkness to radiant light.

The chancel is situated in the middle of the central nave with two masterpieces by Esteban de Obray: a Plateresque railing with narrow columns, and the late Gothic choir stalls with 86 pews decorated with mythological motifs and flora and fauna. Symmetrically placed on both sides of the chancel are the XVIIIth-century chapels of the Holy Spirit and the patron saint of Tudela, Santa Ana. The latter is lavishly decorated with polychrome plastering and is the most elaborate of all examples of Baroque in Navarre. It has a dome which produces theatrical light that stands out against the semi-darkness of the lower part of the room in contrast to the radiant clarity of the tambour that crowns the work. Tudela once had city walls but they were destroyed in 1516 after the Conquest of Navarre, during which time the city was a redoubt of heroism and loyalty to the legitimate monarchs. The city and its surroundings extended as far as the river Queiles, which represented the boundary of the urban area until 1677 when the *Plaza Nueva* was designed. "A beautiful place for trade and bullfights. Square in shape, regular, with large balconies of brick, and painted in tempera", wrote Jovellanos.

The spirit of the Englightenment had a place in Tudela's 'Royal Society of Promoters of Public Good'. José María Magallón, the Marquis of San Adrián, whose portrait was painted by Goya, was a member. The Society, concerned with the economic and educational progress of the time, intervened in hydraulic projects and road-building as well as in the construction and management of a building that would last a long time, the *Real Casa de Misericordia*, the façade of which was designed by Ventura Rodríguez.

Today Tudela is a service centre with an active electronics and metal industry, as well as an agrofood sector accounting for 6% of agricultural employment. The siutation of the Ebro, a real barrier, has determined the eastern growth of its residential neighbourhoods, some of which are fine examples of social planning programmes.

an image of the Assumption of the Virgin Mary, commissioned by the Chapter and carried out by Juan Bascardo in 1606.

Other chapels in the apse contain the stone image of Santa María la Blanca (the church's original protector), the Gothic altarpiece of Santa Catalina with 21 panels painted with great skill in the XIVth century by Juan de Levi, and the flamboyant polychrome alabaster sepulchre containing the remains of the French Chancellor of Villaespesa and his wife, Isabel of Ujué.

The 'Elvira España' State School is an attractive complex consisting of three buildings. The oldest, built in the 1930s, is one of the few examples of Second Republic school architecture remaining in Navarre. Next to it, a second building was built to the design of Rafael Moneo of Tudela, the Pritzker prize-winner for architecture, who in 1968 designed an accessible building with a large amount of light achieved by eye-catching skylights and a structure that is not supported by columns but by the main walls. The third building is the work of Antonio Blasco, an architect who was also responsible for the design of other works in the city such as the Plaza de la Judería, the refurbishing of the Seminary, and the Paseo del Queiles.

The Bajada del Ángel on Easter Sunday. A child dressed as an Angel slides slowly down a cable as if descending from the sky.

FESTIVALS, MUSICIANS AND FOLKLORE

At the end of Easter Week, two centuries-old ceremonies are held in Tudela's Plaza Nueva. The 'Volatín', a wooden articulated model that is made to do somersaults performs a ridiculous dance at the the Clock House at ten o'clock in the morning on Easter Saturday. The following day, on Easter Sunday at the same place but an hour earlier, the ceremony of the 'Descent of the Angel' takes place. A child dressed as an angel climbs down a rope as if descending from the sky, and removes a black cloth that covers the face of the Virgin Mary with his teeth. The statue is then carried in procession to the 'meeting' with her Resurrected Son.

The festival of Santa Ana is famous for its Bullfights and the processions of 'Gigantes' (traditional figures of giants) that dance around the bandstand in the main square, in the same way that the *Tudelanos* do every night of the festivity to the lively rhythm of the 'Revoltosa' music.

Folklore groups display their creativity at carnival time in dances, *paloteados* (a dance involving criss-crossing poles), and *jotas*.

The *jota*, a song accompanied by mandolins, lutes and guitars, has a tradition in irrigation farming areas. It begins with a lively instrumental prelude followed by slow song in just one voice or a duet, and the instruments then play a very lively ending as if they were the voice of the people displaying their happiness. The central point is the sung melody, an opportunity for the 'joteros' to show off their virtuosity and style. There are impressive musical ranges and words loaded with lyricism and popular flavour. The origins of the *jota* and the name itself are uncertain. The oldest reference to a song called *jota* dates back to the end of the XVIIth century (although it could be even older) and there are similar musical forms in other Mediterranean countries.

The Ribera has produced three prominent musicians in recent centuries. Blas de la Serna, born in Corella in 1751, a renowned author of popular songs, was the most prolific. The *tonadilla* was a brief scenic genre for one or several characters and a small orchestra to accompany the voices. Joaquín Gaztambide, born in Tudela in 1822, stood out as a composer and impresario of another lyrical style, the operetta or 'zarzuela'. Fernando Remacha, also from Tudela, won the National Award for Music in 1932 for his 'Cuarteto con piano'. He wrote the soundtrack for films that were praised by Luis Buñuel and Federico García Lorca. He was also the composer of a 'Concierto para guitarra' and the cantata 'Jesucristo en la Cruz', first performed in 1964 during the religious music festival *Semana de Música Religiosa* in Cuenca.

THE TOWNS OF CASCANTE AND CORELLA

The *cierzo*, a cold, gusty north-east wind often blows across the Ribera. The Montes del Cierzo separate two valleys of olive groves, vineyards and crops irrigated by the rivers Queiles and Alhama. The waters of these two rivers have been the subject of countless disputes. According to the ancient writers, the waters of the Queiles served to temper iron, whilst the Arabs refer to a hot spring with the name *Alhama*. Islamic geographers talk of the two valleys as an area full of market gardens and orchards. This has been a land of border conflicts, settlers and strong mediaeval defences. Its inhabitants, according to Julio Caro Baroja, "maybe feel more Navarrese than any other inhabitant. However the characteristics of their culture were and still are more similar to those of their neighbours from Aragon than those within Navarre." The border location meant risk for many centuries, but it also presented an opportunity for economic development. Each valley is crowned by a picturesque town and both are agricultural, wine-growing and industrial.

Cascante is situated on a height,
Corella on a south-facing slope..."

Cascante, as stated by the motto on its coat of arms, was originally a Roman town with a Christian community, the oldest on record in Navarre. A brick gallery of arches goes from the town centre to the top of the hill, which is crowned by the *Basílica del Romero*. The church conserves a Gothic chapel complete with the original altarpiece, fine plasterwork and a unique Baroque organ. An excellent view of the whole of the Tudela area can be enjoyed from the gardens. A monument preserves the memory of the Golden Age friar, Pedro Malón de Echaide, a native of Cascante, who wrote an ascetic pastoral work, 'La Conversión de la Magdalena' (The conversion of Mary Magdalene) in elegant prose.

In Corella everything has a Baroque air, and the brickwork inherited from the Mudejars reaches its highest decorative expression here, not only on the churches or the large houses of the highborn

with their upper arched galleries, but also on the modest houses with their cornices projecting over wooden struts, depressed bricks and bonds of lime and pebbles. The excellent work represented by the *Museo de Arte Sacro de la Encarnación* must be added to the artistic heritage of the Parish and Conventual Churches. The museum contains canvasses by Claudio Coello, Vicente Verdusán, and the native of Corella, Antonio González Ruiz, the first director of the Academy of Fine Arts of San Fernando. The journalist Ramón García Dominguez explained that "one day back in the XVIIth century, the people of Corella, *los corellanos*, saw the wreathed column, the great hanging bunches of grapes, the rubicund angels, the golden loaves of bread, the dramatic gesticulating images of the saints, and they said: This is ours!" This Baroque extravagance is also seen in key religious and festive events. Each Good Friday the *"Función de las Siete Palabras"* ends its literary and musical oratorio with tempests and earthquakes. In the *'Procesión del Santo Entierro'* a double cortège walks behind *'la muerte calaña'* (the Reaper) with live representations of Biblical characters, virtues and the Fathers of the Christian Church, alongside hooded penitents, *'cadeneros'* (penitents dragging chains), *'dolorosas'* (Madonnas), *'mariíllas'* and *'nazarenos'* (penitents). The festival of San Miguel offers the opportunity to run the bulls and to taste fine wines and muscatels. In 1615 the Carmelite monk, Diego de San José, wrote that for him Corella was the Andalusia of Navarre.

Corella is the Baroque town of Navarre, full of XVIIIth century palaces where brickwork and grisaille stand out. This church tower shows the splendour of the Mudejar tradition.

The Bardenas is a desolate area, but it is not a desert. It rather presents a grandiose scene where water, wind and human activity have worked the land on three fronts. It is a large area of common land where traditional pasture and crop activities, the origin of disputes, have given way to new forms of exploitation. The area is an historical frontier marked by watchtowers and castles built to keep out enemies and bandits. The local community retains its own particular legal system here. As a landscape it needs to closely observed in order to discover the rich diversity which lies behind its bare, inhospitable façade. Its flora and fauna are typical of coarse grassland steppes.

THE BARDENAS
An eroded steppe

In the middle of the steppes of the Bardenas you find pools that store rainwater for a short time where livestock come to drink.

SCENERY AND NATURAL RESERVES

The discovery of the natural and scenic value of the Bardenas is a relatively recent one. Scientific studies have refuted a number of myths about the area. Society's increasing environmental awareness, the excellent work of many photographers and good road communications have meant that thousands of tourists have visited this large territory (425 square kilometres), one which aspires to the status of Natural Park and where three Protected Nature Reserves are located.

The Bardenas described by travellers and writers in the past was an 'ugly' one. In *L'Espagne inconnue* the Romantic Cenac Moncaut wrote about "the horrible solitude of the Bardenas… You would think that Spain, in its desire to take everything from the Arabs, has also taken a corner of the desert from them." In *La Ruta del Aventurero* the novelist Pío Baroja noted that "The sun lit up the desolate, deserted land ... We walked for a couple of hours until we reached the Bardenas. It was a solitary, poor place, monotonous, sad and unpleasantly ugly, made worse by the sultry weather. The ashen earth spread out like a sea, and in front of us there were hills eroded by the rain." Observers from Navarre who have visited the area in this century have variously described the Bardenas as a "grim, inhospitable" landscape, "horrendous but imposing."

Nowadays we have a different vision of materials and forms, of vegetation and skies illuminated by changing shades of light. We appreciate the different tones of golden sandstone, wine-hued clays, grey and olive-coloured loams, chalk shining bright like glass. The Bardenas are always beautiful, whether it be in a (rare) snow-storm or under a blazing sun, hidden in the mist, or vivid when the

[PREVIOUS PAGE] *Clayey soil. The landscape of the Bardenas and its natural environment have only recently been discovered.*

cierzo (north wind) blows, when the green of Spring appears in the ploughed fields, and also at night when ghostly shapes emerge under the full moon or the stars. Like a shepherd, it makes a space for silence.

The Bardenas is not a desert, nor has it ever been one. Water courses and vegetation abound, and it is even inhabited according to the season. Archaeological studies reveal that the area had a more favourable environment four thousand years ago. The flora, unthinkable nowadays, consisted of linden, alder, and hazel-nut trees, with populated villages and shelters on the hillsides overlooking the traditional transhumance routes. Many ancient sites have been discovered: 82 Neolithic, 91 Bronze Age and 31 Iron Age. Colonisation increased considerably in the first two centuries AD (up to 31 Roman sites). Medieval fortified towers still stand. Nowadays many huts are found next to animal pens and arable land. These are leisure areas which cannot only belong to those who built them, as there is no private property in this communal territory. A door must always be left open, offering shelter to whoever needs it.

In Spanish we speak of in the plural of "las" Bardenas. Folk wisdom anticipated what the geologists would later say, distinguishing two main parts —*Blanca* (white) and *Negra* (black)— and a third flat one.

The flat *Bardena* is good agricultural land lying to the north. It is an old fluvial plain which ends in steep escarpments where vultures prowl. The vantage points of Cornialto and La Estroza offer excellent views over the 'Blanca'.

The *Bardena Blanca* surely gets its name from its salt and chalk deposits. The arid climate favours the evaporation of ground water. When it rises and evaporates, especially in the high temperatures of summer, the salt deposits flow over the clays and limes to form a kind of white crust. In the *Blanca*, constantly depressed and moulded by strong erosion, there is a stark contrast between its high ridges and deep gullies. The ridges which mark out the old level of the land are called 'cabezos'. They have fantastic shapes: square, round, like trunks, and resist the erosion which tries to devour them, opening up water-formed gullies on their sides thanks to their 'hats' of compact sandstone. Many *cabezos* have their own name: la Ralla, el Rallón, Sanchicorrota, el Bercho, Pisquerra, or the often-photographed Castildetierra. At the bottom of the cabezos there is an inextricable network of gullies of different sizes. They are almost always dry, and if you walk along their beds you will come across an endless series of fantastic shapes: vertical, floating cornices, arches and windows.

In the southern part of the *Blanca* there is a cliff of reddish clay and black limestone. The 'Balcony of Pilate' is where it starts, leading to a succession of great layered plateaux: the flats of Nasa, Alfarillo and la Negra. The gully of Tudela runs between flats and *cabezos*. La Negra faces southwards down its *Caídas* (drops), where almond and pine trees grow alongside agricultural land. Overlooking the Ebro, the *Barranco de Novillas* hollows its bed and forms incredible sculptures, among them the so-called *Juego de Pelota* (ball game). *El Aguilar* and *Sancho Abarca* face each other, challenging each other like fairy-tale castles. The solitary *Cabezo del Fraile* (monk's head) stands at the edge of the Bardenas.

acts as a brake to erosion. *Artemisia hierba alba*, saltworts, salt-marshes and esparto grass determine the existence of a rich steppe-type fauna. A curious sight is the flight of the 'flying witches', the saltworts which whirl around in large numbers blown by the wind.

A good indicator of the high natural quality of the Bardenas is the large number of steppe-dwelling birds from the Ebro valley which shelter in it. Worthy of note are the bustard, with a gait similar to that of the ostrich, the untrusting, brown-coloured grouse, the sand curlew (which only breeds on bare, uncultivated land) and various others, especially the Dupont lark. This bird hides in the scrub and rarely flies, except when it is breeding, when it takes to the air and sings to mark out its territory. There is a rich variety of fauna in the area, including the largest population of vultures in Navarre and large concentrations of owls and golden eagles. The *culebra bastarda*, our longest

The first reference to the name "Bardena", *Yabal al-Bardí* in Arabic, is in a Muslim chronicle of the year 915. The origin of the word is unclear; it resembles the Aragonese term 'pardina', which means low hill pasture, an area where sheep usually graze and are herded in enclosures. In the search for its origin, the historian and geographer Julio Altadill stretched its meaning to combine two Basque words, *abar* and *dena*, to mean "all branches." This fuelled a belief for many years that this large tract of land had been completely covered by leafy forest at some time in the past. The scientific opinion is that there was always some kind of mixture of forest and desert in the Bardenas. Before Man appeared on the scene the vegetation consisted of holm oak groves, of which a few remain in the *Negra*, kermes oak, the odd Aleppo pine wood (a typical tree of the Bardenas) and also juniper, savin and rosemary.

Nowadays the Bardenas is greener than fifty years ago because tree and bush cutting has ended. There are plenty of *garrigas* (brushland) and coarse grassland near the pinewoods. Rosemary and thyme groves take up most of the surface. In the clearings of the rosemary bushes a dense pastureland called 'lastonar' appears which

snake, takes refuge in brush and pinewoods. The rabbit, the main prey for many species, is fundamental to these ecosystems, as it has always been hunted. Until the end of the 18th century hunting was a privilege of the nobility, the peasants only being allowed to hunt with sticks. Many took to poaching dressed as esparto grass reapers. They would trap the rabbits with ferrets and wait for them to emerge from their warrens to catch them with string.

The wildlife of the area seems to have adapted to the overflying fighter jets and blank bombs dropped on the military firing range covering two thousand hectares in the heart of the Bardena Blanca. The Armed Forces rent the firing range, and it is only at the weekends that the scream of jets is not heard overhead. An ever-growing citizens' movement and also the Parliament of Navarre have asked for the firing range to be closed.

In the meantime, the *cierzo* wind from the north-west is the most common 'music' in the Bardenas. A writer from the area, Francisco Escribano, described it well: "the wind which rides like a devil pursued, a waving blade which groans through the gullies and cabezos." It is a fast, turbulent wind which easily reaches speeds above 40 miles and hour, dragging clouds along with it, drying out

the air and leading to sudden temperature changes. The wind, the summer heat and the irregular rainfall give the area a dry climate. Precipitation, however, is not particularly low (between 400 and 500 litres per annum) although it all falls in just sixty days of the year.

There are three Natural Reserves in the Bardenas, spaces which have been preserved owing to their great ecological value. The first, a small cirque covering 500 hectares, is *El Vedado de Eguarás*. In the Middle Ages it was called *El Vedado de Miraflor*, like the castle whose ruins it contains, a place where only the Kings of Navarre came to hunt deer, at least until the end of the XIVth century. It is now private property with many pine trees, which are accustomed to heat and drought and can live up to two hundred years. They reach a height of 20 metres and are easily distinguished from afar by their rounded, light green top of fine needles which last for two years. The thin trunk has a whitish bark. In the rich heaths there are junipers and mastic trees of considerable height. Common reed-grass and other reeds grow around the lakes, and white outcrops of chalk appear along the paths and tracks. A range of high, spectacular cliffs separates the Vedado de Eguarás from the plain in the form of a stunning line of eroded columns.

The second Reserve has the poetic name of *El Rincón del Bú*. The "Bú" evokes the owl, which breeds in the steep cliffs and takes to the air at night, marking out its territory with a gentle *"uhu"*, hence its name. The 'Rincón' is not small, it covers 460 hectares, and its main interest lies in that it provides a good example of shapes of land erosion. It is a countryside of gullies, cliffs and *cabezos* covered with saltwort, clay and limestone, loam and sandstone in colourful horizontal layers. It has entry and exit points such as *El Balcón de Pilatos* ('the Balcony of Pontius Pilate') an excellent vantage point for birds of prey and other steppe species.

The third natural reserve is the *Caídas de la Negra*. This area, with its 1,926 hectares, is the second largest in Navarre, with drops of 270 metres in the surface of the land. Crops and corrals mingle among thick pinewood with kermes oaks which cover the twisting, steep slopes. The wildlife is that of a Mediterranean wood, with boar, wildcats, dormice, eagles and wood-pigeons.

So much for Nature. In geological terms the Bardenas are a recent creation, an area of fluvial origin which is still subject to a fierce process of erosion. From the many vantage points you can see an imposing, changing panorama of high hills and deep gullies. The geology, climate and vegetation have led some people to claim that

the Bardenas is a sub-desert, but the reality is that it contains attractive life forms and resources which have interested Man since time immemorial. In the XIVth century the Navarrese historian José Yanguas y Miranda wrote: "The Bardenas is a great land of pasture, firewood and arable land."

The area has not always been exploited peacefully. Its history reflects ambition and violence, but also that good sense and understanding can make life easier, with justice and culture creating a harmonious way of living with Nature.

Photographers, painters and film-makers have fallen in love with the Bardenas. They like its distances, plains, marked contrasts, delicate colours and hues, and even its sometimes blinding light. Also its solitude, which is neither static nor completely silent.

A couple of surfaced roads penetrate the Bardenas, together with a complex network of tracks, routes and sheep-paths from north to south across its 30 miles length and 15 miles width. Three gullies drain it. The largest, *Las Limas*, twists for 30 miles and acts as a collector for the Bardena Blanca before petering out among rice-fields. Marshland crabs, frogs and storks now abound on land where the fighting bulls of Guenduláin and Carriquiri were once

The area of Pisquerra in the Bardena Blanca. The vegetation has disappeared and the accelerated erosion leads to spectacular land forms.

raised, bulls which even fought in Paris and were the basis for famous bull-ranches in America.

HISTORY AND HUMAN ACTIVITY: SHEPHERDS AND FARMERS

Sancho Garcés I, who founded the Kingdom of Pamplona, massacred the Muslim army of the Banu Quasi in a fierce battle in the Bardenas on 20th July 915. The frontier remained very unstable, however, for at least another 150 years. It was certainly not an impenetrable border, as it seems that Christians and Muslims crossed it frequently and transhumance continued even during times of great tension.

Julio Caro Baroja says that trashumance has been documented since Roman times. He also states, however, that the origin of the descent from Roncal to the Bardenas cannot be exactly established, although some date it back to Prehistoric times. With the arrival of Autumn the flocks come down from the Pyrenees, where the snow covers the pastures above the tree line in winter. At the end of Spring the flocks return to the mountain passes, as two traditional *jotas* (traditional Navarrese folk songs) bear witness:

Ya ha llegado San Miguel,	San Miguel has arrived
pastores a la Bardena,	shepherds to the Bardena
a beber agua de balsa,	to drink pond water
y a dormir a la serena	and sleep outdoors.
Ya ha llegado Santa Cruz,	Santa Cruz has arrived
pastores a la montaña,	shepherds to the mountains
a comer migas con magra,	to eat breadcrumbs and ham
y a dormir en buena cama.	and sleep in a good bed.

Since 882 the Roncal valley has held the right to put flocks out to graze and make pens and huts. Moreover, the Salazar valley, 19 villages from the South of Navarre, and the Monastery of La Oliva now have equal access to the pastures, arable land, woods, hunting and other uses of the Bardenas.

About three hundred thousand head of sheep used to spend the winter in the Bardenas. Now that most of the flocks are from surrounding areas (transhumance has dropped considerably) the numbers are probably only a third of that figure. The pressure on sheep farming is very much felt, however, because since the end of the last century large tracts of land have been turned over to crops, and pastures now occupy about half the area they did previously.

Two major livestock routes cross the Bardenas. The main route is 75 metres wide, and that of the byways 50 metres wide. About twenty thousand sheep still pass along the *Cañada Real de los Roncaleses*, and those which do the entire route (130 kilometres from Vidángoz, in the Roncal valley, to the Bardena Negra) take six or seven days to make the journey. The sheep move at a leisurely pace, never stop grazing along the way, get excited when they reach the watering-holes and only move at a 'top speed' of 3 kilometres per hour. The *Cañada Real* from Tauste to the mountain ranges of Urbasa and Andía is less used. Ten thousand head of sheep from nearby villages still use it to this day although no flocks take its entire diagonal route across Navarre; the disused hill huts are now in ruins. Not only sheep have passed along the paths, however. Many heads of cattle have been led along them by mountain livestock rearers from the Salazar and Roncal valleys. Caro Baroja says that this is surely the reason why they were nicknamed *chalabardanos*, because in the Basque language the calf is called *txahal*.

The Rasa sheep, known in some areas as 'churra', an edgy animal which eats grass, stubble and plants, is closely linked to this area. The archaeologist Blas Taracena joked that the "the sheep is to the Bardena as the camel is to the Sahara." The Rasa sheep, producer of good lambs and fine wool, is also the mother of Roncal cheese, the first to obtain its own Designation of Origin in Spain.

It is interesting to watch the movement of livestock when the summer hunting season is over. The flocks of sheep, guided by calves carrying enormous bells, spend the night near El Paso, the natur-

Cereals in the Bardenas. The low and irregular rainfall means that crops in these non-irrigated lands are very erratic.

al entry 'gate'. At dawn on 18th September the *Cabo de Guardas* fires his rifle to signal the start of the pasture season.

Near El Paso a well-deserved monument to the shepherd has been raised. Since the Neolithic Age no human figure has been so closely associated with Las Bardenas. The shepherd, with his clever and obedient sheepdog as sole company, is used to the sun and the rain and often acts as a watchman. He is used to an austere diet, all his protein coming from some sheep in the flock which have died or from the frogs and rabbits he catches. He made necessity a gastronomic virtue and invented 'migas' (dried bread and suet) and added potatoes and beans to taste. In his book *La Cocina Popular en Navarra* ('Popular Cuisine in Navarre'), Víctor Manuel Sarobe picks up a strange recipe from shepherds in the Bardenas. It stems from the *cholent* of the Jewish community from the Tudela area, a dish they prepared over a slow fire on Friday nights so as to respect the Sabbath: beans and water in an earthenware pot which is covered and left to cook over the burning embers of a fire.

Living conditions for the shepherds have improved considerably. There are now about eighty new, large and well-ventilated stock-yards in the Bardenas, some of them with comfortable living accommodation. The shepherds rarely spend the night there, however. At sunset they close in the sheep and head off to the nearest village to spend the night.

For many centuries the pastures were the main form of human exploitation of the area. The jurist Francisco Salinas Quijada has written how "the conflict of interests between farmers and livestock rearers is one of a sad series of violent disputes, vicious brawls, and even horrific massacres. It was a struggle for survival. Because the basic problems were so serious, discussion usually ended up in bloodshed; the farmers almost always suffered more than the shepherds." This continued until a verdict was passed at the end of the XIVth century. Many official regulations followed, but they always gave pasture rights precedence over ploughing the land.

Agriculture in the Bardenas has been practised for little over a century. Indeed, it hardly existed before. The geographer Alfredo Floristán, whose work is a landmark in scientific knowledge of the area, has compared (on a smaller scale) the era of creating new farmland at the end of the XIXth century with the period of colonisation. He has collected verses from *jotas* of the time which reflect the tensions between the two disputing sides: the 'corraliceros' (shepherds) and the 'comuneros' (farmers). The controversy continues to the present day between the 'partitionists' and 'antipartitionists': The villages on the edges of the Bardenas possess over eighty per cent of the cultivated land: other villages further away proposed dividing the Bardenas so that each village could have exclusive rights to its particular area. The lawsuit was a long one and has led to far-reaching verdicts.

Since 1979 the right of the Community of the Bardenas to full and direct control over the territory has been recognised, and the rights of the villages have also been ratified. A farmers' trade union maintains that it is the people and not the municipal councils which hold the working rights to the area, and points out that in practice the farmers are the owners of the land they work. As far as the trade union is concerned the Community is no more than an administrative entity. The municipal councils, on the other hand, defend the structure and functions of the *Junta* which governs the Bardenas and are opposed to what they consider to be the privatisation of an area which has always been common land. Behind this dispute is the difficult economic situation of agriculture and livestock rearing, and the rational exploitation or abandonment of the land and animals. The Government of Navarre insists on the need to put local resources and practices in order before dealing with the possible declaration of the territory (4% of the surface area of Navarre) as a Natural Park.

Apart from grazing, agriculture, forestry and hunting, the Bardenas offers other curious examples of economic activity. Throughout the centuries stone, limestone and chalk have been extracted for construction, and charcoal has been produced in large quantities in the pine forests. Pitch to make leather, baskets and ceramics impermeable has been made in ovens since the Bronze Age, from sap from the pines. A place name bears witness to this: the 'Barranco del Horno de la Pez' ('pitch oven gully'). Likewise, the 'Barranco del Viso' conjures up images of the *visco* (mistletoe) found there in abundance. It was used to make the sticky *liga* (strip) to catch birds. Esparto grass was used to make rustic footwear, receptacles and string.

CASTLES AND BANDITS

In the Middle Ages the frontier territory of the Bardenas was dotted with castles, heirs to the Roman *turres*. They were basic watchtowers which sometimes served double duty as prisons, and more often as points which sent smoke signals by day and fire signals by night. Good examples remain, some of them perched on inaccessible hillocks, or at least a reminder of those that King Sancho el Fuerte ordered built at the beginning of the XIIIth century: Aguilar, Mirapex, Peñaflor, Peñarredonda and Sanchoabarca.

The Bardenas is a desolate, rugged land with woods which villains used as hiding places, particularly in times of political crisis. The phrase "echarse a la Bardena" (run for the Bardenas) came to mean dedicating oneself to pillage or fleeing from the Law. The remains of the 'Torre de la Estaca' (Stake Tower) are visible near the Passage of Santa Margarita, on the border of the kingdoms of Navarre and Aragon. In 1204 a Fraternity of Aragonese and Navarrese was established to defend themselves against bandits. When the bandits were caught, a chain was tied around their necks and they had to defend their cause themselves. Capital punishment was carried out nearby because, according to Fernando Videgáin, there were four gallows in the Bardenas: at Poyo Redondo, Cabezo de Puy García, Puy de Sancho and Peña Pasarera.

During the civil war in the XIVth century between the rival factions of the 'Agramonteses' and 'Beaumonteses' a certain Sancho Rota (nicknamed "Sanchicorrota") lorded over the area, committing all manner of plunder and kidnapping with his gang of thirty horsemen. King Juan II ordered two hundred knights to stop Sancho's antics, and, despite being outnumbered, the bandit stood his ground hard and managed to wound and capture some of his adversaries. Towards the end of the fight, however, his group was split up and almost all his companions died. Realising it was all over, he took out his dagger and plunged it into his chest. His corpse was hung up and shown in Tudela.

During later centuries stories still abounded of villains who attacked travellers and post coaches. Angel Morrás wrote a romantic novel about Álvarez from Tudela (known as 'Moneos'), a stagecoach robber who behaved in a gentlemanly manner to the ladies of his victims.

From the highest point of the Codés mountain range, the rocky mass of Yoar overlooks a group of villages and dominates the alluvial plain that slopes down like a fan towards the river Ebro. This land, inhabited since ancient times, is a busy frontier crossroads. Viana stands on a hilly outpost 'like a fossilised stone vessel with its stern and bow, masts and spars which have no sails, and the worn masts of two watchtowers. This vessel, after a cruel and difficult voyage, remains anchored, stranded, now that the tide of history has ebbed. A city-island, a city-countryside, a city with a pleasant sounding name', says the writer Pablo Antoñana.

VIANA
AND THE LITERARY
REPUBLIC OF YOAR

In the South-west corner of Navarre, the Codés range forms the final barrier to the Ebro depression. It is an isolated spot, as beautiful as it is unknown. In the centre the grey and bluish rocks of Yoar rise up, flanked to the East by the Costalera Cliffs and to the West by the Chiquita range. These two ridges then spread out in a chaotic series of crags, ravines, and stony slopes. The geological unity is broken by the massive silhouettes of the rocky pinnacles of *Los Penitentes*, which line up their undulating crests above the dense holm oak wood. To the North, a leafy beech wood conceals the steep slope of the land while Peñalabeja, a 24-hectare Nature Reserve, protects a cluster of cypress oaks, which are very rare in Navarre. Attractive plants grow amongst the rocks in the sunny spots, and eagles and Egyptian Vultures nest in the limestone cliffs. Kermes gall oaks intermingle below with boxwood, broom, junipers, strawberry trees, and a few vineyards and scattered olive trees are to be found on the edge of the *Sierra*.

The source of the Linares and Odrón rivers is in Codés. They are really small streams and, at their lowest, become mere scars suppurating water. They join after draining the moisture from the Aguilar and Berrueza valleys. The Aguilar valley is a very fertile, sheltered, narrow strip, ideal for growing market-garden vegetables. The rock rose found on the rugged low ridges may have given *La Berrueza* its name, or it may be from the tilled wine-red earth which produces cereals, vegetables, oil and wine.

From 'El Alto de los Bojes' in Aras, through wild, rural scenery of abandoned fields, olive groves, almond trees, asparagus fields, vineyards and cereal plantations, the district of Viana gradually descends to the small market gardens of the plain and reaches the banks of the Ebro, where groves of trees and an irrigation system dating back to ancient times are to be found. The plain is fertile and provides delicious green vegetables, red peppers and delicate fruit.

On the boundary with La Rioja there is a Nature Reserve which has been declared of international importance: the reservoir of Las Cañas. It covers 100 hectares and must have originated as a lagoon. In the XVIIth century it was flooded with salt water for irrigation. A long dam increased its area and capacity, giving a depth of around 6 metres in the deepest areas. Today it has returned to Nature, with a beautiful belt of vegetation. The marsh species spontaneously form concentric borders depending on the time they live underwater. Bulrushes, reeds, rushes, tamarisks, willows and black poplars cling to the wetland. The dense colony of night herons has brought international recognition. Las Cañas is also the wetland with the greatest variety of nesting species in Navarre, and is the second in terms of density of birds. From the nearby observatory of El Bordón there are sightings of mallards, red crested pochards, purple and grey herons, bitterns, bitterns, black winged stilts and grebes. During the winter months flocks of up to 100,000 starlings arrive, flying in formation and gathering in the reedbeds.

[PAGE 213] *The Church of Santa María de Viana has the size and air of a Cathedral.*

[OPPOSITE] *On the heights of Piñalba, in the heart of la Berrueza, stands the basilica of San Gregorio Ostiense.*

The 1st of February is a holiday for the schoolchildren of Viana. A roll of drums and a peal of bells summons them to the Church of Santa María. The mayor reminds them that on this same day in 1219 the first stone of their town was laid; each child is given a coin and they leave the church, 'one by one and through just one door' to spend it on sweets.

The origin of the name 'Viana' has been discussed at length. It may be related to the names of other European cities with similar names. Some consider it to be of Celtic-Iberian origin and relate it to archaeological findings in the area or to words that indicate a military position. Others resort to legend and affirm that the Romans, surprised to find a large area of vineyards there, named it *vinetum*. In the XVIIIth century, according to Caro Baroja, the great vineyard of Viana was widely acclaimed.

The town boasts some important prehistoric sites. In the middle Palaeolithic period the settlement of La Custodia was initiated. This was a prosperous place that reached its splendour in the second half of the Iron Age but was destroyed in the first century BC. The *Hypogaeus* of Longar belongs to the end of the Neolithic and Calcolithic periods. It is a long, corridor-type tomb with over one hundred corpses. It remained intact until excavation work began in 1991, as its heavy covering caved in during prehistoric times. There are other Bronze and Iron Age sites and at least a dozen Roman villas, some of which survived until mediaeval times.

The XIth and XIIth centuries saw an increase in the number of pilgrims along the Way to Compostela. As they passed through the walkers and horse-riders caught a glimpse of those ancient settlements and even went through two of them. Today a fountain surrounded by pinewoods is to be found in the depression where the village of Cornava once stood. The remains of Cuevas, cited by Aymeric Picaud in his travel guide, are more clearly visible. The author of the Calixtine Manuscripts could not imagine the present hermitage dating back to the XVIIIth century but he may well have seen the image of the Virgin kept there, and he would definitely have observed and might even have been received by 'La Orden', a convent of the Order of the Holy Trinity under the patronage of Roncesvalles whose robust Gothic ruins still stand. Many legends and stories still exist about some wicked monks who hid all they robbed from travellers in holes, or about a hen that hid nearby with her twelve golden chicks.

At the beginning of the XIIIth century, with the appearance of the frontier with Castile, the strategic value of a small hill was noticed. Viana, a decisive part of a line of fortifications, was created by King Sancho VII el Fuerte by joining various neighbouring villages together, either willingly or by force. Each village was a separate district within the new walled enclosure and was allowed to maintain its historical records.

Juan Cruz Labeaga has studied the history of Viana's art and town planning in depth. The streets were arranged in a straight line: "The map of the construction, a 450 by 125 meter rectangle, is a very regular parade ground. Placed on the highest point of a hill, it follows the arrangement of a Roman camp. Its main street, La rúa Mayor, is on a longitudinal axis, and another is on a transversal axis. The square is located at the crossing point of the two axes. The narrow streets and high buildings are a result of defence requirements and the lack of land. The wall was built slightly away from the blocks of houses since, according to the laws of the time, there had to be sufficient space for a horse and rider to pass. Surrounded by a double enclosure with towers built at intervals, its accesses were, and still are, six main gates and two side gates. The castle and the churches of San Pedro and Santa María were built in the corners. The poor quarter, inhabited by the poor and the Jews, developed next to this fortified enclosure." The quarter of Torreviento, close to the walls, was one of the most thriving Jewish communities in Navarre; it had as many as 45 houses, and, like the rest, was assaulted and razed to the ground in 1328.

As well as fulfilling a strategic objective, King Sancho must also have thought about promoting a corner of his kingdom and opening up a trade route, so he gave a charter to the people for the defence of the town. The walls were built in just four months, and the King granted the 'Privilegio del Aguila' when they were completed in April 1219, evoking the ancient coat of arms of Navarre. The Privilege determined that the Gate of San Felices would be where justice would be dispensed and stated that: 'if there were no witnesses, your oath would be sufficient'. It freed the inhabitants from heavy burdens, giving them the right to own goods and buy and sell, and also to make use of communal property: "wherever you find uncultivated land plough it; wherever you find grassland, graze it and sow it; wherever you find water to water animals, small vegetable plots, or mills, use it."

Viana became a resting place along the Pilgrim's Way, a market, a shelter, an inn and a hospital, and a place of residence for labourers and craftsmen.

The main altar-piece in Santa María de Viana, the apotheosis of the Virgin Mary in the Assumption, is given a strong personality by its excellent decoration.

it was bought for 14,000 silver ducats. This was a period of prosperity and splendour, after some very hard years.

When the kingdom was in its death throes, Viana became the scene of a struggle between the Beamonteses, allied with Castile, and the Agramonteses, who favoured the Navarrese dynasty. In this climate, a man who embodied the Renaissance spirit came to die at the gates of Viana. César Borgia, son of Pope Alexander VI, had been named Bishop of Pamplona when he was 16, but he was never even ordained as a priest. His father made him a cardinal and an instrument of his policies. He had spoken impeccable Latin since he was a boy, studied theology and law, had a good income, and was ambitious and arrogant. In short, he lacked nothing. Machiavellian in nature, those who knew him and had dealings with him said that 'there was nothing so great that it would not appear small beside him'. The turbulent politics of Europe brought him to Navarre. After escaping from prison at Medina del Campo, he reached the Court of his brother-in-law, Juan de Albret, and the King appointed him Chief of Army Operations in Navarre. He died, speared by a lance, in an area which cannot be precisely located on 11th March 1507.

The tomb of Cesar Borgia has, like the personage himself, an uneasy history. His remains were placed in a Gothic alabaster mausoleum in the High Altar of the Church of Santa María. The monument, a gift from the King of Navarre, was dismantled in that same XVIth Century by the presumed decision of a Bishop of Calahorra who ordered the body to be put out onto the street 'in order that, in payment of his sins, men and beasts should trample on it', as it was the corpse of an excommunicated person. Since 1953, after certain studies of identification, the bones found where tradition indicated he had been buried now rest in front of the church porch under a white marble tomb stone, and 'the people from Viana softly tread on them, with care' according to the mayor at the time.

CÉSAR BORGIA AND HIS TOMB

In 1423 King Carlos III established the Principality of Viana for his grandson Carlos and the future heirs to the crown of Navarre. However, it did not receive the status of 'ciudad' until 1630, when

THE RENAISSANCE AND BAROQUE STYLE IN VIANA

After the conquest of Navarre by Castile the walls of Viana underwent major modifications although the castle itself remained intact, saved from the general destruction ordered by Cardinal Cisneros in 1516. The great fortress survived until the beginning of the XXth century. Next to it, a large area was flattened in the XVIth century in order to hold bull festivals. It was called the 'Plaza del Coso' and is still used for the same purpose.

The town has two large churches. The ruins of the Gothic parish church of San Pedro reveal the strangeness of the front of the church, with five radiating chapels, the square tower as a look-out post and defence, and the stonework and sculpture of the Baroque doorway.

The church of Santa María resembles a cathedral in size and appearance, with three large naves, chapels, clerestory and ambulatory. The grandiose facade is like an altar-piece in stone with themes from the Passion and Christ's infancy. Fernando Chueca Goitia said that it was: "one of the most daring attempts of the XVIth century to organise a classic façade", and, according to José Camón Aznar:

The reliquary of the apocryphal bishop saint, San Gregorio Ostiense, who has protected the fields from locusts and plagues for centuries, is shown here in front of the Baroque façade of his sanctuary.

the Baptist by the royal sculptor Jehan Lome de Tournai, who also made the tomb of Carlos III and his wife for the cathedral of Pamplona.

In addition to this Gothic carving, the chapel of San Juan del Ramo, built from 1781 onwards, also holds the best collection of XVIIIth century paintings in Navarre. They are refined oils and temperas in the Rococo style, corresponding to a programme conceived by its author, Luis Paret y Alcázar. He was an elegant artist but with a popular wit and, amongst his contemporaries, was second only to Goya. Remaining faithful to the biblical environment and with a preference for a range of blues and greens, Paret illustrated scenes from the life of John the Baptist in oils of minute detail and temperas with a loose brush. The critics, who always preferred the painting of the 'Announcement of the Angel to Zaccharias' as his most complete work, coincided with the tastes of the author himself who wrote 'I very much like this work, it is the best

'the composition of the façade is most audacious and shows the greatest architectural genius of our Renaissance period, being one of the few conceived coherently as a single unit with great style'. Its main creators were four artists, all named 'Juan': Juan de Goyaz, Juan de Orbara, and two Juan Ochoa de Arranotegui (father and son). Inside there are several Baroque altar-pieces, all made in a local sculpture workshop. The excellent decoration gives a strong character to the high altar piece, the apotheosis of the Virgin in her Assumption. The vestry has a beautiful collection of liturgical ornaments from the XVth, XVIth and XVIIth centuries.

Inside the imposing church of Santa María, the Chapel of San Juan del Ramo is worthy of attention. The name itself is noteworthy, referring to a Franciscan convent which changed its location to the centre of Viana from the extinct medieval settlement at Soto, near Aras, where the ruins of an early hermitage are to be found.

There is a wonderful legend which says that Carlos, Prince of Viana, was out hunting one day when he was caught in a heavy storm. He sought refuge in the church of San Juan de Soto but it was locked, so he decided to shelter under an oak. A flash of lightning reduced the tree to ashes except for one branch, under which the hunter remained unharmed. It has been demonstrated that the Foundation was created in 1440 by Prince Carlos, who supposedly made a gift of a beautiful Gothic-Flemish image of John

I have done'. Paret, who designed the beautiful fountains which brought the first water to Pamplona, also stood out in Santa María as a designer of furniture and accessories: some as beautiful as the tabernacle of the high altar, the altar tables or the processional cross.

The entire Old Part of Viana has been declared of Cultural Interest. XVIIth and XVIIIth century palaces and houses of the nobility abound. The Town Hall, a Baroque building with arcades, has a great stone coat of arms on its facade and two brick turrets. The old Pilgrims' Hospital of *Nuestra Señora de Gracia*, a Gothic structure with Baroque additions, has a sober dining room where the members of the brotherhood of Veracruz dispatch the typical Maundy Thursday supper: *Migas* (cooked breadcrumbs), broad beans, wine served in earthenware pitchers and raisins and figs for dessert.

VIANA AND ITS WRITERS

In October 1833, to cries of 'Long live Don Carlos!', Santos Ladrón de Cegama passed through Viana at the head of a group of volunteers armed with cudgels. A short time later, he was taken prisoner and his execution in the Citadel of Pamplona marked the beginning of the first Carlist war, a cruel war with hand-to-hand bayonet battles.

A young writer from Viana who hated the war and the Carlists read some fiery verses before the victorious General Espartero. However, Francisco Navarro Villoslada, a convinced Catholic, soon abandoned liberalism and became part of the Ultramontés band. He directed fundamentalist newspapers and earned the trust of Charles VII, the Carlist pretender. He was one of the promoters of the romantic historic novel. His best works were written during his youth: 'Doña Urraca de Castilla' was a narrative of surprising speed, and 'Doña Blanca de Navarra' was published in three editions in a very short space of time. At the age of 50, obstinate and shut away in his house in Viana, he would walk about the rooms reciting aloud what would then be put to paper. This is how 'Amaya or the Basques of the VIIIth century' was created. The musician Jesús Guridi performed the work for the first time as an opera in 1920, and a film of it was made in 1952.

The house of Navarro Villoslada is at number 26 in the street bearing his name. An inscription in Classical Latin, 'siste gradum, viator' attracts the passer-by's attention and causes him to stop and remember the 'poet of the Basque race'. The traveller who loves literature may have two reasons for halting because, in the same bed and room where Don Francisco died, another writer of our times was born: Pablo Antoñana, another writer marked by the trauma of a war he hated. He is a modern-day chronicler of an expressive rural language, columnist, author of prize-winning novels and tales, and the creator of a harsh but endearing literary universe.

THE 'REPUBLIC' OF YOAR

Ethnographers classify the local scenery as one of 'transition between the mountains and the plain, a producer of grain, vegetables, oil and wine'. For Antoñana, it is a group of "small villages, with a fountain of just one spout, and saints with very strange names which are called upon to remedy any wrong. My 'Republic of Yoar', small and deep, full of bandits, outlaws, bishops of Havana and alchemists like Joanes, the sorcerer of Bargota."

It extends as far as Los Arcos, which XIIth century documents call *Urancia* and *Arqueta* in the regional language. Its long Calle Mayor is a harmonious ensemble of strong houses and unassuming cottages built from a mixture of stone blocks and bricks. The coats of arms of the nobility and the magnificent ironwork of the balconies add beauty to the facade of the *Plaza de la Fruta*. There is a Renaissance Tower by Martín and Juan de Landerrain, considered by many to be the most beautiful bell tower in the whole of Navarre. The church of Saint Mary has a Plateresque facade and Gothic cloisters.

[OPPOSITE AND ABOVE] *Visitors are invariably impressed by the Romanesque church of the Holy Sepulchre at Torres del Río. It is octagonal and covered with star-shaped cross ribs.*

For reasons of war, Los Arcos belonged to Castile for almost three centuries, as did the other small villages around it. In El Busto there are large stone houses and Armañanzas has a large house with a wide staircase used by the owner to go up on horseback to his rooms. Desojo is close by where, according to the Madoz Dictionary, 'the most common ailments are colds'. Sansol received its name from its patron saint Zoilo, whose bust on the altar-piece carries a kidney on a tray as he waited to cure the urinary and bladder complaints of the faithful. In Torres del Río, visitors are always astonished by the small Romanesque church of the Holy Sepulchre, with its octagonal ground-plan and vaulted roof with star-shaped cross ribs.

Azuelo is located on a high point in the Aguilar valley. Very close to the village the parish of Saint George is to be found. This was a Benedictine monastery which appeared in chronicles in 992 and even succeeded in collecting more relics than Leire. The church was built in the first quarter of the XIIth century with Romanesque influences from Jaca and Loarre in Aragon. The original wooden roof was replaced in the XVIth century by the vaults which are still in place today, as is the rich Romanesque doorway of the façade. The interior is high and well-lit and is powerfully built. From the outside a singular play of volumes can be appreciated between the cubic bodies of the transept, the polygonal shape of the roof and the rounded forms of the apse.

In 1375 the Franks and noblemen of the small town of Torralba founded the brotherhood of St. John the Baptist to defend the inhabitants from malefactors: It was organised into three groups during combat: crossbowmen, lancers, and a third one which included the remaining inhabitants with spears, shafts and slings. According to legendary tradition, in the XVIth century there was a group of bandits who had their hideout in Punicastro, close to the rocky summit of Yoar. There was a chase and a long, hard battle and in the end, Juan Lobo, the captain of these outlaws, was speared by a lance and fell dead. To celebrate this, the brothers agreed to kill a lamb every October and accompany the festivities with the *gaita* (bagpipes) and drum. The festival has been repeated ever since and the Dance of the Crossbowmen of San Juan is still performed in Codés.

At Piñalba, in the heart of the Berrueza valley, stands the basilica of Saint Gregorio Ostiense. The saint was an apocryphal bishop who has protected people against locusts, fleas and downy mildew for centuries. Not content with receiving visits, he sent the water blessed in his sanctuary to distant lands and even paraded his relic in royal coaches, to such an extent that it is common to say in Navarre that 'this is going round more times than the head of Saint Gregorio'. Everything is very beautiful in Sorlada: the location, the miraculous arrival of the saint's body on the back of a mule, the wonders, the brotherhood, the reliquary and the basilica with a magnificent doorway, simple paintings and wonderful stuccoes. It is one of the most important Baroque monuments in Navarre.

NAVARRE
The land and its people

Navarre is located at a cultural and geographical cross-roads and is a land of great contrasts and similarities. It covers 10,391 square kilometres (2.1% of the total territory of Spain), and has a population of 520,574. Its low population

density, 50 per square kilometre, is two-thirds of the Spanish figure and only one-sixth of the Dutch. It is region steeped in history which has a very defined personality, its political identity going back to the XIIIth century. It has two official languages (Spanish and Basque) and a high level of self-government, including powers of tax collection and administration which have never been lost. Its GDP per capita is 91% of the European Union average. The region's agriculture is highly developed and its industrial productivity is the best in Spain.

"Some States and nationals were formed and developed on the basis of ethnic, linguistic, religious and geographical unity. Others, however, did so according to their territorial and cultural contrasts. Navarre belongs to the second group. It is a historical region made up of diverse areas which are nevertheless cohesively linked by the thread of history. It is not a geographical region, but a historically coherent one. Historic because history marked out the borders of its territory; not even the Pyrenees are a natural geographic border. Navarre's present-day border is impossible to explain without bearing in mind that for centuries it was a kingdom stretching across the Pyrenees. Coherent because the solidarity and interdependence between the culturally and ecologically dissimilar parts of the territory have played a major role in the formation and consolidation of the ancient Kingdom. The two cornerstones of the 'functional union' that is Navarre are the Pyrenees and the Ebro valley."

These words by the geographer Alfredo Floristán are the key to understanding that Navarre is a complex region whose unity is based on diversity and the exchange of complementary resources. It is a small but varied territory with scenery in the north reminiscent of the Alps or the Atlantic coast of Europe, and in the south large irrigated tracts of land and eroded steppes with gullies which remind you more of the wadis of the Sahara Desert.

Navarre stands at the western end of the Pyrenees and has several ancient mountain valleys and passes. It has a perimeter of 757 kilometres, 163 of them along the French border to the north, the remainder with the other three neighbouring Autonomous Communities: 190 km. with the Basque Country, 149 km. with La Rioja and 255 km. with Aragón.

The *navarros* spontaneously divide their land into two areas, the *Montaña* (the mountainous area in the north) and the *Ribera* ('riviera') in the south i.e. the extended area around the Ebro river and valley, with an intermediate *Zona Media* (central area) in between. This vision of Navarre is a very ancient one, as the ancient Basques distinguished a woody *saltus* in the north and a ploughable *ager* in the south. Transhumance along the *cañadas* (cattle/sheep tracks), general traffic along the roads and paths, and wood transport down rivers in rafts were age-old ways of communication.

Looking at Navarre on a map, the territory is defined by the rivers within the three main areas referred to above. Indeed, the rivers had a greater impact than the mountain ranges when the region's administrative divisions were established. The structure of municipalities, *cendeas* (groupings of villages into one administrative unit), valleys and *consejos* (small village councils) dates back to the Roman era, and the division into *merindades* (similar to counties) took place in the Middle Ages.

The highest point in Navarre is the 'Mesa de los Tres Reyes' (Table of the Three Kings) at 2,434 metres above sea level in the Roncal valley at the western end of the Pyrenees. The lowest point is the bridge at Endarlaza, where the Bidasoa river flows into neighbouring Gipuzkoa in the north near the sea. The town of Bera is the lowest in Navarre (56 metres above sea level), the highest being Abaurrea Alta at 1,032 metres. The highest building in use, however, is the church at Aralar (1,235 metres).

[TWO PREVIOUS PAGES] *The valley of Araiz, protected by the Malloak mountains, is at the northern end of the Aralar range.*
[ABOVE] *The woody saltus to the north and the cultivable ager to the south make up the landscape of Navarre.*
[OPPOSITE] *The new Library building on the campus of the Universidad de Navarra, alongside the Sadar river.*

The rivers in Navarre flow in two different directions. The shorter, faster-flowing rivers Bidasoa and Urumea (1,300 cubic hectometres per year) end up in the Bay of Biscay. There is a popular saying that the south-flowing Ega, Arga and Aragón "make the Ebro a man of a river", because between them they contribute 4,150 cubic hectometres, 23 per cent of the total volume the Ebro then takes to the Mediterranean. The dams in the region regulate the torrential flows to a certain extent, enable irrigation and water supply, and avoid the flood peaks produced by their feared freshets.

In the limited ten thousand square kilometres of Navarre there are effectively three climates: damp Atlantic, cold Alpine, and sunny, dry Mediterranean. This also explains the biological diversity of the region. In Navarre it is possible to find thirty-three plant varieties in contrast to the seven found 200 kilometres north of the region, beyond the Pyrenees. The leafy woods of the northern mountains give way to conifer forests to the east. The change to the Mediterranean climate occurs in the Central Area and marks a transition from standard and gall oak to holm and kermes oak. There are still rosemary and thyme groves in the Ribera on clayey and loamy soils, and esparto grass and tamarinds in the steppes of Las Bardenas. A series of Reserves, Enclaves and Natural Parks protect the region's most valuable lands.

Navarre is particularly interesting from the wildlife standpoint, and it is particularly a paradise for ornithologists. Recent guides have catalogued 26 different species of fish, 16 amphibians,

25 reptiles, 183 nesting birds and 46 mammals. Some species at risk such as the bear and the Lammergeier, which are emblematic for ecologists and nature lovers, are specially protected. Hunting is organised on the basis of rigorous scientific criteria in order to regulate the strong pressure represented by 33,000 weapon licences.

Animal husbandry, particularly cattle in the Pyrenees and *latxa* and *jaca* sheep from Navarre have received special attention in recent years because, in the opinion of the experts, improvements in animal science create a greater need for indigenous animals. Historians have also shown interest in studying these domestic animals, whose evolution can shed light on human migration.

THE POPULATION

In May 1996 Navarre had a population of 520,574, half of it in Pamplona and its surrounding area.

It is a stable population which, as in the whole of the European Union, is ageing. Two decades ago young people under 15 years of age represented 26 per cent of the entire population of Navarre, but now they only account for 14.4 per cent. In contrast, the proportion of people over 64 years of age grew from 11.1% to 17.3%.

The age pyramid tends to resemble a screw which is narrow at its base and vortex. There are more pensioners in the region (94,548) than schoolchildren. This is due to longer life expectancy and many early retirements. Around one thousand nonagenarians live in

Pamplona, one fifth of them leading a completely independent life and another fifth being totally dependent on the care of others. A study by Dr. Sánchez-Ostiz shows that previous cases of longevity in a family and being a woman are the two decisive factors in reaching such a ripe old age.

The towns which have grown most over recent years are those around Pamplona and in the Ebro valley. Estella, Tafalla and some places near the Arakil and Bidasoa rivers have also expanded. The Pyrenean valleys are losing population, together with the villages in the Estella area and those located on the northern edge of Las Bardenas.

Navarre has 900 populated localities, of which 67% have less than one hundred inhabitants. Small villages are increasingly present in the administrative 'mosaic' of 272 population centres, and moreover they are getting smaller all the time. The 258 municipalities with less than 5,000 inhabitants account for 95% of all localities, but they only hold 37% of the population. Eight have a population over 5,000, and six more than 10,000: Pamplona, Tudela, Barañain, Burlada, Estella and Tafalla. Thirty-two per cent of the population lives in the capital, Pamplona.

Navarre is a bilingual Community, the official languages being Spanish and Basque. The first is official all over the region, and the second has this status in the Basque-speaking areas. Statistics for 1996 show that 87,846 navarros speak or understand euskara (Basque). It is considered that 53,823 are euskaldunak (people who usually speak the language), of whom 92% are literate in Basque. There is also a group of 34,023 people who are almost native speakers, with a lower level of proficiency. In Pamplona and the 15 municipalities around it there are 16,477 native Basque speakers and 18,023 from the second group i.e. 40% of all the people of Navarre who speak Basque or state that they can to a certain extent.

Many visitors to Navarre have written about the character of the men and women of this land. In Ancient times and the Mediaeval period they were portrayed in rather negative terms, but the opinions expressed became rather subtler from the Renaissance onwards. Observers have considered that the people of Navarre have always been opinionated, fairly inarticulate, not given to verbal excesses, proud of their past, rather stubborn, good eaters and drinkers, ingenious and efficient when it comes to work, honest with themselves, hospitable and trustworthy. Those who know them best say that their greatest asset is their solidarity with causes, whether they be close to home or not, and the problems they have reaching consensus and understanding. These observations are both stereotyped but also offer insights into the character of the people of Navarre.

THE ECONOMY

Navarre's GDP was valued at 1,151,116,000,000 pesetas in 1996, accounting for 1.5 per cent of the total for the Spanish State. Production per employed person is 4.3% above the national average.

Navarre is a pioneer community in the use of renewable energy sources. The wind farm on the Perdón range was the first of many now in operation in the region.

The region's *per capita* GDP is equivalent to 91% of the European average, the fourth highest among the Autonomous Communities of Spain.

Active population figures for 1996 show that Navarre is clearly an industrial region (38% of all jobs), this sector contributing 41.7% of the GDP of the region. The agricultural sector (9% of employment) is largely made up of family-run smallholdings and accounts for 5.3% of the GDP. The service sector completes the picture with 53%, both in terms of employment and contribution to GDP.

There are 17,400 jobs in Agriculture, 54,800 in Industry (16,600 of them in Construction), and the Service sector employs 101,400 people. Of the total of 15,552 companies, 24 have over 500 employees, 329 between 51 and 500, and the rest are small and medium-sized companies with between 1 and 50 employees. The largest, Volkswagen, located near Pamplona, employs 4,565 people. There are 22 Industrial Estates in Navarre.

The sectors which make the greatest contribution to the industrial economy of the region are: automotive, electronics, household appliances, agro-processing and paper-making.

Multinational companies have a strong presence in Navarre: over 109 companies of this type have set up operations here.

The Social Economy Sector includes 356 Co-operatives and similarly-structured companies, representing 4,000 jobs. There are 179 agricultural co-operatives.

Within agriculture, animal husbandry and forestry are extensively practised on common land (464,850 hectares), i.e. 45% of the territory of Navarre. Twenty per cent of this common land is cropland, 33% pasture, and the rest woodland. These areas complement agricultural family income, help local tax collection, enable work of interest to the community to be undertaken, help in the improvement of social services, and provide leisure areas of great ecological value.

In 1997 the public sector in Navarre had a budget of 271 billion pesetas and employed 17.000 people. It invested 61 billion pesetas and the average sum spent per capita (not including money given to Municipal Councils) was 464,379 pesetas. Navarre spent 65.7 billion pesetas on Health, 54.2B on Education and Culture, 28.6B on Public Works, and finally 27.3B on Social Welfare and Protection.

In 1995 the 'Mancomunidades' (transmunicipal entities) and other local entities were allocated 58.6 billion pesetas, of which 64% were for current expenses and 36% for investment. At municipal level (employees: 4,500) average spending per capita was 109,283 pesetas.

The percentage of active population over total population grew from 34.1% to 42% in the period between 1976-1996. The level of male employment remains stable, with the large rise in women in work accounting for the overall increase.

Average unemployment in 1996 was 11.4% compared to the Spanish level of 22.2%. Of the 24,053 people out of work at the end of 1996, 40% were men and 60% women.

In the European context Navarre is a small, peripheral region belonging to the Atlantic Euro-Region. In terms of population, it is number 154 among the 179 regions of the fifteen countries of the EU. However, if its GDP *per capita* is considered, it is in position

105, and its unemployment rate puts it in 118th place.

In terms of Spain, Navarre is in the 'top group' of regions in terms of Regional Income, Family Disposable Income, and social, health and educational facilities. There were over 25,000 students enrolled in the courses of its three Universities (Public, Private and Open) during the 1996-97 Academic Year.

Exports from Navarre in 1996 reached 503 billion pesetas, representing a positive trade balance of 216 billion pesetas for the region. Eighty-four per cent of trade (exports and imports) is with other countries in the European Union.

The economists Manuel Rapún and Vicente Leoz have analysed the strengths and weaknesses of the regional economy: "It has a low level of specialisation in agriculture and a high level in industry. Its agriculture has one of the highest levels of productivity in Spain, although the productivity of the land is relatively low. Navarre has a developed, but not rich, agricultural sector. Its industrial productivity is the highest among the regions and is 11% above the Spanish average. In terms of industrial weak points, it is too dependent on the automotive sector and the concentration of foreign capital is very high. Nevertheless, Navarre has the advantages of good availability of natural resources, the level of qualification and skill of its workforce and the existence of a regional government with autonomy in tax collection and administration and many years of experience. Navarre should continue to increase the quantity and quality of its infrastructure."

Of its 3,511 kilometres of roads, 500 are main (national) 528 main (regional), and 2,483 country, with a 'spider's web' structure. A toll motorway links Pamplona with Zaragoza and there are two toll-free expressways to San Sebastián and Vitoria. The Belate tunnels facilitate communications to France. There are 175 kilometres of railway line in Navarre along the Alsasua-Zaragoza corridor. Pamplona (Noain) Airport has daily scheduled flights to Madrid and Barcelona, plus other services.

THE MARK OF HISTORY

The earliest evidence of human life in Navarre goes back to the Early Palaeolithic era, in the form of open-air stone workshops in the Urbasa mountain range. They data back over one hundred million years and correspond to pre-Neanderthal man. The caves of Alkerdi at Urdax have objects made by Cro-Magnon Man in the Late Palaeolithic Age.

During the Neolithic revolution most of the people in the territory spoke euskara (Basque) a pre-Indo-European language which still survives today. Dolmens appeared around 3000 B.C, and more

than 250 are preserved in Navarre. In the thousand years before Christ Indo-European migration brought the culture of iron to the area, together with hill villages and circular cromlechs, where the ashes of the dead were deposited.

The impact of the arrival of the Romans was not uniform but led to an excellent road system, a eries of small agricultural settlements, cities, the technical innovations of ploughing and using animals for pulling, and the new crops: wheat, vines and olives. Long before the idea of the 'territory' came about, early historians underlined the existence of a group, the vascones, which was described by Greek and Roman chroniclers.

The first Christian communities were set up in the south in the second half of the IIIrd century. It is sure that the town of Cascante had Bishops at that time, although the Bishopric of Pamplona came about later, possibly at the end of the 'Bajo Imperio', although its first known Bishop, the Visgoth Lilíolo, lived in the VIth century.

The name 'Navarra' is of Mediaeval origin and was not originally applied to the whole territory but just to the central western part. Julio Caro Baroja thinks it is a specifically Basque name. The philologist Mikel Castillo believes it comes from nabar, which means 'brown colour' in Basque, and was a widely used surname in the Middle Ages. Others think that the name is related to the pre-Roman name nava (plain between mountains). Eginhardo, a chronicler of Charlemagne in the IXth century, is the first writer to describe it: "Hiberum amnem apud Navarros ortus."

Given the scarce and unreliable documentation from the early Middle Ages, attempts have been made to explain the origins of the kingdom of Pamplona through later accounts of traditions and legends. The Mediaeval expert Angel Martín Duque speaks of a kingdom in a 'latent condition' with a later 'epiphany'. "It is accepted that the kingdom of Pamplona was fully instituted under Iñigo Arista, its first sovereign, before the IXth century. It seems reasonable to wonder if Iñigo Arista, his son García Iñiguez and even his grandson Fortún Garcés were really aware that they were at the head of a political framework in a geographical area of almost ridiculous size." The kingdom, explains Martín Duque, was born as a replica of Asturias and León, with the same anti-Islamic message behind it. There were various dominant noble families. It was only under Sancho Garcés I at the start of the Xth century that military success and expansion took place. A large part of the Ribera

[ABOVE] *One of the first remains of human presence in Navarre: the Portillo burial ground at Artajona.*
[OPPOSITE] *The Library of the Universidad Pública de Navarra, the most emblematic building on the campus.*

was dominated by the Arabs and people were converted to Islam until well into the XIIth century.

Sancho III el Mayor, who reined at the start of the XIth century, joined Christian land from Sobrarbe (Aragon) as far as León, built great public works, was a pro-European who established contacts with the monks of Cluny, opened up the Pilgrim's Way to Compostela and started town-building in a way which would attract the Franks.

In the summer of 1612 Sancho VI el Sabio (the King who called Basque the *lingua navarrorum*) changed the title 'King of the people of Pamplona' to 'King of Navarre'. Sancho VII el Fuerte, a huge man, behaved both as a covetous money-lender and a generous helper to those who took part of his kingdom away. In 1212 he led the troops of Navarre in the decisive battle of Navas de Tolosa.

French royal dynasties reigned in Navarre from the XIIIth century. Theobald I of Champagne, a Crusader king, was a great

The sculpture titled 'Momento espiritual' by Jorge Oteiza stands in Pamplona's Yamaguchi Park, the new 'green heart' of a city that is expanding westwards.

troubadour, and also elegant and courteous. During his reign the task of compiling the ancient laws (the 'Fueros') began. Over 44 years the Capets, Kings of France, also wore the Crown of Navarre. They were years of cruel civil conflict.

The House of Evreux brought with it French methods of administration. Carlos III, a pacifist and lover of the Arts, built the cathedral of Pamplona and the palaces of Olite and Tafalla, and was the architect of the union of the three warring and walled boroughs into which Pamplona was divided.

A deep crisis followed which divided the nobility of Navarre into two factions, *agramontés* and *beaumontés*. This situation continued through the reign of the houses of Foix and Albret, and Navarre, a small State between two great powers, ended up conquered by the troops of Fernando el Católico in 1512. The legitimate kings attempted to recover the territory and finally maintained their kingdom of *Ultrapuertos* (the territory to the north of the Pyrenees that is now in France). a Renaissance Court where art flourished and dissidents were welcomed. Fortifications and castles were demolished by the Castilians. Navarre lost its monarchy as such but, converted into a viceroyalty, it kept its institutions until 1841: Parliament (*Cortes*), Regional Administration (*Diputación*) and Courts, its special municipal administrative structure, and a border with Customs along the river Ebro.

Many *navarros* took part in the conquest and colonisation of America, providing soldiers, civil servants and priests. In return,

new crops and the money from Navarrese settlers flowed into Navarre, seen in the form of their noble houses. At the end of the XVIIth century, during the so-called 'Hour of Navarre of the XVIIIth century', some prominent families such as the Olavide, Múzquiz or Goyeneche held key posts in the Administration and businesses.

The XIXth century was characterised by wars, which put an end to the old regime and the political system of Navarre. It lost its status as a kingdom and became a 'provincia foral' (province with a special charter) within Spain. A group of moderate liberals, among them José Yanguas y Miranda, were the architects of the Law of 1841, later called the 'Ley Paccionada' (pact law). Navarre maintained its own *hacienda* (Tax Office) and sovereignty in tax collection and administration, in exchange for a 'donation' which it pays the Spanish State every year. It also kept a separate administrative system under the *Diputación Foral*, with powers in areas such as municipal laws, road building and education, and maintained its Civil Law. During the almost 150 years of the 'Ley Paccionada' there were many claims for 'reintegración foral' (independence) and autonomy.

Navarre played a decisive role in the military uprising against the Second Spanish Republic, contributing around 17,000 volunteers to the cause, mainly through the phenomenon of 'Carlism'. It is estimated that 4,500 *navarros* died on the battles, and another 2,700 during retreat in reprisal. In 1937, when the Civil War was at its height, General Franco added the emblem of the Laureate Cross of San Fernando to the chains and emerald of the heraldic coat of arms of Navarre, although it was withdrawn with the arrival of democracy.

What was previously an agricultural region, and one from which people emigrated, took on an air of modernity and the population patterns changed after the Industrial Promotion Plan of 1964. The last years of Franco's regime were marked by trade union strikes and a rising democratic movement claiming freedom.

THE INSTITUTIONS OF NAVARRE

The 'Ley Orgánica de Reintegración and Amejoramiento del Régimen Foral de Navarra', passed on 16th August 1982, states that "Navarre is a chartered community with its own system, autonomy and institutions, indivisible, integrated in the Spanish nation and declaring its solidarity with all its peoples."

This law (abbreviation 'LO-RAFNA') regulates the democratic institutions and, at the same time, integrates and guarantees the political powers and faculties of the region.

The territory is made up of the municipalities in the 'Merindades Históricas' of Pamplona, Estella, Tudela, Sangüesa and Olite. The status of navarro is held by Spanish people who are registered as inhabitants of any of the municipalities of Navarre. This is also applicable to emigrants who previously had their residence in Navarre and their children, if they request the status.

The coat of arms of Navarre consists of gold chains on a red background, with an emerald joining the eight links, and above them

The Throne Room in the Palacio de Navarra, seat of the regional government, recalls the history of the Kingdom and symbolises the self-government Navarre has enjoyed over the centuries.

the Royal Crown (the symbol of the ancient kingdom). The flag is red, with the coat of arms in the centre. The capital of the region is the city of Pamplona. The Institutions of Navarre are: the Parliament (*Cortes*), the Government (*Diputación Foral*) and the Presidency of the Government of Navarre.

The Parliament of Navarre, currently consisting of 50 Members, is elected by universal suffrage every four years. It represents the people of Navarre, exercises legislative powers, approves the Budget and Accounts, and promotes and controls the work of the Government. There is a body known as the *Cámara de Comptos* (Chamber of Accounts) which advises the Government and examines and audits the accounts and management of the public sector.

The Government of Navarre consists of the President and his/her Regional Ministers, who are the executive body. They establish general policies and head the Administración of the region. The President of the Government of Navarre is the highest level of representation of the Community, and also of the Spanish State, in Navarre.

Navarre has powers to maintain, establish and regulate its own taxation system. Tax collection and financial administration is regulated through an 'Economic Pact' with the Spanish State.

PHOTOGRAPHERS

THIS ENGLISH VERSION OF
"NAVARRA POR MIL CAMINOS"
WAS PRINTED
IN THE SPRING OF 2000.